T0323515

Strategic Management and Governance

This book is an investigation into the evolving nature and consequences of strategic management in public governance. It is prompted by the practical as well as the academic interest in the application of strategic management to public governance and to the public sector.

The main features of this book are its management focus, its use of published statistics and expert ratings to develop empirical insights into the capabilities and processes of strategic management in government, and its concern for practical relevance. Although this book deals with governments, it is a management book and not a political book. It is, in fact, a management book that "frames" strategic management in government as a tool of (or enabler of) the public governance process. This is relatively novel. The book's management focus has several themes, which can be summed up as comprising: the use by government of long-term strategic visions and strategies, effective management of the delivery of strategic visions and strategies, the performance of national governments, and the implications of strategic state capabilities for the quality of public services, for sustainability, and for managing strategic crises.

This book will be relevant reading to researchers, scholars, advanced students, policymakers, and public administrators in the fields of strategy, strategic management, and public governance.

Dr Paul Joyce is an Associate in the Institute of Local Government Studies (INLOGOV) at the University of Birmingham, UK. He is also Visiting Professor in Public Management at Leeds Beckett University, UK.

Routledge Critical Studies in Public Management
Series editor: Stephen Osborne

The study and practice of public management has undergone profound changes across the world. Over the last quarter century, we have seen

- increasing criticism of public administration as the over-arching framework for the provision of public services,
- the rise (and critical appraisal) of the "New Public Management" as an emergent paradigm for the provision of public services,
- the transformation of the "public sector" into the cross-sectoral provision of public services, and
- the growth of the governance of inter-organizational relationship as an essential element in the provision of public services.

In reality, these trends have not so much replaced each other as elided or co-existed together – the public policy processes have not gone away as a legitimate topic of study, intra-organizational management continues to be essential to the efficient provision of public services, while the governance of inter-organizational and inter-sectoral relationships is now essential to the effective provision of these services.

Further, while the study of public management has been enriched by contribution of a range of insights from the "mainstream" management literature it, has also contributed to this literature in such areas as networks and inter-organizational collaboration, innovation, and stakeholder theory.

This series is dedicated to presenting and critiquing this important body of theory and empirical study. It will publish books that both explore and evaluate the emergent and developing nature of public administration, management, and governance (in theory and practice) and examine the relationship with and contribution to the over-arching disciplines of management and organizational sociology.

Books in the series will be of interest to academics and researchers in this field, students undertaking advanced studies of it as part of their undergraduate or postgraduate degree and reflective policymakers and practitioners.

Pandemics and Public Value Management
Usman W. Chohan

Strategic Management and Governance
Strategy Execution Around the World
Paul Joyce

For more information about this series, please visit: www.routledge.com/Routledge-Critical-Studies-in-Public-Management/book-series/RSPM

Strategic Management and Governance

Strategy Execution Around the World

Paul Joyce

Routledge
Taylor & Francis Group

NEW YORK AND LONDON

First published 2022
by Routledge
605 Third Avenue, New York, NY 10158

and by Routledge
4 Park Square, Milton Park, Abingdon, Oxon, OX14 4RN

Routledge is an imprint of the Taylor & Francis Group, an informa business

Library of Congress Cataloguing-in-Publication Data
A catalog record for this title has been requested

ISBN: 978-1-138-48633-1 (hbk)
ISBN: 978-1-032-27678-6 (pbk)
ISBN: 978-1-351-04579-7 (ebk)

DOI: 10.4324/9781351045797

Typeset in Sabon
by MPS Limited, Dehradun

This book is dedicated to Ava, Aoife, and Keira.

Contents

Figures

Tables

Acknowledgements

My sincere thanks to Geert Bouckaert, Paul Corrigan, Kate Mooney Joyce, Caitlin Joyce, Louis Meulemann, and P. S. Reddy for their feedback and suggestions. My special thanks to Theresa Joyce for her help and support.

Preface

The main features of this book are its management focus, its use of published statistics and expert ratings to develop empirical insights into the capabilities and processes of strategic management in government, and its concern for practical relevance. Although this book deals with governments, it is a management book and not a political book. It is, in fact, a management book that "frames" strategic management in government as a tool of (or enabler of) the public governance process. This is relatively novel. The book's management focus has several themes, which can be summed up as comprising: the use by government of long-term strategic visions and strategies, effective management of the delivery of strategic visions and strategies, the performance of national governments, and the implications of strategic state capabilities for the quality of public services, for sustainability, and for managing strategic crises.

The book was written with four groups of readers in mind. These were public administration and public management students on postgraduate courses, public administrators working in government, policymakers (politicians), and researchers in the field of public administration and management.

It was intended to offer these four sets of readers three key benefits. The first of these, which if successful would be both important and unusual, is to make it as genuinely concerned with the experiences and circumstances of governments throughout the world as realistically possible. This was intended to be a book about a world of different governments developing and using strategic planning as part of their public governance function.

The second benefit was to offer the fruits of analysing statistical data and databases of expert ratings. This was seen as necessary to make breakthroughs in understanding the nature, context, and consequences of governments' having strategic capabilities. This was not intended to be an advanced statistical exercise. It was hoped that using simple analysis techniques (scatterplots, bivariate correlations) patterns could be found that would provide some empirical testing of simple models of how strategic management enabled governments to serve their citizens. Obviously, it was (and is) hoped that the analytical insights would be of interest to researchers in the field of public administration and management and that they would through their own research corroborate or correct them.

The third intended benefit was to offer a book of practical relevance to current and future practitioners (postgraduate students) as well as policymakers. This was envisaged as requiring a book that would either draw lessons or would make it easy for the reader to draw lessons. The final chapter of the book speculates on some of the lessons for practice that emerged in the book.

* * *

Almost by definition, we can say that governments need strategic capabilities to deliver visions and strategies. But what are these capabilities? It might be guessed that governments operate within official constitutions and in circumstances that vary enormously. Does this mean that strategic management processes and capabilities would be quite varied? In advance of analysing the data that were available and writing the book, it was difficult to be sure how much progress was likely to be made in understanding these capabilities and contingent factors, but it was hoped to make significant progress.

This book was much influenced by the existing literature on strategic management in government, especially the management theories proposed by writers specializing in studying and understanding the public sector. A specific influence on the book was an earlier book on the role of strategic management in the governments of European countries (Drumaux and Joyce 2018). A final influence, of fundamental importance, was the practical advice on public governance given by the OECD. This advice is based on several years of reviews commissioned by governments and has from time to time been presented in OECD publications, including a publication on sound public governance published in 2020. These OECD documents were particularly useful in forming anticipatory ideas about how strategic management processes interacted with public governance.

Most of the analysis presented in this book uses a sample of 63 countries. They were chosen to include countries with a large proportion of the world's economic activity, with large and small populations, and with at least some coverage of Africa, East and South Asia, Europe, Latin America, Middle East and North Africa, and North America. A key dataset for this book was the Institutional Profiles Database for 2016 published by the French Government (http://www.cepii.fr), which is an expert-ratings database. This proved of critical importance for the analysis of the strategic policy process which formed a key component of the conceptualization of the strategic execution capabilities of governments.

The analysis relied heavily on simple techniques such as scatterplots and bivariate analysis. There were probably many different paths the analyses could have taken. The paths taken at times involved striking a balance between insights grounded in data and connecting the analysis to parsimonious and meaningful models of the "strategic state" and public governance. One key inspiration during the analysis of the data on the "strategic state" was the model of strategic management in government developed by Philip Heymann (1987). In hindsight the key developments in the analysis of the execution of long-term strategic visions and strategies by governments were as follows:

1   Three core "strategic-state" capabilities were aligned to components of an existing theory of strategic management in government (Heymann 1987).
2   A national outcome variable was composed consisting of just two indicators, which were the United Nation's Human Development Index and the Environmental Performance Index.
3   Contextual factors identified as pertinent were societal characteristics relating to democracy and "internal conflict" within society.
4   Public governance was operationalized as "strategic policymaking" plus two flanking processes (which were first the judicial system and second a representative process comprising a national body and elections).
5   A "quality of public services" factor was fitted into the analysis and linked to both national performance and to core capabilities for the execution of strategic policies.

The key findings presented in this book include the finding that national outcomes correlated strongly with the average subjective well-being of citizens. The variations in national performance were also found to be correlated with the degree of development of "strategic state" capabilities and the quality of public services, with these two factors being strongly interrelated. And the operation of executive government and the work of the civil service were placed in a public governance context and linked to societal conditions. By the time the analysis was complete, the full model that emerged in the book was strongly grounded in the data used.

Arguably, while the ideas on strategic state capabilities in this book can be linked back to the work of previous writers on strategic management in government, and even though we have the best practice advice on good governance published by the OECD, the book is very unusual in academic literature in treating strategic management as a tool of public governance rather than as an organizational analogue of private-sector strategic management.

In the next decade, it will be critical for practitioners to think creatively and act innovatively if the challenges of the climate crisis and of the 2030 Agenda of the United Nations are to be met. This book will have delivered a little on a desire to be relevant if it encourages some experimentally minded practitioners of public governance to take new initiatives thereby contributing to the required creativity and innovation.

Paul Joyce
UK, October 2021

References

Drumaux, A. & Joyce, P. (2018) *Strategic management for public governance in Europe*. London: Palgrave Macmillan.

Heymann, P.B. (1987) *The politics of public management*. New Haven, CT: Yale University Press.

OECD (2020) *Policy framework on sound public governance: Baseline features of governments that work well*. Paris: OECD Publishing.

1 Strategic Management and Governance

Introduction

If you are a politician or civil servant and you ever read a business management book, did you try to apply it to a public sector environment? Did it work? There is a great deal written about managing private sector companies. If you browse a bookshop, online or in-person, you will find thousands of books about how businesses should be built, managed, run, adapted, the list goes on. When you look for that same theory and understanding for government or for the public sector, it tends to feel like private sector management theories have been shoe-horned into the public sector world. While it may seem that the theory is transferable, it isn't. In fact, blindly applying private sector theory to the public sector and expecting it to work is, in my opinion, rash and irresponsible. The public sector is distinct from private companies in so many ways, in structure, funding, impact, objectives, so it needs distinct and separate theories.

But this isn't the first book to attempt to deal with the processes of government and management. Obviously, management is important for all manner of bodies, public and private. Objectives should be set, plans formulated, directions given, departments and individuals managed, decisions implemented, lessons learnt, and adjustments and adaptations made. But management in the government sector is different from that in the private sector. The circumstances are massively different, and the purposes and consequences of management in government are enormously important and special for communities and societies. This book is not following in the tracks of some previous attempts to relate management to government, where the effect was to recast government in the image of management. Burnham (1962) outlined his ideas of a managerial revolution in which "managers" would rule all sectors of society, and parliaments would be replaced by administrative bureaus. The dominance of government by managers is not envisaged here. As a glimpse of the analysis and arguments to come, it might be said that this book is about the development of a new type of public governance that is modernized and reformed around strategic management as a tool of sound public administration. In this analysis,

DOI: 10.4324/9781351045797-1

politicians remain in their key roles in political processes, but the credibility and effectiveness of government are reinforced through the growth and use of strategic capabilities.

A recent book on how to be a civil servant summed up the function of civil servants as one of advising ministers and helping them to deliver their long-term goals (Stanley 2016). Several duties assigned to senior civil servants appeared to be consistent with this definition of the function: they were to agree strategic aims with ministers, agree and provide financial and human resources needed to deliver the strategic aims, carry out project management, and troubleshoot. This statement of the role of senior civil servants seems to me to imply that strategic management is a key tool of public governance.

People have been thinking about, and writing about, strategic planning by governments for more than thirty years. It is not a new topic. There is now a lot of advice about how to do strategic planning in public sector organizations and what part it can play in sound public governance (Bryson 2011; OECD 2020). The case for governments to become more strategic in how they function and the importance of them making use of long-term strategic visions and planning as tools of public governance have been made cumulatively in a series of authoritative statements (OECD 2013, 2020; Osborne and Gaebler 1992; United Nations 2019; World Bank 1997).

An argument for embedding strategic planning in public governance could go something like this. First, public governance is a process that has the aim of serving citizens (OECD 2013, 8). Second, an effective governance process can be used to steer public services and national development and make it more likely that governments serve the interests of citizens effectively. Third, competent public governance can be built around a process of formulating long-term strategic visions and strategic plans and implementing them.

But, still, it is not easy to use strategic visions and plans as tools of public governance and the usefulness of much of the advice given really ought to be empirically tested.

In this opening chapter, the aim is to introduce the idea of strategic decision-making and examine some key philosophical ideas about the nature of reality and the meaningfulness of predictions of the future. This will set the foundations for thinking about strategic management processes. We have moved a long way from the early days of strategic thinking for the corporate sector when strategic processes were largely conceptualized in terms of the setting of objectives, analysing situations, and choosing options. This phase of expert opinion made it seem that the key moments in strategic management were intellectual and analytical. The subsequent work of implementation of a strategy just did not receive much attention in the classic texts of this period. In a later stage, there was a realization that strategic implementation had to be taken more seriously. Some took this too far and even went as far as to belittle the ability of corporate leaders to set objectives and determine strategies. One expression of this was a low opinion of headquarters staff engaged in analysis and planning and a recommendation that corporations should do their way into strategy (act first, think later?).

The initial view taken here would rebalance the view of the strategic management process by proposing that all stages of the process matter. I would suggest that each, and every, stage is critical, and we should not pick one stage and give it all the importance of the whole process. We can suggest the stages are: setting the strategic vision, designing strategies, then implementation, and, finally, monitoring and evaluation of strategies. Do any one of them badly and successful execution is put at risk. Even monitoring and evaluation is essential since strategic learning leads to revisions and adjustments.

What we think about the knowability of the future will affect how we configure the whole process of strategic management. For example, if we believe that we can make very accurate and infallible long-term predictions of the future, we might feel that implementation can be done by creating a programme of change, designing new budgets, systems, and roles, and allocating people to the roles and training them to carry out the new roles very precisely. But if we think knowing the future is inherently problematic for various reasons, we will decide that we need implementation to be more experimental and to provide sturdy opportunities for evaluation and learning. We will also put more emphasis on adaptability and flexibility in organizational matters, and so will not expect to slot individuals into a new structure in a single move. We might instead say we will pilot new structures and ways of working and only confirm them or roll them out more generally when we are sure we have learnt all the lessons that need learning.

How we think about the knowability of the future, and how we think about this in the sense of what we might anticipate or expect in the future, matters not just at the stage of first agreeing strategic visions and goals and strategies but also in how we approach strategic implementation and learning.

The ubiquity of strategic decision-making

Should we be surprised that we now expect governments to be strategic and use strategic planning? Back in the 1950s, one of the earliest management gurus, Peter Drucker (1955), prophesized that strategic decision-making would become increasingly important. Drucker's idea of strategic decision-making did not seem simple or easy to execute in practice. And yet he saw strategic decision-making as growing more significant, and intuitive and tactical decision-making being less important for tomorrow's managers.

His conception of strategic decision-making was multi-dimensional. The situation of a strategic decision-maker was neither known nor simple and the facts known to the decision-maker were normally incomplete. It was important that strategic decision-makers took great care when formulating the questions to be considered in decision-making – they needed to address the right questions in their decision-making. He stressed that it was not obvious in the case of strategic decisions what alternative actions might be taken. Further, strategic decision-makers had the difficult task of making sure strategic decisions were effectively delivered. Finally, it was important that strategic decisions were made that fitted in with decisions being made elsewhere in the organization and that were aligned to the goals of the whole organization. Drucker clearly anticipated the concerns sixty years later of many of those giving advice to leaders in public governance systems about the challenges of implementation and the challenges of ensuring whole-of-government coordination.

The nature of strategic thinking

What can be said in a concise way at the outset of this book about the character of strategic thinking? As a preliminary orientation to the nature of strategic thinking, we might say that it is like doing social science and like doing a puzzle. Why is it like doing social science? Because seeing strategic thinking in this way emphasizes that it is akin to scientific experimental thinking in which the strategy is equivalent to a hypothesis and implementation is the testing of the hypothesis. Like social science, strategic thinking requires observing what happens when strategy is implemented and valuing the facts that can be observed. Finally, as in social science, the correctness of an individual's strategic thinking can only be established by empirical verification.

There is also something useful in thinking of strategic planning as like doing a "puzzle". The key thing about a puzzle is that its solution normally requires some ingenuity. We can think of this ingenuity in strategic thinking as taking the form of an intellectual journey of discovery when we first formulate strategy and second learn from implementation. During this journey, we think through, and revise, what we think will be the essence of the best possible strategy. Strategic thinking for the individual, to the extent that it is like solving a puzzle, can be very engaging and stimulating and, maybe, on occasion, exciting.

Context matters

Ferlie and Ongaro (2015) have emphasized that context matters in strategic management. We can think of contexts as made up of an infinity of conditions or factors, some of which are pertinent to matters under consideration and an infinity that are not pertinent. If we think of the public sector as a specific context, then we should be sensitive to the need to investigate how causal relationships and social processes may be affected by pertinent conditions in the public sector context.

To take a simple example, let us look at how some specific types of strategy document will be affected by being produced in a public sector space. The documents in question are called "issue briefs" and "issue position papers" (Heath 1997). The first of these types of documents – the issue brief – is a clarification and an exploration of a strategic issue. It does not suggest a strategy to solve the issue but establishes the seriousness of the issue, sets out some options, and outlines the power and interests of relevant stakeholders. The structure of the brief can be as follows: the consequence of not doing anything about the strategic issue (how important is the issue), timescales (how urgent is action on the issue), strategic options, stakeholders (who are they, how powerful are they, and what are their interests). The second document – the issue position paper – can be seen as building on the work of strategic analysis done in an issue brief. It evaluates strategic options (ideally giving a lot of attention to feasibility) and then recommends that strategic decision takers choose one of them. Evidently, these two specialist strategy documents can be written by advisers to a strategic management team or a board or a strategic leader.

This may seem very logical and very technical. It may seem that the main constraint on the usefulness of these documents is the availability of information or data. What happens when now we think about the equivalents to these documents being produced by civil servants? To keep this simple, we can think about the UK civil service. In the UK, civil servants are not, formally speaking, responsible for setting the strategic aims of government or approving the strategic plans of government departments. Civil servants are expected to help government ministers. Civil servants are advisers to ministers. They advise ministers on how to achieve long-term goals. Civil servants write "submissions" and "briefs". They must do this, in theory, without compromising their "impartiality".

Impartiality is a key norm in the UK civil service. This refers to political impartiality. This proves on closer examination to be a complex norm to uphold. The UK version of political impartiality includes two distinct ideas. First, for a civil servant to be impartial requires he or she has a concern for objectivity in the sense that is meant in science – that is, claimed facts must be verifiable. Second, a civil servant can support government's policies but he or she cannot explicitly or implicitly criticize the government's political opposition. Thus, political impartiality is a peculiar mixture that creates a partisan and one-sided objectivity. Civil servants are on the side of government but must be objective and must not attack political opposition parties. It is worth stressing that this means that civil servants do, in fact, take part in adversarial politics to support the government's actions and policies.

Civil servants imbued with accepted norms of the UK system of public governance cannot approach the writing of submissions or briefs relating to government strategies and their implementation as a purely analytical or technical exercise. They must always keep in mind their political impartiality.

Is the future already determined?

Given the scope of this book, it would not be right to stray too deep into philosophical discussions, but it is important for a book on strategic management to appreciate the shortcomings of a view that assumes a total state of determinism dominates all experiences and the future. Determinism says everything is caused and all events in history are linked together in a web of cause and effects. This is a problematic perspective if you believe people have free will and can think and act purposively, making use of means to secure ends. Strategic management assumes the purposive nature of people who can act intelligently in the circumstances they find in existence around them. How does the appeal of determinism work its magic to such an extent that many politicians and public officials look for authoritative predictions of the future, with prediction not being equated to a guess but equated in some secular sense to a scientific prophecy? One answer might lie in the way our minds reflect on and process change. This is set out in three points:

First, a possible future may become an actual future, but this is not inevitable.

Second, if a possible future becomes an actual future, it does so at the cost of an alternative possibility for the future failing to become actual.

Third, when a possible future becomes an actual future, it may feel very difficult to imagine that it was originally only a possible future. It may seem to our minds in a process of reflection that it was always inevitable.

William James expressed the third of these ideas as follows (James 1995, 279):

> Do not all the motives that assail us, all the futures that offer themselves to our choice, spring equally from the soil of the past; and would not either one of them, whether realized through chance or through necessity, the moment it was realized, seem to us to fit that past, and in the completest and most continuous manner to interdigitate with the phenomenon already there.

If we reject a belief in a totally deterministic universe, then we can turn our attention to an alternative belief, which is that we always have some ability to choose what we do next. This rejection of determinism clears the way not only for strategic thinking – which is only meaningful if we can make choices – but also opens the question of whether governments and civil servants make morally good choices. Do public sector leaders exercise choices in favour of good ends and not bad ends, do they pursue strategies aimed at good outcomes and not bad ones? One sign of the existence of a moral dimension in public leadership would be the fact that individuals and governments can and do experience regrets for missed opportunities to deliver better lives (James 1995, 292):

> What interest, zest or excitement can there be in achieving the right way, unless we are enabled to feel that the wrong way is also a possible and a natural way – nay, more, a menacing and an imminent way? And what sense can there be in condemning ourselves for taking the wrong way, unless we need have done nothing of the sort, unless the right way was open to us as well? I cannot understand the willingness to act, no matter how we feel, without the belief that acts are really good and bad. I cannot understand the belief that an act is bad, without regret at its happening. I cannot understand regret without the admission of real, genuine possibilities in the world. Only then is it other than a mockery to feel, after we have failed to do our best, that an irreparable opportunity has gone from the universe, the loss of which it must forever after mourn.

Surprises and uncertainty

Recently, a management consultant outlined his ideas of business trends but began with the warning that "business forecasting exists to make astrology look good" (Huber and Sneader 2021). Daniel Kahneman in his book about how people think reviewed studies of expert predictions and concluded (Kahneman 2011, 221): "… you should not expect much from the pundits making long-term forecasts – although they may have valuable insights in the near future".

Long ago leading writers on strategic management appreciated that our ability to anticipate the future had its limits. Some of them highlighted the existence of surprising events. No matter how good organizations were at trend analysis or forecasting, the future continued to produce surprising events. Some surprises occur because of nature. One of the biggest earthquakes in recent history, with an epicentre at sea near northern Sumatra, Indonesia, triggered a tsunami in 2004. A massive earthquake off the Japanese coast in 2011 created a tsunami and then a nuclear disaster (BBC News 2021):

The 9.0-magnitude quake was so forceful it shifted the Earth off its axis. It triggered a tsunami which swept over the main island of Honshu, killing more than 18,000 people and wiping entire towns off the map. At the Fukushima nuclear power plant, the gigantic wave surged over defences and flooded the reactors, sparking a major disaster.

We are in a period with a rising incidence of unexpected extreme weather events. The weight of scientific opinion is behind the theory that this trend is caused by the climate crisis and policy-makers are generally concerned that if climate change cannot be managed then even more surprises because of extreme weather can be expected.

Some surprises are created by economic activities. In 2007 and 2008, many economists were taken by surprise as a financial crisis developed in the United States and spread to many other countries in the world. Gus O'Donnell, who was the UK's Cabinet Secretary from 2005 to 2012, and thus the top civil servant in the UK at the time, later reported that the civil service had been taken by surprise when this financial crisis struck. When interviewed, he admitted that it had not even been on the national risk register and such a crisis demands an immediate response (O'Donnell 2013):

> If you look back, for example, at the financial crisis, you know, and you look at where was that on our risk register, actually it wasn't there because we were concentrating on non-economic issues actually within the Cabinet Office. ... and there are things that come along like the financial crisis in 2008, you know ... the fact that it moved so quickly, the fact that over a weekend you're faced with a situation where all of the big banks were basically bust, and you're thinking about how do we save that situation? Obviously, Treasury in the lead. But if you've been through something like that before then you realise that financial markets move incredibly quickly. You know then that you can't afford to say, 'well, lets sit back, lets analyse this to death', and actually if you do that the patient is dead before you've prescribed any medicine.

Even when governments attempt to do contingency planning and anticipate emergencies, there can be great uncertainty about their timing. Even if there is a national strategy for preparedness, it can still be a surprise when an emergency happens. A good example would be the COVID-19 pandemic that occurred at the beginning of 2020. A report by officials in the Ministry of Finance in Finland emphasized that the pandemic was both sudden and unpredictable (Holkeri and Nurmi 2020, 275): "The sudden, unpredictable and global nature of the pandemic has caused some unusual difficulties, e.g. on supply chains, when everyone is buying at the same time". It is also the case that even generally effective governments may simply fail to be prepared and, presumably, this can be put down to politicians and officials deciding that they cannot predict the timing of an emergency and decide to take a risk by failing to invest sufficiently in preparedness. Norway is a very well-regarded government, but it appears that it too had failed to prepare adequately for COVID-19 (Christensen and Laegreid 2020, 343):

> The Norwegian authorities were in some ways not particularly well prepared to handle the crisis, because relatively little was done to build up specific capacity to deal with such an epidemic. National risk assessments had warned that the risk of a major pandemic was high but reserves of emergency medicine and infection control equipment were insufficient. The responsibility for such tasks was delegated to the individual regional health enterprises, which were mainly working according to the dominant management doctrine of 'just in time' and lean management, focusing on efficiency and not fit for building up robust emergency preparedness. The main bottleneck was lack of infection control equipment, respirators and testing kits. On the local level, 74 out of 356 municipalities did not have an operational plan for infection control, and training was lacking. But despite all this, as it turned out, it was more important that the Norwegian health care system is very good and overall resources are abundant, so in most important aspects it had enough capacity.

It is possible to flip the view that long-term strategies may get blown off course by surprising events and instead suggest that events can be seen as affecting the evolution of strategies. Of course, it might also be said that long-term strategies and events interact dynamically as leaders attempt to achieve important ends in the prevailing circumstances. Some exploration of the effects of events on strategy is to be found in the study by James Quinn, which was based on experiences in a dozen corporations. He concluded that events "would precipitate urgent, piecemeal, interim decisions which inexorably shaped the company's future strategic posture" (Quinn 1980, 37). And before it is suggested that these corporations were poorly managed companies reacting to events, we should note Quinn's argument that "no organization – no matter how brilliant, rational, or imaginative – could possibly forsee the timing, severity, or even the nature of all such precipitating events" (Quinn 1980, 38). He argued that at the beginning of strategic processes "it is literally impossible to predict all the events and forces which will shape the future of the company" (Quinn 1980, 50). My conclusion, based on his arguments, is that faced by surprises, and not fully understanding the implications of alternative responses, strategic leaders should make decisions incrementally, observing how well their assumptions work, and keeping their options open for as long as possible. In other words, in the face of surprising events, experimentation and learning are the essence of rational and purposive steering of an organization.

But it is not only surprises created by nature or economic activity that make anticipating the future difficult. If a government has a long-term strategic vision and strategies to deliver the vision, it cannot know for sure, nor can it completely know, how different societal stakeholders will respond to their actions. According to Friedberg (2007, 49):

> The first and most fundamental task of any strategic planning operation is to develop alternative courses of action and to assist policymakers in conducting a systematic evaluation of their potential costs and benefits. Because the responses of the opponent and the unfolding of events can never be predicted with assurance, this kind of calculation is always imprecise and becomes even more so the farther into the future it attempts to project. Yet, for nations as well as individuals, some attempt to identify and evaluate different paths forward is the sine qua non of rational behavior.

Therefore, the consequences of government action inevitably have an uncertain element to them. This conclusion is self-evidently true to anyone who believes in free will and believes that societies are made up of a plurality of interests. Even for a government determined to make a better future for its citizens, its anticipation of the future will be based very heavily on guesswork about how others will react.

One implication of the assumptions that we live in a pluralistic universe and that people have free will is that overconfidence in forecasting is a mistake. If there are limits to our ability to forecast accurately, humility in a forecaster is an asset. It is better for a forecaster to be one who makes tentative forecasts. Tetlock et al. (2012) discussed two types of forecasting in relation to countries exiting the eurozone by a certain date, one they called fox-style forecasting and the other hedgehog-style forecasting. The former was more "eclectic" in the factors considered. The latter is bolder and, I would say, more reliant on a simple model. Tetlock et al. made comments that were more favourable with respect to fox-style forecasting, and they also noted the possibility of forecasting that took account of countervailing variables and accepted the limited understanding of interactions between variables that existed. Consistent with this discussion of styles of forecasting, Tetlock et al. summed up what was known about forecasters with a consistently better record of forecasting (Tetlock et al. 2017, 482):

> Their personality profiles revealed above-normal scores on measures of active open-mindedness (a willingness to treat one's beliefs as testable hypotheses, not sacred possessions), on measures of

cognitive growth mindset (a willingness to treat forecasting as a skill that can be cultivated and is worth cultivating), and on measures of acceptance that chance plays a key role in shaping life outcomes (a skepticism of efforts to imbue life-altering coincidences with deep meaning, such as fate).

Scenarios

Since the late 1960s and 1970s, there has been growing interest in the idea of scenario planning. It has been used by many governments. Sometimes it seems to me that when scenarios are presented to civil servants and public managers for discussion and consideration, the actual scenarios immediately grab all the attention, while little thought is given to their production or whether any attempt has been made to verify their possibility.

One succinct introduction to scenario planning suggested the fabrication of scenarios from trends and events (Government Office for Science 2009, 5):

> Scenario planning is a futures technique used for medium to long-term strategic analysis and planning. It is used to develop policies and strategies that are robust, resilient, flexible and innovative.
>
> Scenarios are stories (or narratives) set in the future, which describe how the world might look in, say, 2015 or 2050. They explore how the world would change if certain trends were to strengthen or diminish, or various events were to occur. Normally a set of scenarios are developed (between two and five) representing different possible futures, associated with different trends and events.

Sometimes the justification given for doing scenario planning is that it causes civil servants and public services managers to be more alert to what is going on in their environment, more ready to notice and spot a significant new trend or development. It has also been said that scenarios are good because they challenge our implicit assumptions about the future. Perhaps they serve to challenge any tendency we might have to think that the future will be a continuation of the present and that much in the future will be the same as it is now.

How do scenario planners decide on the selection and definition of trends and events to make the building blocks of their scenarios? One option is to look for the uncertainties in the environment. If these are then identified, clarified, and finally assimilated into a small number of scenarios around major axes of uncertainty, then, in effect, the inspiration for scenatio planning is the desire to triumph over uncertainty rather than to create desired futures.

Do those who write or use scenarios ever inquire into the possibility of verifying the possibility of the scenarios? Some method of verifying the possibility of a scenario is conceivable. For example, there could be a method which answered the question: has the combination of trends and events imagined in a specific scenario ever occurred in a stable form in history? This method would be essentially one based on analysis of historical situations. This might provide some degree of reassurance of the possibility of the scenario. If that combination has never existed before, however, it might be argued that there is no way of verifying that it is really a possible scenario. There would also be a danger that causal relationships identified in the historical situation would become the basis of predictions about what might happen in an imagined scenario; this extrapolation would be founded on the "resemblance" of the scenario to a historical situation (Kahneman 2011). Presumably, such extrapolations of causal relationships would be an example of the bold hedgehog-style forecasting that Tetlock et al. (2012) suggested was over-confident.

If verifying that scenarios created for purposes of scenario planning are "really" possible is rarely attempted in practice, why do scenarios have so much appeal as a means for anticipating the future? We can turn once more to Kahneman (2011), who suggests that when questions demand reasoning involving difficult issues, one response is to substitute a simpler question. So, instead of asking is this scenario possible, we can ask: is this scenario plausible? In fact, Kahneman also had some opinions on "plausibility" as a criterion for judging forecasts (Kahneman 2011, 159–160):

> The uncritical substitution of plausibility for probability has pernicious effects on judgments when scenarios are used as tools of forecasting. Consider these two scenarios, which were presented to different groups, with a request to evaluate their probability:
>
> A massive flood somewhere in North America next year, in which more than 1,000 people drown.
>
> An earthquake in California sometime next year, causing a flood in which more than 1,000 people drown."
>
> ... plausibility judgments were higher for the richer and more detailed scenario, contrary to logic. This is a trap for forecasters and their clients: adding detail to a scenario makes them more persuasive, but less likely to come true.

The second scenario is included within the first scenario and thus the probability of the second scenario is less than the total probability of the first scenario. But we are told that it was the second scenario that was the more plausible story. We are, it seems, persuaded by details.

The second scenario has more details and is more persuasive but less probable. The lesson? Scenario planning by governments may produce plausible scenarios but the scenarios are not necessarily possible. I wonder how many of those government officials directly participating in contemporary scenario planning are aware that they may be reacting to scenarios based on their subjective plausibility?

Singapore's experience of scenario planning

Peter Ho, formerly Head in the Singapore Administrative Service, named scenario planning as one of the foresight tools used in Singapore (Centre for Strategic Futures 2018, 1):

> Since its beginnings in the 1980s, the practice of foresight in Singapore has matured but it is constantly evolving. Against the backdrop of growing complexity, we have tapped on a growing range of foresight tools to help the government manage threats and capitalise on unpredictable opportunities.

> This means we need to keep warm ties with thinkers and policy-makers around the world to keep a pulse on changes around us, rely on diverse sources to pick up weak signals through emerging strategic issues and challenge policy-makers through thoughtful scenario planning and foresight-to-strategy translation.

By 2018, the civil service in Singapore had built and evolved an infra-structure for futures work. It had much experience of scenario planning under its belt. It had been using scenario planning for some twenty years. While scenario planning was partly justified as a tool for enabling officials to reflect on their mental models, the intention was to consider possible futures. Scenario planning was specifically seen as producing a set of plausible futures, thereby facilitating discussions of future risks and challenges. For example, a set of scenarios was produced in 2017. These scenarios were based in part on identifying several troubling trends:

- Nationalism rising in other countries causing more global uncer-tainty
- Reduced rates of economic growth
- Greater incidence of technological disruptions.

Logically speaking, any government identifying such trends should feel the need to audit its plans and policies and check what changes in priorities are needed. But the point here is that by 2017 these trends could be seen as issues requiring immediate attention. It did not escape the notice of the Singaporean civil servants that identifying current issues was one of the benefits of doing scenario planning (Centre for Strategic Futures 2018, 28):

> While scenarios are meant to explore possible futures over a 15 to 20 year horizon, they also reflect the salient issues of their time. The evolving themes in Singapore's National Scenarios exercises closely track the evolving concerns of the day.

So, the civil servants in the Singapore Government had noticed that its scenario planning had been good at identifying immediate strategic issues. This seems to suggest that in trying to imagine the future we are heavily influenced by our current experiences. It would be an irony if scenario planning turned out to be more useful as a way of drawing attention to current strategic issues requiring immediate attention, then it is in creating scenarios that allow governments to anticipate possible futures.

From plausible scenarios to possible utopias

Ideally, politicians and civil service futures' experts would be good at identifying and clarifying desirable futures, good at checking that desirable futures were also possible futures, and good at planning how to make the possible and desirable futures real. Desirable futures may be described as "strategic visions". They carry a strategic intent. They may be written up as though they were scenario statements, but they should not be confused with the scenarios produced by scenario planning based on trends and events, which do not carry a strategic intent.

An early example of a formal design for a strategic management approach that used a vision statement was proposed by Nutt and Backoff (1987). They suggested not only analysing the historical context of a public sector organization in terms of past trends and events, and any changes in direction (e.g., changes in programmes or resources), but also creating idealized images of the future of the organization. The idealized image was to be produced by a strategic management group that implemented the process of strategic management. The group was required to "describe attributes that would make up an ideal vision of their organization" (Nutt and Backoff 1987, 46). The attributes – ideal attributes – provided a target for strategic change. Looking back now it might be commented that their guidance on how to do a strategic management process was focused on a better organizational future. This can be refocused. For example, the strategic vision in a public governance process could be an idealized image of the future of a society or a community.

The character of strategic visions for a society may vary between very technocratic ones, in which well-meaning experts rely on their capacity for empathy and their understanding of the needs and desires of citizens, through to populist ones in which politicians try to decipher the "will of the people" to define a vision for the future. And this leaves plenty of scope for approaches between these two extremes. Strategic visions for a society might be based on party manifestos and election campaigns. Both of these may reflect the judgements of politicians about the concerns and priorities of ordinary members of the public, although some political parties may be very ideological when preparing manifestos and campaigns. They can be based on consulting the public and on large-scale surveys of the public.

One view on creating strategic visions of a better and desirable future is to be found in the writing of John Dewey, an American philosopher. John Dewey invited people to think about designing a future that had more of what was desirable (good) in the present. His idea of projecting into the future the desirable in the present is contained in the following statement supporting "practical idealism" (Dewey 1993, 9):

> We pride ourselves upon being realistic, desiring a hardheaded cognizance of facts, and devoted to mastering the means of life. We pride ourselves upon a practical idealism, a lively and easily moved faith in possibilities as yet unrealized, in willingness to make sacrifice for their realization ... All peoples at all times have been narrowly realistic in practice and have then employed idealization to cover up in sentiment and theory their brutalities. But never, perhaps, has the tendency been so dangerous and so tempting as with ourselves. Faith power of intelligence to imagine a future which is the projection of the desirable in the present, and to invent the instrumentalities of its realization, is our salvation.

Even if we accept that we can write strategic visions by identifying what is good in the present and then imagining a future in which lives are lived with even more experiences that are good, pluralism makes writing strategic visions difficult. One of the challenges, therefore, in formulating strategic visions for the future is that governments need to do so with empathy for the diversity of values and expectations among members of the public and concern for social justice in balancing one set of sectional interests against another. Given an empathy for diversity and a concern for social justice, governments then might make the case for reforms and national development that can mobilize as much public support as possible and as much consensus as possible for long-term strategic visions of societies and communities.

Societal and community reforms and developments may be accompanied by arguments in society about proposals that are deemed "utopian". For some of those arguing, utopian proposals are foolish dreaming. But utopianism that is hopeful and possible is not foolishness. It may be ambitious and optimistic, but it is not foolish. Liking utopian proposals may be dreaming but it is not necessarily foolish dreaming (Rorty 1998, 101):

> You have to describe the country in terms of what you passionately hope it will become, as well as in terms of what you know it to be now. You have to be loyal to a dream country rather than to the one in which you wake up every morning. Unless such loyalty exists, the ideal has no chance of becoming actual.

The governance of societal action enjoying widespread public support to bring about utopian futures could be a form of "pragmatic idealism". This would be public governance to turn "possibilities" into actuality. The possibilities depend on current realities. Thus, it has to be hard-headed governance as well as dreaming, steered by experiments rather than bold bet-your country or bet-your community plans.

Utopias do not escape unaffected by the existence of pluralism. Bouckaert and Jann (2020) have argued that one person's utopia is another person's dystopia. So, if we accept their point, we cannot conclude this chapter by assuming that the contents of utopias are easily agreed by all members in society or in a community. They also point to the dangers of utopias (Bouckaert and Jann 2020, 34):

> Yes, trying to realise utopias may create severe problems. We have ample experience of this in the last century. But it would be a strange lesson that we therefore should stop thinking about possible futures and how to achieve them.

Conclusions

When thinking about the use of strategic management in public governance a good starting point is the implication in strategic thinking that there are choices for a society or a community in how it moves forward. Strategic management presupposes that choice really exists and can be evaluated even though the prediction of the future is inevitably problematic because of the existence of free will and the importance of plural interests and perspectives.

A second conclusion is that strategic forecasts are more like guesses than divinely inspired prophecies. In some religious worldviews, there is a belief in prophets who are inspired by a deity to make revelations that are guaranteed to be infallible predictions of the future. Within a strategic management frame of reference, the infallibility of forecasts cannot be warranted by science or statistics or anything else. As a result of the blatant failures of many economic forecasts inthe 1970s, no doubt because of high levels of volatility in the global economic system, the fallibility of forecasting became abundantly clear.

Another key conclusion for this chapter is that scenario planning has not solved the problems of knowing the future; nor has it transcended the limitations of forecasting. The popularity of scenario planning may rest more on the scenarios being plausible than on the scenarios being possible. Maybe we like scenario planning because it appears to have accepted that uncertainty cannot be avoided when forecasting the future. Scenario planning makes a virtue of uncertainty by generating a set of scenarios based on axes of uncertainty, all of which are supposed to represent possible futures. But if the individual scenarios are not tested to check their status as possible futures, they are just narratives about the future, albeit that they are presented as being the result of methodical analysis.

Embedded in the notion of scenario planning is the proposition that society and communities need to adapt or adjust to the future. Leaders can consider the scenarios and then can take decisions so that organizations can adapt to the challenges and circumstances of the future. Adopting this perspective would mean for political and administrative leaders that they were pinning their hopes on reacting to what the future promises or threatens. The alternative orientation is to set about making a desirable future. This does not have to be aiming at foolish utopian ideas, but may be practical and idealist, taking account of facts in moving towards hoped for improvements. It probably means finding the future experimentally, rather than believing that change can be completely programmed in advance and errorless.

Guide to the chapters

It usually helps a reader to have an initial sketch of of the book they are reading. To the extent that there are linkages between the chapters and later chapters build on earlier ones, then the reader can relate what they are reading in a chapter to the whole and this should aid comprehension of the significance of what they are reading. In this final section of this first chapter, a sketch is provided of the book on a chapter-by-chapter basis, starting with Chapter 2.

In Chapter 2, we look at some tried and tested ideas about "delivery". These ideas are not specific to delivering strategy. They can be applied to any ministerial promises, priorities, departmental policies, government strategies, as well as to the delivery of long-term strategic visions for the development of a country. At its heart will be a map of a government delivery process, devised for looking at the mechanics of making something happen when there is political will to drive through change. The delivery challenge may be framed as a problem because the government is struggling to do something it had intended to do or it may be positively framed as an opportunity to realize a political aspiration to make improvements on the current state of things.

In Chapter 3, the focus is on long-term strategic visions of government. One of the issues addressed in this chapter is this: can we assume clear prioritization when a government has a strong long-term strategic vision? It might be assumed that governments can and should have both long-term strategic visions and clear prioritization. But governments can be stronger on one than the other. And this chapter will, among other things, highlight some of the contingent factors that appear to be in play. Another issue is the degree to which stakeholders are conscious or aware of long-term strategic visions. After all, if governments are to be backed by stakeholders, surely those stakeholders need to know and agree the vision?

Chapter 4 addresses strategic capabilities of government as a whole-of-government phenomenon. It looks, as might be expected, at the issue of whether governments actually act in accordance with government long-term strategic visions; after all, it is not much use having a long-term strategic vision if government then ignores it when it is taking action or delivering public services. It examines the amount of co-ordination and collaboration within the civil service and within public administration generally. And finally, it looks at how policymaking is executed in practice. Together these attributes can be seen as essential attributes of a capacity for delivering strategic policy.

There is much talk these days of governments not trying to do everything by itself and working in partnership. There is also much thought been given to open government and how members of the public can participate in government decision-making (in addition to engaging the political system through voting for parliamentary representatives). Chapter 5 looks at these matters and provides an analysis of a whole-of-society dimension to the delivery of long-term strategic visions and government strategies.

It is said in relation to strategic management that context matters. This seems obvious in the case of strategic management and the large corporate sector. Strategy texts may pivot analysis around customers, competitors, and the competitive advantages of the business in question. In times gone, business gurus taught generations of business students how to analyse the competitive forces that formed the environment or context of an individual business. The strategic management theory of the corporate sector is clear: the context is the "market" and competitive pressures are of paramount significance.

There does not seem to be the same clarity in the literature on strategic management for government on the nature of the context and the pressures on government, despite many discussions of "publicness", which can produce quite an array of dimensions to distinguish public and non-public organizations. One line of analysis pursued in Chapter 6 is a Hobbesian view of internal conflict in society, with its emphasis on the presence of a potential for violence and the desire for peaceful lives.

Internal conflict in a society takes a variety of forms. For example, economic cleavages in society – between rich and poor – were emphasized by Aristotle. Global bodies nowadays are fully aware of divisions on ethnic lines and the persistence of ethnic conflicts in society. There is also criminal as well as political violence. So, maybe the context that matters for government is about violence and peace in society. A recent hint that this is of continued relevance to the discussion of public governance is to be found in Levi's (2006, 9) statement:

> In virtually every state – or government – building project, it is necessary to "tame the violence" within the country's borders, to stop the "roving bandits", to halt ethnic violence and build a national identity, and to offer powerful constituents enough in the way of benefits to retain their loyalty and to desist from violent predation.

In Chapter 7, the strategic management process of government is directly related to the quality of public services. The issue is this: are public services of a better quality when there are long-term strategic visions, capabilities for strategic management, and a whole-of-society approach? The answer from the analysis presented in this chapter is that there is a strong alignment of high-quality public services and these factors.

Chapter 8 looks at the 2030 Agenda and the efforts of individual governments within their own national borders to deliver it. The chapter presents evidence to evaluate the importance of strategic state capabilities in enabling the national delivery of sustainable development. It indicates that governments with stronger strategic capabilities were not clearly outperforming other governments. This indicates the need to examine the conditions under which the effect of strategic state capabilities operate. These include the strategic autonomy of national governments in delivering the 2030 Agenda and its complexity because of strategic issue tensions in the 17 sustainable development goals.

Chapter 9 explores the strategic management of crises. This is first considered through a case study of the coronavirus pandemic. One of the aspects of crisis management explored in this chapter is the use of strategic preparedness and strategic agility to minimize mortality rates. International cooperation in a crisis is explored through the crisis of climate change. Towards the end of the chapter, the focus is broadened to include insights into crisis management generally and concludes with some ideas on national strategies for crisis management.

The first section of Chapter 10 outlines three types of leaders, transformational leaders, democratic populist leaders, and adaptive leaders. It then looks at leaders as re-designers of institutional capacity and changes. It ends by building a picture of the work of strategic leadership and then discussing country leaders, ministers, and civil servants.

In the final chapter, which is Chapter 11, we will consider some issues connected to the challenge of renewing strategic state capabilities for the 2020s and 2030s.

References

BBC News (2021) Fukushima disaster: What happened at the nuclear plant? Available at: https://www.bbc.com/news/world-asia-56252695 [8 August 2021].

Bouckaert, G. & Jann, W. (2020) The EPPA project. In: Bouckaert, G. & Jann, W. (Eds.) *European perspectives for public administration: The way forward.* Leuven, Belgium: Leuven University Press, pp. 21–42.

Bryson, J.M. (2011) *Strategic planning for public and nonprofit organizations: A guide to strengthening and sustaining organizational achievement.* 4th edn. San Francisco, CA: Jossey-Bass.

Burnham, J. (1962) *The managerial revolution.* Harmondsworth, UK: Penguin Books.

Centre for Strategic Futures (2018) *Conversations for the future.* Volume 2. Singapore: Prime Minister's Office. Available at: https://www.csf.gov.sg/files/media-centre/publications/conversations_vol2-publication-web.pdf [22 March 2019].

Christensen, T. & Laegreid, P. (2020) The Norwegian Government response to the COVID-19 pandemic. In: Joyce, P., Maron, F. & Reddy, P.S. (Eds.) *Good public governance in a global pandemic.* Brussels: IIAS-IISA.

Dewey, J. (1993) *The political writings.* Indianapolis: Hackett Publishing Company.

Drucker, P. (1955) *The practice of management.* London: Pan Books Ltd.

Ferlie, E. & Ongaro, E. (2015) *Strategic management in public services organizations: Concepts, schools and contemporary issues.* Abingdon: Routledge.

Friedberg, A.L. (2007) Strengthening U.S. strategic planning. *The Washington Quarterly*, 31(1), 47–60.

Government Office for Science (2009) Scenario planning. Available at: http://webarchive.nationalarchives.gov.uk/20140108140803/http:/www.bis.gov.uk/assets/foresight/docs/horizon-scanning-centre/foresight_scenario_planning.pdf accessed [13 February 2016].

Heath, R.L. (1997) *Strategic issues management.* London: Sage.

Holkeri, K. & Nurmi, J. (2020) Finland – The National Government experience facing the COVID-19 pandemic. In: Joyce, P., Maron, F. & Reddy, P.S. (Eds.) *Good public governance in a global pandemic.* Brussels: IIAS-IISA.

Huber, C. & Sneader, K. (2021) *The eight trends that will define 2021 and beyond.* McKinsey and Company, 21 June 2021. Available at: https://www.mckinsey.com/business-functions/strategy-and-corporate-finance/our-insights/the-eight-trends-that-will-define-2021-and-beyond?cid=other-eml-alt-mip-mck&hdpid=4c13cd69-ac45-49ef-8d88-8e68339a7eb8&hctky=9940921&hlkid=29605cf314ee4ec19bed0d436338924d [11 August 2021].

James, W. (1995) 'The dilemma of determinism' (published in September 1884). In: *Selected writings.* London: Everyman, pp. 271–297.

Kahneman, D. (2011) *Thinking, fast and slow.* UK: Penguin Books.

Levi, M. (2006) Why we need a new theory of government. *Perspectives on Politics*, 4(1), 5–19.

Nutt, P.C. & Backoff, R.W. (1987) A strategic management process for public and third-sector organizations. *Journal of the American Planning Association*, 53(1), 44–57.

O'Donnell, L. (2013) Interview with Lord Hennessy Wednesday 30th February 2013 at 10 Downing Street. Available at: http://www.cabinetsecretaries.com [9 August 2021].

OECD (2013) *Strategic insights from the public governance reviews: Update.* GOV/PGC(2013)4, 12 April 2013. Paris: OECD.

OECD (2020) *Policy framework on sound public governance: Baseline features of governments that work well.* Paris: OECD Publishing.

Osborne, D. & Gaebler, T. (1992) *Reinventing government: How the entrepreneurial spirit is transforming the public sector.* Reading, MA: Addison Wesley Publishing Company.

Quinn, J.B. (1980) An incremental approach to strategic change. *The McKinsey Quarterly*, Winter 1980, 34–52.

Rorty, R. (1998) *Achieving our country: Leftist thought in twentieth-century America.* Cambridge, MA: Harvard University Press.

Stanley, M. (2016) *How to be a civil servant.* London: Biteback Publishing Ltd.

Tetlock, P.E., Horowitz, M.C., & Herrmann, R. (2012) Should "systems thinkers" accept the limits on political forecasting or push the limits? *Critical Review*, 24(3), 375–391.

Tetlock, P.E., Mellers, B.A., & Scoblic, J.P. (2017) Bringing probability judgments into policy debates via forecasting tournaments. *Science*, 355, 481–483.

United Nations (2019) *United Nations World Public Sector Report 2019. Sustainable Development Goal 16: Focus on public institutions.* New York: United Nations.

World Bank (1997) *The state in a changing world.* Washington, DC: Oxford University Press.

2 It's Not Easy

Introduction

Governments need to get both strategic vision and execution right. Light's (2014, 8) comment in a study of federal government failures in the United States chimes with this: "Vision with execution is the clear driver of success, just as its absence is an equation for failure". He expanded on this in another paper on federal government breakdowns (Light 2015, 2):

> It is one thing to develop grand visions of a future good; it is quite another to craft effective policies and provide the resources, structure, leadership, and organizational cohesion necessary to honor the promises made.

Strategic visions, planning, and execution are not easy to get right, but it is not obvious how the following claim that government agencies rarely excel at strategic planning and execution can be stood up (Boland et al. 2019):

> Smart planning and sustained execution are needed to anticipate and navigate the increasing complexity and challenges facing government leaders around the world. ... public-sector agencies commonly fail to value strategy, and they rarely excel at strategic planning and execution. The result: government leaders struggle to change their organization's behavior and to drive progress toward the most important policy outcomes.

In this chapter, an open-minded view is taken of successes and failures in the public sector. It is assumed there are both many successes and many failures. Just as there are in the private sector.

A long-term strategic vision is an intellectual construct and is invariably presented as a written statement on the future. (It is curious that we use the word "vision" even though we expect a strategic vision to be expressed through words rather than an actual picture!) If we see a

DOI: 10.4324/9781351045797-2

strategic vision as useful for the purpose of steering or guiding strategic action, then it makes sense to equate it to a strategic intent. Because of the nature of human beings and the presence of a plurality of interested parties, a strategic vision that is a statement of intent is constructed as possibility and not inevitability.

A strategic vision may be intended to help bring about a better or a desirable future, with the future specified as containing things that are wanted. Where visions come from is sometimes taken for granted. This can happen when it is assumed that strategy is the province of a bold leader who has a personal vision for the future of their organization. The leader's vision may be seen as a blueprint of the future that will be realized through his or her decisions. In contrast, it may be assumed leaders can deliberately create strategic visions (and strategic goals) for society and consciously design them to mobilize support for government by a variety of stakeholders (Heymann 1987). Leaders can, for example, imagine a future in which there are evident benefits for the public, where there is more of the good things and less of the bad things. This implies that leaders have a capacity for empathic understanding of the public, understanding how they see things and what they expect and desire, and may be an understanding of what the public's latent desires may be (Hamel and Prahalad 1994). A World Bank's (1997, 14) report seems to have had such leaders in mind when talking about successful political leaders of reform:

> They were successful because they made the benefits of change clear to all, and built coalitions that gave greater voice to often-silent beneficiaries. They also succeeded – and this is crucial – because they spelled out a longer-term vision for their society, allowing people to see beyond the immediate pain of adjustment.

A better future indicated by a strategic vision can only be a possibility. There is surely always at least one moment in government when political leaders espousing a long-term strategic vision must wonder if it can be brought into existence? Some, but not all, of the uncertainty can be explained by the inherent indeterminism of human activity, which arises from the existence of free will and from the plurality of interests and expectations at work in the world (Chapter 1). Some more of the uncertainty arises from fallibilities of intellectual processes (jumping to the wrong conclusions, vagueness, oversimplifications, fallacies, etc.) and from leadership failings (incompetence, untrustworthiness, dishonesty, etc.). It seems safe to say at the present time that many factors can contribute to the uncertainty that is an inevitable aspect of the delivery of long-term strategic visions and plans. Between our own shortcomings as thinkers and the fact that how things turn out also depends on others who have free will, we cannot be 100% certain about what the future will bring. Thus, we assume that there is always and everywhere some uncertainty, or doubt, about whether a vision can be made a reality.

Some strategic visions and associated strategies are supranational or global. Some are produced by individual governments and are very long-term or very comprehensive in their scope (comprehensive in the sense of covering a multitude of policy sectors). Some government strategic visions relate to specific policy sectors such as the economy, poverty, health, education, urban planning, infrastructure, the natural environment, regional integration, and international integration. Not all government strategies are necessarily seen as equally important by country leaders. Some strategies might be seen as more central to the government's political agenda or its government programme. In the period 2001 to 2007, in the UK five-year strategies were developed for all government departments but it was clear that strategies in four policy sectors were treated as of greatest importance by the government cabinet; they were health, education, criminal justice, and transport.

Global visions

Since the late 1990s, Secretary-Generals of the United Nations have formulated and promoted ideas for a global effort to deliver sustainable development. In 1997 when Secretary-General Kofie Annan articulated a vision for the world's development and proposed new governance arrangements for the United Nations, he described a vision in these words (Annan 1997, 9):

> The United Nations is a noble experiment in human cooperation. In a world that remains divided by many and diverse interests and attributes, the United Nations strives to articulate an inclusive vision: community among nations, common humanity among peoples, the singularity of our only one Earth. Indeed, the historic mission of the United Nations is not merely to act upon, but also expand the elements of common ground that exist among our nations – across space to touch and improve more lives and over time to convey to future generations the material and cultural heritage that we hold in trust for them.

In the year 2000, the United Nations got support for the international pursuit of what were named the millennium development goals. Fifteen years later, national leaders decided to build on this experiment in global cooperation. In September 2015, the United Nations General Assembly formally adopted what Secretary-General Ban Ki-moon labelled a transformative vision of a better world. It was a long-term vision, titled the 2030 Agenda for Sustainable Development, to be delivered over a 15-year period. It was a vision that country leaders representing nearly 200 member states formally committed to and which contained a set of global goals. Adopting it meant that leaders of national governments were agreeing to pursue action to reduce poverty and inequality, to get inclusive economic growth, to counter climate change, and to deliver results on many other progressive ideals by the year 2030. The countries of the world were to work together, in a global partnership, to deliver the transformative vision. Ban Ki-moon advocated the vision and stressed the requirements for global solidarity, partnership, and a long-term focus (UN News Release 2015):

> The 2030 Agenda compels us to look beyond national boundaries and short-term interests and act in solidarity for the long-term. We can no longer afford to think and work in silos.

The vision was bold in identifying issues and seeing them as amenable to capable collective global action (United Nations 2015, 3–4):

> In these Goals and targets, we are setting out a supremely ambitious and transformational vision. We envisage a world free of poverty, hunger, disease and want, where all life can thrive. We envisage a world free of fear and violence. ...

> We envisage a world of universal respect for human rights and human dignity, the rule of law, justice, equality and non-discrimination; of respect for race, ethnicity and cultural diversity; and of equal opportunity permitting the full realization of human potential and contributing to shared prosperity. ...

> We envisage a world in which every country enjoys sustained, inclusive and sustainable economic growth and decent work for all. ... One in which democracy, good governance and the rule of law, as well as an enabling environment at the national and international levels, are essential for sustainable development, including sustained and inclusive economic growth, social development, environmental protection and the eradication of poverty and hunger. One in which development and the application of technology are climate-sensitive, respect biodiversity and are resilient. One in which humanity lives in harmony with nature and in which wildlife and other living species are protected.

National visions

China's government has long provided an important example of an individual government with a long-term strategic perspective, not least because it achieved a record of economic development since the late

1970s that meant its economy, as measured by gross domestic product (GDP), leap-frogged many of the world's major economies.

A key aspect of its long-term strategic vision since the late 1970s has been the idea of Chinese people being financially better off. The concept of a national development agenda aiming at creating a "well-off society" or a "moderately prosperous society" emerged in the arguments that went on in the leadership of the Chinese Communist Party in the period after Mao Zedong – in the late 1970s and 1980s. The rationale offered in the following comments by Deng Xiaoping for giving great priority to the economic prosperity of China and the living standards of the people was a political one (Deng 1978):

> In today's world, our country is counted as poor. Even within the third world, China still rates as relatively underdeveloped. We are a socialist country. The basic expression of the superiority of our socialist system is that it allows the productive forces of our society to grow at a rapid rate unknown in old China, and that it permits us gradually to satisfy our people's constantly growing material and cultural needs. After all, from the historical materialist point of view correct political leadership should result in the growth of the productive forces and the improvement of the material and cultural life of the people. If the rate of growth of the productive forces in a socialist country lags behind that in capitalist countries over an extended historical period, how can we talk about the superiority of the socialist system?

The focus on living standards was reaffirmed by President Xi Jinping, elected in 2013, when speaking at the annual National Party Congress meeting of 2015. He presented a political slogan, which was to "comprehensively build a moderately prosperous society". In 2017, he suggested that delivering such a society would involve "defusing major risks, relieving poverty, as well as preventing and controlling pollution" (Government of China 2017). He linked delivering the vision to the mission of the Chinese Communist Party. He told the 19th National Congress of the Communist Party of China (Xi 2017):

> Never forget why you started, and you can accomplish your mission. The original aspiration and the mission of Chinese Communists is to seek happiness for the Chinese people and rejuvenation for the Chinese nation. This original aspiration, this mission, is what inspires Chinese Communists to advance. In our Party, each and every one of us must always breathe the same breath as the people, share the same future, and stay truly connected to them. The aspirations of the people to live a better life must always be the focus of our efforts. We must keep on striving with endless energy toward the great goal of national rejuvenation.

In early 2019, the focus of attention was still on delivering the vision of a moderately prosperous society by the target date of 2020. The National Development Reform Commission reported to the National People's Congress that it was important to "be prepared for worst-case scenarios, identify key problems, adopt targeted policies, and tackle major difficulties to ensure all tasks are accomplished on schedule" (National Development Reform Commission 2019, 29).

Assuming that the vision of a moderately prosperous society was accomplished by 2020, what next for China? Xi Jinping set out a two-stage vision for the development of China beyond 2020. From 2020 to 2035, the vision was of a modernized China that was a global leader in innovation, with the rule of law in place, people living more comfortable lives, social etiquette and civility enhanced, modern social governance, and improvement in the environment. The vision from 2035 to 2050 was of a "great modern socialist country that is prosperous, strong, democratic, culturally advanced, harmonious, and beautiful".

A second example of a government of a country with a long-term strategic vision is Saudi Arabia. At a time when Saudi Arabia was evolving its development planning system, in 2004, its vision for the future (Government Saudi Arabia: Vision 2025) continued to emphasize a move away from dependence on oil to a more diversified economy:

> By the will of Allah, the Saudi economy in 2025 will be a more diversified, prosperous, private-sector driven economy, providing rewarding job opportunities, quality education, excellent health care and necessary skills to ensure the well-being of all citizens while safeguarding Islamic values and the Kingdom's cultural heritage.

And in 2016, the year after the United Nation's General Assembly adoption of the 2030 Agenda for Sustainable Development in 2015, the leadership of Saudi Arabia published "Saudi Vision 2030". A key feature of this vision statement was the strategic intent of ending the country's economic reliance on oil. This vision statement has been frequently seen as the work of the Saudi ruler's son, Mohammad Bin Salman Bin Abdulaziz Al-Saud. The published vision statement identified three underlying themes: a vibrant society, a thriving economy, and an ambitious nation. The economy theme in the vision included the aim of diversifying the economy away from dependence on oil, an aim that had been important to the Saudi Government for a number of decades leading up to 2016. Mohammad Bin Salman's foreword to the vision statement provided some interesting messages on the transformational developments intended. He wrote (Kingdom of Saudi Arabia 2016, 7):

> We are determined to reinforce and diversify the capabilities of our economy, turning our key strengths into enabling tools for a fully

diversified future. ... Our ambition is for the long term. It goes beyond replenishing sources of income that have weakened or preserving what we have already achieved. We are determined to build a thriving country in which all citizens can fulfill their dreams, hopes and ambitions. Therefore, we will not rest until our nation is a leader in providing opportunities for all through education and training, and high quality services such as employment initiatives, health, housing, and entertainment. ... Our Vision is a strong, thriving, and stable Saudi Arabia that provides opportunity for all. Our Vision is a tolerant country with Islam as its constitution and moderation as its method.

Sector visions

Some government visions and strategies relate to specific policy sectors. The examples that follow relate to poverty, infrastructure, relationships with other countries, and sustainability.

Until the mid-years of the 1980s, Vietnam had a system of central economic planning, but then its government introduced economic reforms (the Doi Moi policy). Vietnam went on as a country to achieve fast economic growth and a massive reduction of poverty over a twenty-year period beginning in the early 1990s. This success in poverty reduction was especially linked to urban areas. The percentage of households living below the national poverty line had been nearly 60% in 1993; twenty years later, in 2013, it was less than 10%. This was a major achievement by any standards.

How did it happen? The usual sources of effectiveness ratings of governance of different countries, even in very recent years, do not prepare us for the fact that such a positive change had occurred. The Vietnam government is still not regarded as particularly effective compared to governments generally. Nor is the government reckoned to be especially future oriented nor to have established long-term strategic visions for economic, environmental, and social development. However, government strategies had existed and did exist. In 2002, the Government of Vietnam started the Comprehensive Poverty Reduction and Growth Strategy (CPRGS). Just four years later, in 2006, Vo Hong Phuc, the government minister responsible for planning and investment, reported that national performance against employment and poverty targets were either satisfactory or better than planned. The minister summed up matters as follows (International Monetary Fund 2006):

> These social and economic achievements in the context of price fluctuations, epidemic occurrences and natural disasters over the recent time have highlighted great efforts of the people, enterprises, the Government of Vietnam and authorities of different levels ... .

This victory is a vivid reflection of the fact that Vietnam is pursuing the implementation of Doi Moi policy, opening its economy, moving towards international integration, and improving the investment and business environment in order to promote the economic growth for poverty reduction.

In more recent years, the Vietnamese Government formulated a 2010–20 Socio-Economic Development Strategy and a 2016–20 Socio-Economic Development Plan. And in 2016, the Vietnamese Ministry of Planning and Investment, together with the World Bank Group, produced *Vietnam 2035: Toward Prosperity, Creativity, Equity and Democracy.*

Over the twenty-year period from 1993, there was a high rate of economic growth and a trend to urban living, both of which occurred without a large increase in income inequality in Vietnam's society. It is possible that factors such as improved education and more and better paid employment in cities were big causal factors in the drop in the rate of household poverty.

At the very least, the record of Vietnam's poverty reduction and the existence of a government intent and strategy together must create a presumption that the strategy had been successful. Pham Huu Chi, Vietnam's ambassador in Korea, in a lecture to the Asia Society during 2014, indicated that the transformation of the poverty figures was no accident. It was an achievement, a success. And at least from 2002, he made clear that there was a strategy in place to steer the reduction of poverty (Asian Society 2014):

> Ambassador Pham Huu Chi started his talk by explaining how poverty reduction is now a comprehensive strategy in Vietnam … In 1986 the Vietnamese government mandated the DoiMoi (open door) policy, shifting from a centrally planned economy to a market oriented one, achieving great economic and social success. This was followed up in 2002 with the launch of the Comprehensive Poverty Reduction and Growth Strategy (CPRGS) as it was recognized that poverty was the root cause of social and political unrest.

So, as we have seen, the scale of the reduction of poverty in Vietnam was remarkable between 1993 and 2013 and, while it was achieved in the context of a high economic growth rate, it was achieved without a marked increase in income inequality. And from 2002 onwards there were government strategies and plans in place to reduce poverty and spur economic growth. As of 2016, the government was still committed to the pursuit of reducing poverty, but it now faced a challenge of reducing poverty among members of the ethnic minority population, where much poverty was still concentrated.

The achievements of the Singapore Government's development of its infrastructure have long been praised. One study underlined the transformation that was managed in a period of about four decades (Lim 2008, 29):

> Just 40 years ago, Singapore faced the problems of overcrowding in the city, poor living conditions and a severe lack of infrastructure. Today, Singapore is a thriving city and international business hub characterized by a high standard of living in a clean and green environment, but the success did not come about by chance but through a process of proactive and farsighted planning.

Singapore's reputation for success in developing its infrastructure has been maintained and has been credited to the existence of a long-term vision, persistence in delivering the vision, and forward-looking planning (World Bank 2016).

The vision is not just about buildings, transport hubs, and logistics. The Singapore Government's Ministry of National Development (MND) published the following statement on the physical and non-physical infrastructure of the country (Ministry of National Development, Singapore Government 2019):

> Our Vision
>
> An Endearing Home, A Distinctive Global City
>
> MND's vision reflects MND's growing emphasis not just on physical infrastructure, but also on the softer aspects of creating emotional attachment in our people, the global talents and corporations whom we attract here. At the same time, it articulates MND's goal of building upon Singapore's unique distinguishing characteristics to develop Singapore as a global city of knowledge, culture and excellence.

In 2018, the Norwegian Ministry of Foreign Affairs published a vision and a strategy to guide its European cooperation strategy. It said, "The Government's European policy is designed to promote the realisation of an ambitious vision: a secure, free, economically strong Europe that takes joint responsibility for common challenges" (Norwegian Ministry of Foreign Affairs 2018, 6). The strategy for cooperation covered a wide range of strategic topics: security, defence, the rule of law, trade, labour markets, climate change, energy, and much more.

The Norwegian Ministry was clearly recognizing that the countries in its global region are of special importance for the well-being of Norway. And, implicitly, it was saying it wanted a point of view about how to influence its regional context and therefore how it wanted to see the European Union develop. It was, therefore, articulating through the strategy document what it saw as an effective European policy (Norwegian Ministry of Foreign Affairs 2018, 20):

> Pursuing an active European policy has been a priority for successive Norwegian governments since the referendum on Norwegian EU membership in 1972. There has been broad political agreement that, even though Norway is not a member of the EU, we should be an active participant in, rather than a passive observer of, European integration. Norway will continue to participate in and contribute to European integration, and we will make full use of the opportunities we have to express our views.

The fact that national governments can and do formulate strategies about how they will relate to other countries in their region and what ends they would like to see supranational bodies for the region embrace should be recalled when we think about the national differences and contexts that exist in the world. Some structuring of the world politically and strategically through regional associations of countries – association that may exist more or less formally – could be a significant factor in how the world develops economically and socially.

Sweden provides us with an example of a government taking a strategic approach to the natural environment. The government took a proactive interest in national environmental objectives as early as the1990s. In 2002, the Swedish Government presented a national strategy for sustainable development, which it revised in 2003 and in 2006. "Sustainable development was adopted in 2003 as an overall objective of Government policy" (Ahlberg 2009, 161). The European Union's Guiding Principles for Sustainable Development (Commission of the European Communities 2005) was, apparently, an influence on it and it has been suggested that there was a degree of correspondence between the European Union's strategy and the Swedish national strategy on sustainable development. The Swedish approach at this time went a long way beyond a concern for the protection of the natural environment. According to Ahlberg (2009, 162), the Swedish thinking at this time was that sustainable development concerned social, economic, and environmental aspects of national life:

> Furthermore, SD [sustainable development] is considered as a holistic approach to society's needs and problems. The approach is based on the insight that a well-functioning economy is the basis of social justice and environmental protection. Hence, policy decisions should be properly balanced regarding their long-term social, economic and environmental consequences.

The Swedish Government at this time tended to see the possibility of a beneficial interaction between economic and environmental developments. The Minister of the Environment, Carlgren, was reported to have made the argument for this possibility in 2008 (Ahlberg 2009, 168):

> At a symposium on renewable energy in Portugal in 2008, Carlgren argued in line with Reinfeldt that it is possible to protect the environment and to stimulate the economy at the same time. In his view, sustainable urban development is an important part of the transformation into a global, competitive and welfare-producing zero-carbon economy.

In terms of the governance of the Swedish national strategy, the government specified sustainable development indicators, including a small number of headline indicators, and it planned to monitor and evaluate these indicators.

Did the strategy of the Swedish government bear fruit? According to European Union statistical comparisons approximately a decade after the first version of the Swedish national sustainable development strategy appeared, the country was in the forefront of performance on various dimensions of a broadly conceived sustainable development agenda. It was in the top three of European Union countries in the following: it had a small percentage of people at risk of poverty, a low percentage of its population that could not afford to keep their home adequately warm, a high percentage of people engaged in lifelong learning, a high percentage of seats held by women in the national parliament (women had nearly half the seats), a high employment rate, a low long-term unemployment rate, a high gross domestic expenditure on research and development, a high percentage spend on official development assistance, a high percentage share of renewable energy in its final energy consumption, a low percentage of population exposed to air pollution by particulate matter, a big percentage of its area under organic farming, a low percentage of its area that was built up or had artificial land cover (European Union 2016).

The Swedish Government announced, in 2017, an ambition to be a leader in implementing the United Nations' 2030 Agenda for sustainable development, and it was proposing to set national indicators and to create a national action plan for achieving the sustainable development goals of the 2030 Agenda. Reflecting on the country's societal model, it described its sustainable development approach as "about developing the partnership-driven processes with innovative thinking about strategic and operational steering" (Swedish Government 2017, 4). It believed it was starting out on this future endeavour highly ranked as a country in global comparisons of sustainable development achievements. In fact, an early effort to use available data to show how countries were performing in relation to the 2030 sustainable development goals identified Sweden as the top-performing country in the world (Sachs et al. 2016).

The government's own estimate, in 2017, was that it was already meeting about 20% of the global indicators set by the United Nations as part of the 2030 Agenda. Given its relatively good past performance, compared to both other European countries and to countries everywhere, it seems likely that Sweden will be in the forefront of the global sustainable development movement in the 2020s. If this proves correct, it seems possible that this will be a result of its model of governance, which had involved not only partnership but also strategic steering.

Reflections

Statements of strategic visions are not normally book-length descriptions of better futures and better lives but are frequently very short statements consisting of a few sentences and phrases, maybe even just a short listing of top priorities. Evidently, modern statements of strategic visions by governments have to be understood in a fairly intuitive way and, pre-sumably, by readers making spontaneous sense of what can be quite sparsely worded statements.

Second, strategic visions often imply a strategic intent. Governments are saying that they will work to build better futures, to make the long-term strategic visions happen. Long-term strategic visions should not be equated with prophecies or predictions that merely describe a future. As Wen Jiabao, Premier of China's State Council, put it in 2004 when talking about the government of China's long-term vision of society: "The government bears heavy and demanding responsibilities in the effort to build a moderately prosperous society in all respects" (Wen 2004).

Third, long-term strategic visions may well extend over several planning cycles and be the work of successive governments and leaders of a country. This may seem a challenging thing to do – to sustain a long-term vision over more than one political cycle and despite changes of leadership – but, as was seen above in the case of China, it does happen.

Fourth, it appears that new vision statements can have significant continuities with past vision statements. This was the case with Saudi Arabia Vision 2025 and Vision 2030. Both featured a future with a more diversified economy. It was also the case with the Europe 2020 strategy (approved by the European Council in 2010) and the Lisbon strategy (that was approved in 2000). The Lisbon strategy featured priorities in respect of research and innovation, investing in people, modernizing labour markets, increasing business potential, energy, and climate change. The Europe 2020 strategy had similar priorities. One clear in-dication of continuity was reuse by the later strategy of two targets found in the Lisbon strategy: these were targets for an employment rate of 70% and for research and development investment of 3% of GDP. It appears that long-term strategic visions may have their roots in issues that persist over long periods, issues that are of continuing concern to governments and other stakeholders.

Difficulties of strategy implementation

There is no shortage of things that can go wrong when a government implements a strategy. As you read the implementation issues below bear in mind that major events of strategy implementation are often organized through a project format.

1   Failure by government officials to do the work needed to understand projects that are highly complex

In fact, much criticism of government implementation of projects focuses on delayed delivery and over-budget costs of major strategic projects that can take ten or more years from their appearance as an idea in a strategic plan to their realization. This definition of failure is based on comparing the planned implementation date and the planned budget and the outturns. In some cases, the label of failure may be contested; hindsight may have a different definition of success and failure – the long-run costs and benefits in terms of public value from the delivery of a government strategy may suggest it was a success. For the rest of the cases, there may be an optimism bias causing the poor estimation of costs and risks and exaggeration of benefits.

2   Officials underestimate costs and risks and exaggerate benefits because of excessive desire to get authorization and budget allocations

The problem of bias may not be one of naivety or ignorance but of deliberate over-optimism. To get the necessary authorization and budget for a strategic project, officials may be tempted to knowingly make an over-optimistic case.

3   Failure of officials to challenge (mistaken) views of more senior officials

For many years, UK civil servants have been surveyed about their attitudes and perceptions on a range of matters. The findings of a survey in 2018 made for dismal reading. Only about a half (49%) of the respondents had confidence in senior management decisions, and slightly less than a half (47%) considered it safe to challenge the way things were done (Cabinet Office 2018). So, it may well be that implementation failures occur because there is a culture in which there is reluctance on the part of civil servants to provide feedback to more senior officials about the existence of problems or errors in their thinking.

4   Failure to properly assess feasibility of proposed change

The simple step of carrying out an evaluation of the feasibility of a proposed strategic action before it is authorized improves the impact of strategic planning (Poister and Streib 2005). If that step is omitted, then the rate of implementation failures can be expected to increase.

5   Government officials complacent about coordination of and coop-
     eration of delivery partners

     Failures can occur when the execution of a government strategy depends on other parts of the public sector or on private sector providers of public services. For example, a UK Government Ministry was recently criticized in part because of its approach to implementation of a major change in probation services. The services were provided by private-sector Community Rehabilitation Companies. A report by the National Audit Office (2019) noted that they had frequently missed contractual targets, were not fully compliant with professional standards, and often were rated as doing work that was "inadequate" or "requires improvement" by government inspectors looking at the quality of their activities. Where government strategies depend on coordination and collaboration in multi-organizational systems, they can fail if government does not coordinate and manage partners effectively.

6   Failure to pilot proposals and thus to test their realism

     The probation services just mentioned may have also failed because of poor piloting of implementation (National Audit Office 2019, 9):

> The Ministry designed and implemented its reforms too quickly and without sufficient testing. Tight deadlines meant that the Ministry did not adequately test how the transformed system might work before letting contracts. It did not have a good understanding of probation trusts' delivery models, working practices and governance, and relied heavily on their information about costs. Although it began some pilots, these ended early and others were abandoned before they started.

7   Not clear who has overall responsibility for delivery

     The need for governments to be clear about who is responsible for making sure a strategy is successfully implemented was highlighted by the National Audit Office of the UK. It said (2013, 11):

> In our work on Online Tax returns by HM Revenue & Customs, we found that governance of the expansion programme followed good practice. This included having a Senior Responsible Owner accountable for its success, clear roles and responsibilities for those involved, and board meetings at programme development and operational levels. Board meetings, attended by key personnel, were held as scheduled and reported on achievements, risks and issues. As a result, HMRC was able to increase take-up rates, within expected timescales and within budget.

Governance attributes affecting how implementation is done

Governance systems can have a range of attributes in terms of the legitimacy claimed by political leaders, the type of professionalism exhibited by civil servants, and the credibility and accountability of government. All of these seem to be likely to affect how strategies are developed and implemented.

The type of legitimacy claimed by political leaders can vary over time and from one country to another. Populist leaders rely on the "will of the people" for legitimacy and are likely to see civil servants as part of the "establishment". Liberal-pluralist leaders like democratic populists get a mandate to govern from elections but will also enlarge their capacity for governing by negotiating and seeking compromises. Leaders in some socialist societies base their legitimacy in the leadership and educational roles of a political party seeking to build post-class societies. As a final example, some leaders are kings and claim the right to rule acquired by birth into a royal family.

The key thing about legitimacy is that it indicates the existence of a willingness on the part of the public to accept leadership. The argument made here is that the type of legitimacy that is claimed and is accepted has implications for how governance is manifested. Take the case of populist political leaders, they are, in democratic systems, legitimized by carrying out the "will of the people". Populist leaders also distrust "establishment" civil servants. They are, it might be inferred, unlikely to want to take the advice of civil servants, especially if this advice is for government to take strategic action that compromises the delivery of the will of the people. Hence, it seems likely the populist political leaders will operate, in a democratic system, by creating or maintaining a "command and control" relationship between ministers and civil servants. Populist leaders will promote policies attuned to the section of the population that has concerns and attitudes that are defined as within the scope of the "will of the people". These same policies may well antagonize the other sections of the public who disagree with the politician's definition of the will of the people. It might even be imagined that this approach to policymaking will heighten public awareness of policy winners and losers among the public. This will create the circumstances – difficult circumstances – in which civil servants planning the delivery of public policies will have to seek support for policies among stakeholders.

Liberal-pluralist leaders may stand more chance of creating irreversible strategic changes if they are able through negotiation and compromise to create durable consensus. Countries in northern Europe seem at times to have managed this creation of political consensus (Barber 2015, 244):

I agree [with Stein Ringen] that in consensual democracies such as Norway, the chances of irreversibility are higher assuming there is systematic implementation. ... the solution is for them [Britain and America] to become like Norway, I don't see that happening, because of the deep, combative political cultures in those places ... Still less is Norway a model that many developing countries and emerging democracies can simply adopt.

Why does political consensus matter? It might matter if it gives a greater chance of sustaining long-term strategic visions and strategies. Even if a government changes and a new government comes to power, presuming a degree of consensus has been achieved through negotiation and compromise, civil servants may find political leaders expecting continuity and persistence.

In terms of the professionalism of the civil service, we can readily identify three dimensions that crop up in discussions of public administration: impartiality (non-political), realism of advice, and can-do motivation (Figure 2.1).

In recent years, in some countries, civil servants have been trying to walk a tightrope between being non-political and having can-do attitudes as pressure increased for governments to become more effective. A common but not necessarily effective incarnation of civil service professionalism can be identified in what Stanley (2016) described as the club-like nature of officialdom (Stanley 2016, 32):

Other constraints on senior officials include the need to avoid annoying ministers, and the club-like nature of senior officialdom. The latter can be a good thing, in that it encourages senior officials to work collaboratively rather than just for their own ministers. It

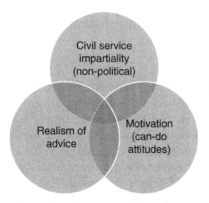

Figure 2.1 Civil service professionalism.

also allows pay levels to be set relatively low, in return for lots of genuine job satisfaction. But the 'clubbiness' of the senior civil service can also lead to senior officials being over-tactful in their dealings with one another, which can delay change, lead to poor annual appraisals, and create confused expectations.

Such a civil service culture, epitomized as not wishing to rock the boat and being very tactful, could be seen by politicians as a brake on getting things done.

Public governance systems low on credibility and accountability, as perceived by the public, might be systems that found it difficult to mobilize public support for government strategies, with consequences for the government success rate.

Delivery capabilities

One of the most influential exponents of the principles of government delivery, including delivery of strategy, is Michael Barber. He identified a specific dilemma for political leaders. To paraphrase him, leaders need credibility in the short term as well as the long term (Barber 2015, 6):

> The dilemma for political leaders in the twenty-first century is that people are impatient for results. If they don't come, the pressure from the people (and the media) intensifies, and political support can crumble. Thus, for reforming political leaders, the paradox is that they have to have a long-term strategy if they are to secure irreversible reform; but unless they deliver short-term results, no one believes them. On the horns of this dilemma some politicians (and in the developing world, donor agencies) revert to announcing 'initiatives', which they hope will convey an impression of activity but which do not result in transformation.

His views and advice are too rich to do full justice to them here. Instead, we can select three key principles of delivery.

1   Priorities should be made clear
    According to Barber (2015, 2), "Every successful business leader will tell you that unless a business is clear about its priorities it will struggle to succeed. The same is true for a government". Barber assumes planning is important because we live in a time when change is ever-present. Relatively rare are the moments of stability. To avoid drift, have a vision of the future and create momentum towards it. Plan for systemic change otherwise change is ephemeral. This requires time for discussion. Persistence is important. Therefore, decide on a few priorities and pursue them with will.

2 Delivery chains should be improved

Barber argued that without an effective delivery chain implementation fails. Conceptually, this means looking at all the participants ("actors") in delivery and how they interact to do the work of delivery. Sometimes, the delivery chain is handicapped by actors who lack the will or capacity to play their part in delivery effectively. Sometimes the issue is that some relationships in the delivery chain are damaged or dysfunctional, as was revealed by "stocktakes" that he organized (Barber 2015, 164):

> Looking back at my diary, written at the time [2001–2005], it is notable how my accounts of stocktakes focus on the quality of the relationships as much as the content. This is partly because I knew the formal minutes would capture the content and data, but ... if the relationships are strained, delivery is much less likely to occur than if relationships are good.

So, delivery depends on the quality of the relationships within the delivery system. "Strained" relationships harm delivery. This opinion crops up again in Barber's account of a delivery chain. Perhaps we might say that a delivery chain is a "political-technical" system. Things can go wrong for technical reasons. But they can also go wrong in terms of cooperation because of strains and conflicts in relationships.

3 Governments should learn from mistakes by monitoring the implementation of plans

Monitoring and analysis play a big part in Barber's view of how delivery should be managed. He says (2015, 124):

> The reason for drawing a trajectory [of actual and target performance during the delivery of a change] is that it forces you to think about the connection between the actions you are going to take and their impact on the outcomes. ... as the plan unfolds, those responsible can check whether the actions set out in it have the effect that was intended; and if they don't, they can learn from what actually happens and tweak the plan.

His own assessment of the extent of learning taking place was downbeat. He thought government too often failed to learn from mistakes (2015, 191):

> Moreover, in my experience government bureaucracies are not terribly good at learning. Collective memory is selective and haphazard, and systematic knowledge management usually absent altogether. Furthermore, there is almost no learning across

departmental boundaries, so the chances of a lesson learned, say, in the health department being applied to a similar situation in education are very low indeed.

All these ideas about how governments can become better at delivering long-term strategies imply important capabilities in the government and civil service for steering long-term change, for ensuring delivery is well organized, and for monitoring and learning from the implementation of plans.

Delivery units and centres of government

Michael Barber has been an advocate of the setting up of "Delivery Units" in the centre of government. These are small units that monitor government progress in achieving priority goals, facilitate face-to-face meetings of officials to evaluate implementation of government plans and to enable learning, and regularly review the delivery agenda. He has also warned against combining them with strategy or policy units (Barber 2015, 37):

> Some governments – Australia's, for instance – have [set up] ... a Strategy and Delivery Unit or a Policy and Delivery Unit. I would not say that can't work; I would say that it is less likely to work for the simple reason that, in political systems such as governments, strategy and policy usually trump implementation and delivery ... tracking implementation, checking actions have been taken across a system, exploring data sets for evidence of progress ... these tasks, however essential they might be, are (unless you are a sad graph-lover like me) fundamentally dull. For this reason, my advice is to separate delivery from strategy so as to ensure there is a senior person whose sole focus is delivery, as mine was in the original Delivery Unit [set up in 2001 by the Blair Government in the UK] and as Idris Jala's has been in Permandu in Malaysia.

Barber seemed to be arguing that if strategy and delivery are contained in the same unit then delivery gets neglected because it is boring and only by making it separate can government ensure it is not neglected.

The UK's Delivery Unit also developed (in 2001) and later refined a "likelihood of delivery" chart, which captured several assessments used to decide in advance if it was possible for government to deliver a top priority goal. Three key factors considered were the ambitiousness of the government goal; the quality of management in relation to planning, implementation, and performance management; and the capacity of the delivery chain. In relation to the delivery chain, the questions posed can be paraphrased as follows (Barber 2015):

Do the participants in the delivery chain know there is a priority and what it is?

Do the participants have the necessary skills?

Do the necessary collaborative relationships exist between participants in the delivery chain?

It is worth stressing that the Delivery Unit might have been a threatening top-down enforcer of government priorities. However, Barber was always keen to stress the efforts that were made to connect and facilitate the front-line of government and the centre of government.

The OECD has been prominent in recommending the strengthening of the centre of government to increase the prospects of governments delivering their strategies. The boundaries of the centre of government may vary from one national context to another. In rather formal terms, it has been described as "a body or group of bodies that provide direct support and advice to Heads of Government and the Council of Ministers, or Cabinet" (OECD 2018, 3). Among other functions, such centres are engaged in the work of government strategic planning. An OECD survey carried out during 2013 found that about a third of governments had centres of government that identified strategic planning as one of their top four tasks (OECD 2014). Moreover, this strategic planning was being redefined to be aligned to policy development and resource allocation. This evolution in strategic planning logically appears very significant. Strategic planning could be used to steer policymaking and implementation – hence we might talk about strategic policymaking – and the integration of strategic planning with resource allocation is critical if strategic planning is to be strong and have an impact.

In a 2015 OECD discussion paper, it was suggested that the centre of government should be actively involved in setting: "priorities that are outcome focused and will make a difference to citizens lives", planning monitoring and performance management, organizing the "centre of government and Civil Service to progress the strategic objectives and priorities", and ensuring a "strategy that builds buy-in and support from delivery agents to achieve priorities" (OECD 2015, 10). The language and sentiments were evidently in line with the ideas of Barber on the successful delivery of government strategies and promises.

Conclusions

Long-term strategic visions of governments are usually written declarations of where a society should be at some future date and often include statements about priorities and goals, which are to be used as means of monitoring and evaluating progress in delivering the visions.

Often long-term strategic visions are utopian. This does not mean that they are impractical visions of the future, but rather statements of strategic intent to radically improve the well-being of people in communities and societies. The often-repeated phrase, we must leave no one behind, seems to be an attempt to evoke a spirit of social solidarity for all people.

In this chapter, the special conditions of the government sector have been stressed. The attributes of governance systems are presumed to be critical for how strategic visions and strategies are developed and delivered. The difficulties of delivery have been grounded in the realities of the civil service and its various cultures. The capabilities needed have been drawn from the highly influential work of Michael Barber on how to make delivery effective. This included the importance of learning from errors and failures. Finally, the organizational significance of delivery units and centres of government have been acknowledged.

Successful delivery of good strategic visions – utopian visions of the future – is worthwhile, but this chapter says we should not expect it to be easy.

References

Ahlberg, M. (2009) Sustainable development in Sweden – A success story. *L'Europe en Formation*, 2009(2), 157–179.

Annan, K. (1997) Renewing the United Nations: A programme for reform. *Report of the Secretary-General*. UN Document A/51/950, 14 July 1997.

Asian Society (2014) Poverty reduction in Vietnam: Success, lessons and role of world community. Lecture by Vietnamese Ambassador Pham Huu Chi at the Korea Centre. [online] Available at: https://asiasociety.org/korea/poverty-reduction-viet-nam-success-lessons-and-role-world-community [1 March 2019].

Barber, M. (2015) *How to run a government: So that citizens benefit and taxpayers don't go crazy*. UK: Allen Lane.

Boland, M., Thomas, T., & Werfel, D. (2019) Four steps to high-impact strategic planning in government. [online] Available at: https://www.bcg.com/publications/2018/four-steps-to-high-impact-strategic-planning-in-government.aspx [15 February 2019].

Cabinet Office (2018) Civil Service People Survey: Civil Service benchmark scores 2009–2018. November 2018. London: Cabinet Office.

Commission of the European Communities (2005) Communication from the commission to the Council and the European Parliament: On the review of the Sustainable Development Strategy: A platform for action. 13.12.2005. Brussels: European Commission.

Deng, X. (1978) Hold high the banner of Mao Zedong thought and adhere to the principle of seeking truth from facts. [online] Available at: https://dengxiaopingworks.wordpress.com/2013/02/25/hold-high-the-b...-thought-and-adhere-to-the-principle-of-seeking-truth-from-facts [11 June 2019].

European Union (2016) *Sustainable development in the European Union: A statistical glance from the viewpoint of the UN sustainable development goals.* Luxembourg: Publications Office of the European Union.

Government of China (2017) To revive China, Xi holds high banner of socialism with Chinese characteristics. [online] Available at: http://english.gov.cn/news/top_news/2017/09/28/content_281475890831923.htm [24 October 2017].

Government of Finland (2019) Inclusive and competent Finland: A socially, economically and ecologically sustainable society. [online] Available at: https://valtioneuvosto.fi/en/article/-/asset_publisher/10616/sallistava-ja-osaava-suomi-sosiaalisesti-taloudellisesti-ja-ekologisesti-kestava-yhteiskunta [16 June 2019].

Hamel, G. & Prahalad, C.K. (1994) *Competing for the future.* Boston, MA: Harvard Business School Press.

Heymann, P. (1987) *The politics of public management.* New Haven, CA and London: Yale University.

International Monetary Fund (2006) Vietnam: Poverty Reduction Strategy Paper – Annual Progress Report. IMF Country Report No. 06/70. Washington, D.C.: International Monetary Fund.

Kingdom of Saudi Arabia (2016) Vision 2030. [online] Available at: http://vision2030.gov.sa/sites/default/files/report/Saudi_Vision2030_EN_0.pdf [28 October 2016].

Light, P. (2014) A cascade of failures: Why government fails, and how to stop it. Brookings: Center for Effective Public Management. [online] Available at: https://www.brookings.edu/research/a-cascade-of-failures-why-government-fails-and-how-to-stop-it/ [4 March 2019].

Light, P. (2015) Vision + action = faithful execution: Why government daydreams and how to stop the cascade of breakdowns that now haunts it. The Volker Alliance Issue Paper, December 2015, New York. [online] Available at: https://www.volckeralliance.org/ [1 March 2019].

Lim, H. (2008) Infrastructure development in Singapore. In: Kumar, N. (Ed.) *International infrastructure development in East Asia – Towards balanced regional development and integration*, ERIA Research Project Report 2007-2. Chiba: IDE-JETRO, pp. 228–262.

Ministry of Economic Affairs and Employment (Finnish Government) (2019) Strategies. [online] Available at: https://tem.fi/en/strategies [16 June 2019].

Ministry of National Development, Singapore Government (2019) Our vision & mission. [online] Available at: https://www.mnd.gov.sg/about-us/our-vision-mission [15 June 2019].

National Audit Office (2013) Over-optimism in government projects. London.

National Audit Office (2019) *Transforming rehabilitation: Progress review.* HC 1986 Session 2017–2019, 1 March 2019. London: National Audit Office. (This report can be found on the National Audit Office website at www.nao.org.uk).

National Development Reform Commission (2019) Report on the implementation of the 2018 plan for national economic and social development and on the 2019 draft plan for national economic and social development. *Delivered at the Second Session of the Thirteenth National People's Congress on 5 March 2019.* [online] Available at: http://www.xinhuanet.com/english/2019-03/17/c_137901686.htm [9 June 2019].

Norwegian Ministry of Foreign Affairs (2018) Norway in Europe: The Norwegian Government's strategy for cooperation with the EU 2018–2021. [online] Available at: https://www.regjeringen.no/globalassets/departementene/ud/dokumenter/eu/eu_strategy.pdf [21 August 2018].

OECD (2014) Centre stage: Driving better policies from the Centre of Government. 33rd meeting of Senior Officials from Centres of Government, 8–10 October 2014, Vienna, Austria. Paris: OECD Publishing.

OECD (2015) *Delivering from the centre: Strengthening the role of the centre of government in driving priority strategies*. Discussion Paper. Draft. Paris: OECD. Available at: https://www.oecd.org/gov/cog-2015-delivering-priority-strategies.pdf [17 March 2019].

OECD (2018) *Centre stage II: The organisation and functions of the Centre of Government in OECD countries*. Available at: https://www.oecd.org/gov/centre-stage-2.pdf [13 January 2020].

Poister, T. & Streib, G. (2005) Elements of strategic planning and management in municipal government: Status after two decades. *Public Administration Review*, 65(1), 45–56.

Sachs, J., Schmidt-Traub, G., Kroll, C., Durand-Delacre, D., & Teksoz, K. (2016) *SDG index and dashboards – Global report*. New York: Bertelsmann Stiftung and Sustainable Development Solutions Network (SDSN).

Stanley, M. (2016) *How to be a civil servant*. London: Biteback Publishing Ltd.

Swedish Government (2002) *Sweden's national strategy for sustainable development 2002: A summary of Government Communication 2001/02:172*. Stockholm: Ministry of the Environment.

Swedish Government (2017) Sweden and the 2030 Agenda: Report to the UN High Level Political Forum 2017 on Sustainable Development. [online] Available at: https://sustainabledevelopment.un.org/content/documents/16033Sweden.pdf [21 August 2018].

United Nations (2015) Resolution: Transforming our world: The 2030 Agenda for sustainable development. [online] Available at: http://www.un.org [26 April 2018].

UN News Release (2015) UN adopts new global goals, charting sustainable development for people and planet by 2030. [online] Available at: http://www.un.org/apps/news/story.asp?NewsID=51968#.Vgkt1LSm3QM [28 September 2019].

Wen, J. (2004) Report on the work of government (2004). [online] Available at: http://english.gov.cn/official/2005-07/29/content_18349.htm [24 March 2014].

Wen, J. (2008) Report on the Work of Government (2008). [online] Available at: http://english.gov.cn/official/2008-03/20/content_924600.htm [24 March 2014].

World Bank. (1997) *World development report 1997: The state in a changing world*. New York: Oxford University Press.

World Bank (2016) For a long-term vision, city leaders and urban planners look to Singapore. Available at: https://www.worldbank.org/en/news/feature/2016/03/30/for-a-long-term-vision-city-leaders-and-urban-planners-look-to-singapore. print [18 August 2021].

World Bank, the United Nations Economic Commission for Latin America and the Caribbean, and the International Institute for Democracy and Electoral Assistance (2005) National visions matter: Lessons of success. Available at: http://siteresources.worldbank.org/CDFINTRANET/Resources/nationalvisions matter.pdf [14 March 2019].

Xi, J. (2017) Secure a decisive victory in building a moderately prosperous society in all respects and strive for the great success of socialism with Chinese characteristics for a new era. *Report at 19th CPC National Congress*. [online] Available at: http://www.chinadaily.com.cn/china/19thcpcnationalcongress/ 2017-11/04/content_34115212.htm [6 June 2019].

3 Strategic Visions and Priorities

Introduction

Government officials and others assembled in an international forum held in Chile for two days during 2004 to consider the lessons of economic development. The forum concluded that long-term visions were important for national development (World Bank 2005, 7):

> A Vision is a prerequisite for development. The viability of a country's development strategy increases in proportion to the participation and commitment of all its social and political stakeholders. The experience of the countries represented at the Forum showed that a shared Vision of the future among the country's leading social and political stakeholders is a national asset.

Long-term strategic visions arise or are produced in a variety of ways. The executive branch of government may be the primary instigator of a long-term strategic vision, but the public and business community may also be involved in creating a vision. Visions for the country may be found in written documents, possibly authored by elected politicians and authorized by parliaments. There can also be national visions expressed through speeches and statements by politicians, business leaders, and others. At the forum in Chile in 2004, it was reported (World Bank 2005, 20):

> There is no explicit shared vision in Chile, no document drafted or signed by the social or political actors. Nevertheless, we do have a rather firm, implicit vision that has made it possible for important developments to take place. The major themes that rally the country and are part of this implicit vision are very common in Latin America and the world today: economic growth, greater social inclusion, and institutional improvement.

But visions – whatever their form – depend for their impact on the formulation of strategies, the creation of clear priorities, the allocation of

DOI: 10.4324/9781351045797-3

resources, and actions by a range of stakeholders. They also depend on a capacity for persistence, and this might mean maintaining persistence despite changes of government.

In this chapter, the idea of governments having long-term strategic visions is introduced. The Executive Director of the International Institute for Governance, Catalonia, presented a series of assumptions about strategic visions that are also accepted here (World Bank 2005, 34):

> Let me introduce a series of assumptions. First, countries are not firms, and to develop an effective vision and strategic management a country cannot use the same techniques and methods as a firm. Second, states are not firms, either. They have two dimensions: they are institutional systems and they are also more or less systemic aggregates of organizations. Therefore, it is not the same to establish a vision and a strategic plan for a government organization from within a government organization, as it is to establish a strategic plan for a country. The latter implies distinguishing clearly between institutions and organizations.

Such long-term visions and strategic plans of governments are, at face value, a tool for steering public governance activities. Obviously, they must also be reconciled with traditional ideas of professional government policymaking and evaluation, and they must become the basis of a management agenda within the civil service. At this stage in the evolution of public governance tools, it is probably meaningful to emphasize strategic policymaking as being policymaking and evaluation set within a framework of a long-term strategic vision and government strategies. This places a policy process as an intermediate process linking strategy and delivery (Barber 2015).

This chapter also introduces the idea of strategic priorities. Any modern government has a vast array of responsibilities and activities and government leaders have long been advised to select and focus activities if they want effective government. For the centre of government, this focus may be provided by identifying and maintaining a set of strategic priorities. Many other things still must be done by government outside of these strategic priorities, but these priorities define key results areas for the government, and thus areas that require extra or special attention. Of course, in practice, it is possible to set performance priorities that cut across a long-term strategic vision of government or even to have priorities in the absence of a long-term strategic vision. But one way or another, highly effective governments now often turn to the use of priorities to create a management agenda for delivery (Bublé 2021).

Measuring national performance in a balanced way

The international forum on national development held in 2004, as we have seen, was clear that experience revealed the clear lesson that national long-term visions for a country that were shared by all stakeholders were an important factor in successful development. People often think of economic growth as the obvious indicator of national development. But a more balanced measure of national success would look beyond economic factors alone. The United Nations has been publishing for some time a Human Development Index (HDI). This includes an economic variable and addresses both education and health aspects of national development. Unfortunately, the HDI does not address the question of national performance in protecting the natural environment. But fortunately, there is a measure of environmental performance that has been designed, published, and revised in recent years. Taken together, they offer a simple but broader based view of national development than simply relying on an economic growth metric.

The HDI is a composite index but quite a simple one. It conceptualizes human development as based on people living long and healthy lives, the development of knowledge, and access to a decent standard living. These concepts are operationalized using four indicators: life expectancy at birth (in years), expected years of schooling, mean years of schooling, and gross national income per capita. The index and associated data are published by the United Nations Development Programme.

Throughout this book the sample normally used consists of 63 countries which were purposively selected to include countries with very large economies and accounting for a very large proportion of the world's population. The sample also includes very small countries in terms of populations. The countries were also selected to include ones from all the continents. One other consideration in selecting countries was the availability of statistics on a range of factors and the availability of expert judgements on governance and strategic management characteristics.

Highly ranked countries in 2019 included Norway, Ireland, Switzerland, Hong Kong, Iceland, Germany, Sweden, Australia, the Netherlands, and Denmark (Table 3.1). There was a slight tendency for public authorities in highly ranked countries to have strong long-term strategic visions for the development of human capital (education, health, etc.). The countries that were increasing their score most on the HDI in the years leading up to the global pandemic – specifically, the years from 2016 to 2019 – were disproportionately countries that had relatively low scores on the index. These countries included Bangladesh, Cambodia, India, Indonesia, and Pakistan. Incidentally, all of these "improvers" were countries that had experienced major reductions in the extent of poverty between 2015 and 2020 (Chapter 8). In fact, generally for the book's normal sample of

Table 3.1 Human Development Index (HDI) ranking

Rank	Country	HDI value	Life expectancy at birth (years)	Expected years of schooling (years)	Mean years of schooling (years)	National income (GNI) per capita (PPP $)
1	Norway	0.957	82.4	18.1	12.9	66,494
2	Ireland	0.955	82.3	18.7	12.7	68,371
2	Switzerland	0.955	83.8	16.3	13.4	69,394
4	Hong Kong China	0.949	84.9	16.9	12.3	62,985
4	Iceland	0.949	83.0	19.1	12.8	54,682
6	Germany	0.947	81.3	17.0	14.2	55,314
7	Sweden	0.945	82.8	19.5	12.5	54,508
8	Australia	0.944	83.4	22.0	12.7	48,085
8	Netherlands	0.944	82.3	18.5	12.4	57,707
10	Denmark	0.940	80.9	18.9	12.6	58,662

Note
The source of the data in this table is the Human Development Report Office. It is reported in the 2020 Human Development Report. The data were obtained from http://hdr.undp. org/ [20 August 2021].

countries, the reduction in poverty between 2015 and 2020 was very strongly correlated with the increase in the HDI between 2016 and 2019.

The publication of the 2020 Environmental Performance Index (EPI) provided a snapshot of national progress towards environmental targets. Using data from recent years (e.g., 2017 and 2018), the results showed the best performers were countries in which income per capita was high. These countries included Norway, Switzerland, Germany, Sweden, and Denmark (Table 3.2).

The EPI Score was based on a very large number of indicators, including one indicator on greenhouse gases, which are thought to be a key factor in global warming and climate change. Using data from 2017, greenhouse gas emission per capita was included as a factor in the EPI score. The 2020 Report data provided an interesting insight: countries that performed well on the overall EPI score were the worst countries for greenhouse gas pollution. For example, Norway, Finland, Denmark, and Austria were among the worst for emissions of greenhouse gases per capita even though they were among the best ranked countries for EPI scores. In contrast, Ghana, Bangladesh, Mozambique, and Nigeria were among the countries with the lowest emissions of greenhouse gases but had relatively poor EPI scores. It seems that while the richest countries (as measured by GDP per capita) were generally very highly ranked for environmental performance, when the specific environmental issue of climate change is considered, they were the worst. It would also seem,

Table 3.2 2020 EPI results

	Country	EPI score	10-year change in score
1	Denmark	82.5	7.3
2	Luxembourg	82.3	11.6
3	Switzerland	81.5	8.6
4	United Kingdom	81.3	9.0
5	France	80.0	5.8
6	Austria	79.6	5.4
7	Finland	78.9	6.0
8	Sweden	78.7	5.3
9	Norway	77.7	7.6
10	Germany	77.2	1.2

Note
The data were obtained from https://epi.yale.edu/epi-results/2020/component/epi [20 August 2021]. See Wendling et al. (2020).

therefore, that higher GDP per capita led to lifestyles and economic activity that was problematic for the climate.

This climate change point might suggest the existence of a tension between economic development and the state of the environment. This might seem obvious: the more economic development there is the greater the industrial activity and the faster the trend to urbanization. Surely these make environmental despoliation inevitable? Not according to the authors of the EPI Report in 2020 (Wendling et al. 2020):

> … the pursuit of economic prosperity – manifested in industrialization and urbanization – often means more pollution and other strains on ecosystem vitality, especially in the developing world, where air and water emissions remain significant. But at the same time, the data suggest countries need not sacrifice sustainability for economic security or vice versa. In every issue category, we find countries that rise above their economic peers. Policymakers and other stakeholders in these leading countries demonstrate that focused attention can mobilize communities to protect natural resources and human well-being despite the strains associated with economic growth. In this regard, indicators of good governance – including commitment to the rule of law, a vibrant press, and even-handed enforcement of regulations – have strong relationships with top-tier EPI scores, highlighting the importance of managing economic and environmental issues with a commitment to analytic rigor and carefully constructed policies.

It is worth noting that for this book's normal sample of 63 countries the two indexes were highly correlated (the correlation was 0.86). The countries scoring very highly on the HDI also tended to score very highly on the EPI. Countries that rated very highly on both included Austria, Denmark, France, Germany, Norway, Sweden, and the UK. Those scoring lowly on both indexes included Bangladesh, Cambodia, China, Ghana, India, Nigeria, Pakistan, and Mozambique (Figure 3.1).

The best performing countries in Figure 3.1 were countries with high values of GDP per capita. This is partly a result of the inclusion of national income per capita as a component of the United Nations HDI. But this does not explain why the EPI score was higher for the high GDP per capita countries.

A second feature of the data displayed in Figure 3.1 is the geographical dimension apparent in national variations in the HDI and the EPI. It seems geography is a good (but not total) predictor of where in the scatterplot an individual country is placed; European countries, the North American countries of Canada and the USA plus Japan, South Korea and Singapore are in the top right-hand quadrant of the scatterplot; just below them are several South American and Latin America countries (Chile, Argentina, Mexico, Columbia, Costa Rica, Brazil, and Venezuela). Overlapping with this group but more variable in their scores on the EPI is the Gulf States group (UAE, Bahrain, Saudi Arabia, Oman, and Qatar). Towards the bottom end of the scatterplot are East Asian countries, including China, Indonesia, Vietnam, and Cambodia. At the very bottom and with very low HDI scores are a group of South Asia and African countries, namely, Mozambique, Nigeria, Ghana, Pakistan, Bangladesh, and India.

Combining the HDI and the EPI

The HDI and the EPI were combined and equally weighted to give a performance score for national development. It might be hoped that countries with good performance scores were more likely to be countries where people were generally highly satisfied with their lives. This is because they could expect long lives, good educational opportunities, a good income, and government progress in responding to environmental challenges. They might still be living in a country producing a disproportionate amount of greenhouse gas emissions, but the government would be striving to cut its carbon dioxide and other emissions.

Data on subjective well-being was based on large scale surveys that asked people to rate the quality of their current lives. The well-being data was for the year 2018 (Figure 3.2).

The scatterplot of performance and subjective well-being scores suggested that these two variables were highly correlated. The correlation was 0.82. Even so, there were cases where the subjective well-being appeared higher or lower than might be expected based on a country's performance on national development. For example, Costa Rica appeared to have higher subjective well-being than might be expected and

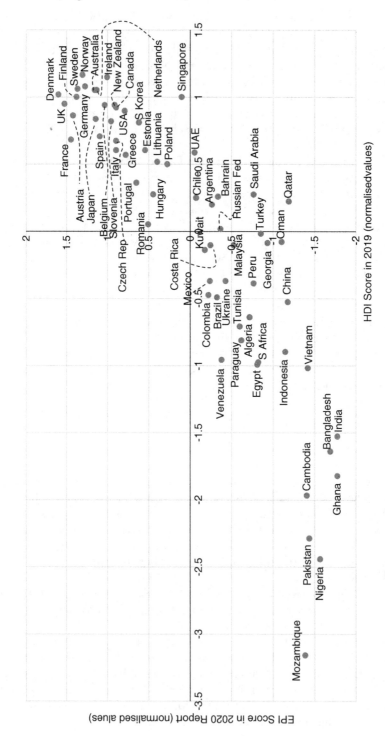

Figure 3.1 Scatterplot of Human Development Index and Environmental Performance Index (normalized values).

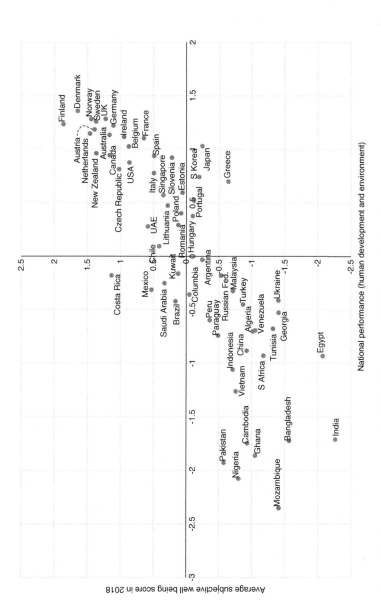

Figure 3.2 Performance on national development is highly correlated with average subjective well-being (normalized values)

Note: The scatterplot data was based on average subjective well-being scores for each country. The data was downloaded from: https://sdgindex.org/reports/sustainable-development-report-2020/ [6 February 2021].

Greece and Japan's subjective well-being was a little lower than might have seemed likely given their national performance.

A geographical dimension to the scatterplot shown in Figure 3.2 was apparent. Countries that were neighbours often (but not always) appeared close together in the scatterplot. The following groups may be identified:

Africa: Ghana, Mozambique, Nigeria, Tunisia, and South Africa

Australasia: Australia and New Zealand

Black Sea: Georgia and Ukraine

East Asia and Southeast Asia: China, Cambodia, Indonesia, and Vietnam

East Asia: Japan and South Korea

Europe – Central and Eastern Europe: Estonia, Hungary, Lithuania, Poland, Romania, and Slovenia

Europe – Northern and Western (and Western central): Austria, Belgium, Czech Republic, Finland, Germany, Ireland, Netherlands, Norway, Sweden, and UK

Europe – Southern: France, Italy, and Spain

Gulf States: Kuwait, Saudi Arabia, and UAE

North America: Canada and USA

South America: Brazil, Colombia, Peru, Paraguay, and Argentina

South and Latin America: Chile, Costa Rica, and Mexico

South Asia: Bangladesh and India

There may be many different possible explanations for why countries in the scatterplot shown in Figure 3.2 appeared grouped together with their neighbours. In a previous chapter, it was seen that the Government of Norway had formulated a strategy for its relationship with the European Union and through this strategy it might be expected that Norway would influence the development of Europe. In other words, neighbours may converge in their aspirations and in their politics and economics because they converge purposively.

In fact, the nature of trading patterns may drive a degree of integration. Economic research suggests that trade tends to be predominantly with other countries in close physical proximity. This fact may have been recognized in or reinforced by mechanisms of regional integration, which occur possibly for both economic and political reasons. Some examples of mechanisms are the Gulf Cooperation Council formed by the

Gulf States, the European Union, the Association of Southeast Asian Nations, the Eurasian Economic Union (comprising Russia, Armenia, Belarus, Kazakhstan, and Kyrgyzstan), and the North American Free Trade Agreement (NAFTA) that was made by the United States, Canada, and Mexico. It might be hypothesized that social intercourse might accompany economic intercourse and lead to convergence in governance systems and social values.

Perhaps we can illustrate some of the factors creating geographical clusters using part of a speech made by the President of the Russian Federation in which he discussed foreign policy priorities in relation to neighbouring countries (Putin 2003):

> Our undoubted priority in foreign policy remains strengthening relations with the countries of the Commonwealth of Independent States. These countries are our closest neighbours. We are united by centuries of historical, cultural and economic ties. The interdependence of our development is also obvious. Among other things, tens of millions of Russians live in these countries.

> And to put it directly, we see the CIS area as the sphere of our strategic interests. We also assume that for CIS states, Russia is within the zone of their national interests. And our country wants to see stability and economic progress in the CIS area.

> I want to stress that the economic integration process taking place in the CIS is bound up with the integration of our countries into the world economy, and will help us carry out this integration more dynamically and in conditions that are more advantageous for all our partners. And we will consistently increase co-operation within a Eurasian economic community that works more and more effectively.

Interestingly, the President positioned integration with neighbours as consistent with integration into the world economy. He did not see them as alternative choices – either integrate with neighbours or integrate into the global economy. This points to a picture of the world's economy as a coalition of locally linked economies that are linked through their economies and much more.

Can we make a link between long-term government visions and national performance?

In Britain, in 2021, it seemed that opposition political parties needed long-term visions to stand any chance of being successful in political terms. Mentioning leaders of the Labour Party who had led the party to electoral success, Keir Starmer, the current leader, argued that it was no accident that in 1945, in the 1960s and in 1997, the Labour Party "glimpsed the future and had a forward-looking programme" (Savage 2021). Starmer, personally, had been criticized for not having a vision for the country. It was reported that in the summer of 2021 he had been touring the country and talking to and listening to voters. It was said he was developing big "themes" with respect to crime, jobs, industry, climate change, and education. He promised to present his view to the annual conference of Labour Party at the end of the summer (Savage 2021):

> For Labour, what I was struck by was that people wanted to talk and wanted to engage. They were open to us. Now I'm not suggesting for a minute that people who voted Tory at the last election are already beginning to switch, but they're open to that discussion ... I think the constructive criticism is, can you show that you've changed? And probably the biggest takeaway, are you listening to me? Conference, obviously, will be our opportunity to set out in primary colours what post-pandemic Britain needs to look like.

So, having a vision for a society's future may be seen as a necessity for opposition party leaders in some countries, but does the existence of a long-term vision for a country benefit it in terms of its human and environmental well-being? Of course, as the forum held in 2004 suggested, it may be that the mere existence of a vision is not enough. It may be that there is a need to mobilize stakeholder support for the long-term vision and produce effective strategies to stand a real chance of delivering progress. But, even so, it might be expected that the presence of a long-term strategic vision for a country is associated with more national development.

The World Economic Forum publishes a Competitiveness Index, and one of its components is based on a survey of executives in various countries and consists of responses to a question about the extent to which the government has a long-term vision in place. The business executives are asked to assess this on a 7-point scale going from not at all to a great extent. Figure 3.3 shows a scatterplot based on the extent of the presence of a long-term government vision and national performance based on the HDI and the EPI.

The strong geographical pattern evident in the scatterplot suggests at least three distinct groupings. At the top of the scatterplot are European countries and countries identified with what in the past might have been termed Western capitalism: the USA, Canada, South Korea, Japan, Australia, and New Zealand. The middle group comprises mostly Latin American and a group of ex-Soviet Union countries (Russian Federation, Ukraine, and Georgia). Also in this group are

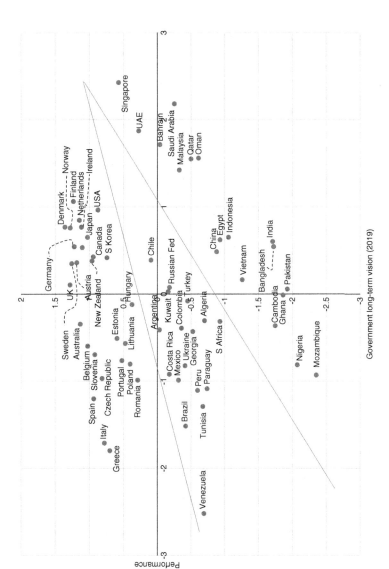

Figure 3.3 Extent of long-term government vision.

Note: Data Source for government long-term vision: World Economic Forum Global Competitiveness Index. Response to the survey question "In your country, to what extent does the government have a long term vision in place?" [1 = Not at all; 7 = To a great extent]. Available at: https://govdata360. worldbank.org/indicators/h5b74eef6?country=B [11 April 2021].

some African countries and Turkey. The third group includes countries from East Asia and Southeast Asia (China, Cambodia, Indonesia, Malaysia, Singapore, and Vietnam), South Asia (Bangladesh, India, and Pakistan), five out of six countries of the Gulf States (Bahrain, Oman, Qatar, Saudi Arabia, and UAE), and some African countries (Egypt, Ghana, Mozambique, and Nigeria).

Within each of the three groups, the extent to which there is a long-term government vision in place covaries with the performance of the country on the HDI and the EPI. One interpretation of this scatterplot is that long-term visions do matter for national performance but that this is affected by conditions. An explanation might be that the three groups vary substantially in their delivery capabilities, with the highest national performance being the result of strong long-term strategic visions and strong delivery capabilities.

But why, if this explanation had validity, are the three groups to some extent geographically differentiated? It is very speculative to say this, but perhaps the pattern of three groups is explicable on the basis of the groups reflecting the results of the history of economic development in the world. To take the last of the three groups, which included countries from East Asia, Southeast Asia, South Asia, the Gulf States, and three African countries, the intensity of modernization and economic development may have increased relatively recently, say in the last forty or fifty years. For example, the turning point for China in its approach to national development began at the end of the 1970s. Another example is Malaysia which launched into national development in 1981 (World Bank 2005, 65):

> Malaysia's vision policy was established in 1981, and seeks ultimately to involve all of Malaysian society in efforts to achieve one main goal: to become a fully developed country by the year 2020. Not only do we aim to achieve development in terms of GDP per capita, but also to reach psychological, political, and spiritual maturity as a nation, focusing not only on economic indicators, but on all dimensions of life, something we refer to as the total development concept.... The policy was instigated by the Malaysian Prime Minister himself, ... development strategies are set out in national development plans. Among these are our long-term development plans, which cover a period of 10 years; medium-term plans, which cover five years; and a short-term plan, which is, in effect, our national budget. This set of plans translates the country vision into programs and policies over a thirty-year period.

Countries that have entered a new phase of development only forty or fifty years ago have had much less time to accumulate resources and delivery capabilities than many other countries in the sample.

In contrast, the European countries included many that began rapid economic development more than a hundred years ago, and therefore may have accumulated extensive resources and many delivery capabilities over this relatively long time?

If this interpretation has any validity, it means that government long-term visions matter for countries with widely varying resources and delivery capabilities, because all governments need long-term visions to mobilize national resources and delivery capabilities. Singapore would then be an outstanding case of a country that used long-term vision and planning to make the most of the resources and capabilities that it possessed. And of course, this is the reputation it has gained throughout the world.

Are priorities implicit in strategic visions?

Michael Barber has been better known for his thinking on priorities and delivery than his thinking on visions and strategy. He, essentially, stressed the importance of having a small number of clear and shared priorities (Barber 2015).

Barber did not see strategy and priorities as rival ways of directing government. He argued for strategy as well as priorities. He had his own distinct perspective on strategy. He tended to think of strategy as an approach to the reform of public services. He saw strategy and implementation as the beginning and end of a process with policy in between the two and connecting both (Figure 3.4). He saw them as, ideally, complementary (Barber 2015, 64):

> … sound strategy is a precondition of a successful delivery. Strategy without delivery is vacuous; delivery without strategy is incoherent.

His acceptance of the need for strategy can also be inferred from a concern he expressed that civil servants might skip strategy and jump straight to policy (Barber 2015, 101):

> Much of government goes straight to policy, forgetting strategy. And then, as we've seen, underestimates implementation. Indeed, many civil servants claim their real expertise lies right here, with policy.

Figure 3.4 Strategy and implementation as the beginning and the end.

But policy without strategy is rarely transformative; and policy without implementation is worthless.

Barber's approach to strategy formulation was more like that of private-sector theorists who propose a set of generic strategies from which leaders could choose. This idea of strategy as a decision-making process in which choices are between known alternatives was also evident in his lack of attention to creative techniques for strategy formulation and in the absence of discussion of strategic issues.

He did worry that attention to strategy might obstruct the government's work of delivery. Indeed, he favoured keeping strategy units and delivery units in the centre of government quite separate (Chapter 2). His worry was that attention to the delivery work of government would be overlooked and so he advocated the existence of a separate unit where there was a single-minded focus on delivery.

The concern Barber had about a focus on delivery being diminished by everyone focusing on strategy (or policy) raises an interesting point. If strategy is led by a long-term strategic vision and the management of delivery is led by a clear set of priorities, could there be situations in which a government was strongly motivated by its vision or strongly motivated by its priorities – but in which it was a challenge to give equal importance to both?

It is not just Michael Barber who stressed the value of having a small number of clear priorities. The following remarks were made by the president of the Russian Federation in 2013 to his deputy prime ministers when work was being done to monitor and prepare and improve action plans for the delivery of long-term targets for economic development (Federal Government of Russia 2013):

I also ask you to identify a few clear priorities for each agency. Colleagues, I draw your attention to this point. We discussed this yesterday in the Presidential Executive Office. There is a lot of routine work to take care of. I know full well what a heavy load the Government has to deal with on a daily basis. I know there is a lot of routine business. Of course it is possible to draw up these plans any old how and fill them with things that look varied and interesting at first glance, but that are unclear and of little need to our people. I therefore ask you to identify 3–4, maybe 5, clear priorities for each agency. These must be objectives that people will find absolutely clear, and specific individuals must be responsible for reaching them. Of course, these priorities must be stated publicly. People must know the steps and resources that will be used to reach them and should be able to follow their implementation in real time.

A recently published study of governance provides expert ratings on the existence of government strategic priorities that can be cross-checked with the data on the extent of government long-term strategic visions produced for the Competitiveness Index (BTI 2020). This study included about two-thirds of the 63 countries in the sample used generally in this book, and Figure 3.5 illustrates four permutations of high and low ratings of strategic visions and strategic priorities.

This shows that it cannot be assumed that strategic planning in government consists of a strong long-term strategic vision, which is translated into strong strategic plans lasting five or more years. Other strategic systems are possible. Another option is where government steering is focused on priorities and the strategic action takes place through projects. This option resembles a system that has operated in Finland (Gerson 2020, 51):

> … the Government Action Plan (GAP, 2017-19) was created to guide the implementation of the key projects and reforms defined in the government's Strategic Government Programme. The five cross-cutting strategic priorities of the government were translated into 26 key projects. Each strategic priority had a ministerial working group, and each key project had a minister accountable for its implementation. The Government Strategy Secretariat in the Prime Minister's Office tracked and monitored implementation,

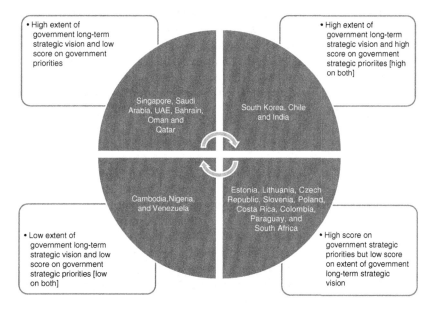

Figure 3.5 Government long-term strategic visions and strategic priorities.

Notes: BTI Dataset downloaded from: http//www.bti-project [10 February 2021]. To what extent does the government set and maintain strategic priorities? Score 1-10. 1=The government does not set strategic priorities. It relies on ad hoc measures, lacks guiding concepts and reaps the maximum short-term political benefit. 10=The government sets strategic priorities and maintains them over extended periods of time. It has the capacity to prioritize and organize its policy measures accordingly.

impact, effectiveness and potential redirection of the key projects. The Government assessed the implementation of the key projects and reforms regularly in its strategy sessions that were held every second week.

No clear or definitive comment is provided here about how governments need to approach creating long-term strategic visions and setting and maintaining strategic priorities, but it is noteworthy that Cambodia, Nigeria, and Venezuela are all countries that scored relatively poorly on the HDI and the EPI. Based on this, the hypothesis is that governments that fail to create long-term strategic visions and do not set and maintain strategic priorities will struggle to perform well in national development terms.

In the next section, the benefits of a strong emphasis on priorities are explored through case studies.

Benefits of priorities: Finland and New Zealand

The case of changes made by Finland's Government to create a new system of governing is interesting because there was a deliberate attempt to move away from wordy government programmes with a huge number of goals. The opportunity to change the way things were done came in 2015 in the wake of a general election. In the words of the Head of the Government Strategy Secretariat in the Finnish Prime Minister's Office, this was the chance to bring in "strategic policy making". There was an attempt to learn from experience elsewhere, with officials exchanging experiences with other countries (Sweden, Austria, the UK, and Scotland). The new system produced a four-year government programme (with relatively few strategic objectives) aligned to a ten-year vision with high-level objectives (Ross 2019):

> The new system set out a common agenda, built around 26 strategic objectives [projects] in five policy areas [priorities], plus a set of structural reforms.... it was supported by a common implementation plan, focusing on budgeting, performance management, and leadership capacity in the ministries.... Ministerial working groups were established for the five policy areas ... and Government Strategy Sessions were held fortnightly. Ministers were strongly encouraged to attend these in person... and to present the themes for discussion themselves rather than delegating the task to officials.

In 2019, a new government was elected in Finland and the durability of the new system was no doubt tested by this event. But, based on the four years from 2015 to 2019, the Head of the Government Strategy Secretariat took the view that the new system had performed well in delivering policy goals and could be improved by closer alignment of resource allocation to the key goals. The lesson of the experience of Finland from 2015 to 2019 appeared to be that prioritization leads to better delivery of the implementation of a government programme.

In New Zealand, a new period of reform of governance began in 2017 with the election of Jacinda Ardern as Prime Minister. The Government established only three priorities:

1   Economic modernization
2   Public wellbeing
3   Governmental reform

Aligned to these three priorities, there were 12 objectives and associated indicators for purposes of monitoring.

To deal with the challenges of inter-departmental cooperation, the New Zealand Government established joint venture structures, which leave the existing structures in place, and intended to foster the skills and culture needed for working across departmental boundaries. New Zealand's Secretary to the Treasury described the joint venture structure created for the government's domestic violence programme as follows (Ross 2019):

> [It is] a joint venture, with its own chief executive and resources. This joint venture's board will comprise the permanent secretaries of all the relevant agencies, and they'll have a mandate to deliver an agreed government programme. The idea is that instead of reorganising and creating new ministries, you have these more agile, more flexible systems focused on particular tasks.

What is apparent from the New Zealand case is that delivering strategic priorities may sometimes be challenging because delivery chains straddle departmental and agency boundaries. For a long-time now, it has been said that strategic priorities should be focused on the problems of the public and these problems may require more comprehensive solutions than are possible if the programme is the property of a single government department (Osborne and Gaebler 1992). If priorities are defined in such a way that they can be addressed through programmes designed and delivered by single government departments, they are allowing the activities of the government to be determined by existing structures, but priorities need to be shaped first and foremost by the needs and problems of the public.

Conclusions

The progressive politicians and civil services of the world appear to be embracing the idea of governance by looking ahead beyond the current term of government and seeking to steer planning using long-term strategic visions. This is even though there can be no guarantee that a long-term vision created by one government will be accepted and pursued by the governments that follow. At the same time, they are continuing to back the idea that effective government is selective government in the sense of governments needing to set a small number of key strategic priorities to provide the basis of a clear management agenda.

The ideas of Michael Barber, an influential thinker on making government delivery effective, point to the assumption that an ambitious long-term strategic vision can lead to much transformation in society if the government execution is a good quality one – if not, if the quality of execution is poor, then a bold vision of change will produce controversy without impact.

Governments that have neither a long-term strategic vision for their country nor a set of strategic priorities seem to be likely to operate as laggards in national development terms. It seems that in formulating priorities governments such as the one elected in New Zealand in 2017 do not believe that the most important priorities can be delivered by single departments or agencies. So, the nature of the priorities being set may lead to the need to develop delivery capability that can encompass multi-organizational arrangements, and presumably needs expert management of the consequent delivery chains.

References

Barber, M. (2015). *How to Run a Government: So that Citizens Benefit and Taxpayers Donat Go Crazy*. UK: Allen Lane.

BTI (2020) *Some reform-minded governments withstand negative trend—Global findings for governance*. Gütersloh: Bertelsmann Stiftung.

Bublé, C. (2021) Biden is moving 'full speed' on management priorities despite key vacancies. Government executive. 23 June 2021. Available at: https://www.govexec.com/management/2021/06/biden-moving-full-speed-management-priorities-despite-key-vacancies/174918/print/ [19 August 2021].

Federal Government of Russia (2013) Federal ministries presented to the President their action plans for implementing the May 2012 executive orders. Available at: http://en.kremlin.ru/events/president/news/18277 [11 March 2018].

Gerson, D. (2020) *Leadership for a high performing civil service: Towards senior civil service systems in OECD countries*. OECD Working Papers on Public Governance No. 40. Paris: OECD Publishing.

Osborne, D. & Gaebler, T. (1992). *Reinventing government: How the entrepreneurial spirit is transforming the public sector*. Reading, MA: Addison Wesley Publishing Company.

Putin, V. (2003) Annual address to the Federal Assembly of the Russian Federation. Available at: http://en.kremlin.ru/events/president/transcripts/21998 [9 July 2019].

Ross, M. (2019) The power of priorities: Goal-setting in Finland and New Zealand. Global Government Forum. 26 August 2019. Available at: https://www.globalgovernmentforum.com/the-power-of-priorities-goal-setting-in-finland-and-new-zealand/?utm_source=Non-Government+Bulletin+Sign+Ups&utm_campaign=81beab56f9-NonGov+email+newsletter&utm_medium=email&utm_term=0_1184a8b56c-81beab56f9–194625861 [28 August 2019].

Savage, M. (2021) Keir Starmer: I'll paint a picture of my vision in primary colours. *The Guardian*. 21 August 2021. Available at: https://www.theguardian.com/politics/2021/aug/21/keir-starmer-ill-paint-a-picture-of-my-vision-in-primary-colours?utm_term=896d5ab16863bcea2924c715dfef8732&utm_campaign=GuardianTodayUK&utm_source=esp&utm_medium=Email&CMP=GTUK_email [22 August 2021].

Wendling, Z.A., et al. (2020) *2020 Environmental Performance Index*. New Haven, CT: Yale Center for Environmental Law & Policy. Available at: https://epi.yale.edu/downloads/epi2020report20200911.pdf [31 October 2020].

World Bank (2005) National visions matter: Lessons of success. Available at: http://siteresources.worldbank.org/CDFINTRANET/Resources/nationalvisionsmatter.pdf [14 March 2019].

4 Taking Strategy Seriously

Introduction

This chapter has two intentions. The first of these is to present advice on strategic implementation based on guides to strategic planning for public sector managers. This guidance is normally wedded to an organizational perspective. The chapter then intends to get beyond thinking in terms of decision flow diagrams and instead to present evidence and analysis that provides insights into some of the factors that may matter for successful execution of government's long-term strategic visions. This will involve looking at long-term strategic visions for policy sectors and at the quality of the execution of the strategic policy process.

Arguably, it would help practitioners if we created and maintained a distinction between implementation and execution, which might seem an odd thing to say if you think these two terms mean (more or less) the same thing. The idea of making a distinction between them is suggested by the phrase "well-executed implementation". We could define implementation as turning strategic plans into action. If there are implementations that are not well executed, what does that mean? It might just mean there was a need for less sloppy management of implementation. But there might be problems caused by a poorly designed "delivery chain" and operational changes may be needed. But another argument for creating a distinction between implementation and execution is that it gives us the opportunity to raise the profile of monitoring, evaluation, and learning as processes useful for correcting and revising delivery. So, we can end up with a special made-up definition that says execution is defined as the successful delivery of a long-term strategic vision through implementation and any learning, refinement, and revision that is necessary.

Governments that are very effective deliverers of long-term visions and strategies may need to be good at the technical know-how of strategic planning, at the formal aspects of planning, budgeting, and at communicating strategic plans. This chapter, however, will also be highlighting

DOI: 10.4324/9781351045797-4

the strategic policy process and the associated capabilities that appear to be core to the strategic performance of government.

Introducing the data used in the analysis

The data analysed in this chapter is from an extraordinarily rich data set produced using expert judgements, which was published by the French Government. In this chapter, the latest dataset was used which was for 2016. The data, for 2016, and other information can be found on a website (IPD 2016).

Only some brief technical notes on the survey are provided here. The official name of the database is the "Institutional Profiles Database" (IPD), which has appeared in several editions since 2001. It was intended to enable researchers to investigate the relationship between economic growth and development and institutions.

The data are perception data collected by the French Directorate General of the Treasury (DG Trésor). The survey was completed by country or regional Economic Services (Services Économiques) of the French Ministry for the Economy and Finance (MEF). It covered 144 countries but data for 63 of them were selected for analysis. These 63 countries are the normal sample used in this book and were selected partly because of data availability in other databases.

The questions in the survey correspond to variables. The data were transformed into normalized values for the analysis conducted for this book. In this chapter, we rely on expert perceptions to provide data for composite indicators of long-term strategic visions for a set of policy sectors and of strategic delivery capabilities.

Guidance on strategy implementation

Bryson (2004) conceptualized implementation as the transformation of strategies into public value. He described the implementation process as involving a few actions. The first action is to get all the parties that need to be involved (the implementers) to accept their role in implementation. The second action, as he puts it, is "the development of a clear under-standing by implementers of what needs to be done and when, why, and by whom" (Bryson 2004, 239). We might call the first action the creation of the necessary commitment to the implementation process by those called on to implement strategy, and the second action might be seen as management setting up accountabilities for implementation.

Strategic vision statements could be seen as important for these two actions. Thus, a strategic vision statement that is expressed in inspiring terms might help with the commitment and motivation of individuals and organizations that need to be involved in implementation. On the other hand, a vision statement, however short it might be, could be quite informative. If individuals think about the vision statement and internalize it, then it might provide them with insights into the role they are expected to play. Presumably, all strategic vision statements can be located on the two dimensions of being inspiring and informative.

Bryson's own thinking on a strategic planning process envisaged a step of preparing "a clear and succinct description of what the organization (or community) should look like as it successfully implements its strategies, achieves its full potential, and creates significant public value" (Bryson 2004, 224). He advised the preparation of this description, which he named a vision of success statement, at a late and optional step in a strategic planning process. The vision of success statement has therefore little to do with a long-term strategic vision that acts as a starting point for strategic planning and mainly offers a target for implementation efforts.

The third action identified by Bryson was what he referred to as debugging. He explained this as follows (Bryson 2004, 239):

> The earliest steps in the strategic planning process are designed to ensure, insofar as possible, that the adopted strategies and plans do not contain any major flaws. But it is almost inconceivable that some important difficulties will not arise as strategies are put into practice. Key decision makers should pay regular attention to how implementation is proceeding in order to focus on any difficulties and plan how to address them.

The word "difficulties" in the context of an ongoing strategic implementation process is an interesting one. It is easy to imagine a formal system of monitoring and evaluation being conducted with a set of milestones drawn from a strategic plan and the managers searching for differences between what is happening and what was planned. In this case, we can think of difficulties as deviations (actual or projected) that trigger management concern and then work to eliminate the difficulties. Bryson defined any conscious evaluation process carried out to effect debugging as being a formative evaluation, that is, evaluation to provide feedback and allow corrections to be made in an ongoing implementation process.

The fourth action is summative evaluation. Summative evaluations can be formally defined as evaluations of a strategy after implementation has ended to decide if the planned strategic goals have been successfully achieved. (This is not the only possible definition of summative evaluation. For example, an alternative one, if there is no wish to link strategy evaluation to strategic goals, is an evaluation carried out at the very end to enable governments or public sector organizations to make judgements about whether a strategy had been worthwhile. This would appear to be a broader judgement than simply one of deciding if the intended strategic goals had been accomplished.) Bryson suggested that formative evaluations, intended to deal with difficulties of implementation, could also be relevant to new cycles of strategy formulation (strategizing).

To avoid confusion, we should note that Bryson (2004) defined the implementation process in such a way that it may include "adaptive learning". In this book, however, evaluation and learning by civil servants are presumed to be important for successful execution of long-term visions and strategies. They may be carried out once implementation has started to produce results that may be evaluated.

As a fifth action, Bryson makes an interesting point, which is paraphrased here, about an implementation action that may be needed when the people involved in implementation change or the situation changes. Sometimes changes require a rethink of strategic intent, but there are times when persistence in delivering a strategic intent is called for in the face of changes. Thus, it may be important to ensure that strategic intent is maintained despite adjusting implementation to accommodate new people or changes in the situation. That is, action is needed to maintain strategic intent while making changes to implementation.

The sixth type of action identified by Bryson is action to make organizational, or interorganizational, or community changes required to stabilize the strategic changes made by the implementation process. He gave the example of an organization that created a new list of its core values. A second example was an organization that made a set of changes, which included a revitalized core competency, a changed relationship with stakeholders, changed training courses, and a changed physical infrastructure (Figure 4.1).

The seventh (and final) action for the implementation of strategy was a review of the strategy. Having suggested there were no "once-and-for-all solutions", Bryson set out the options in a review as follows (Bryson 2004, 242):

> Leaders, managers, and planners must be alert to the nature and sources of possible challenges to implemented strategies; they should work to maintain still desirable strategies, to replace existing strategies with better ones when possible or necessary, and to terminate completely outmoded strategies.

Bryson elaborated further on strategic implementation in the public sector, exploring various issues in relation to links between strategy and budgeting, the form of implementation (new and revised programmes or strategic projects), project management and implementation, and types of approach to implementation.

In his consideration of strategic planning and budgeting, he referred to the idea that budgeting decisions are made in what he called political contexts but equally could have been called pluralistic settings. In other

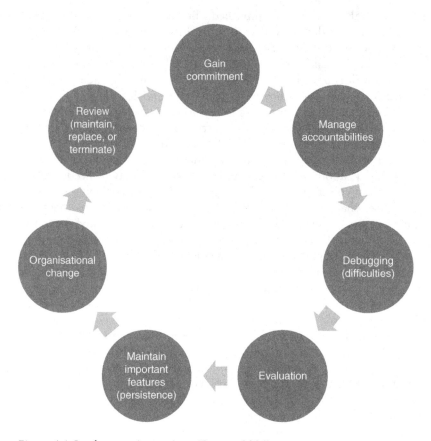

Figure 4.1 Implementation actions (Bryson 2004).

words, the budgetary allocations that get made reflect the interactions of competing interest groups all seeking to exert an influence on the budgetary decisions made. Among other things, Bryson counselled the careful selection of fights over budgets (Bryson 2004, 246):

> Given the number of players the budgeting attracts, particularly in the public sector, you cannot win every battle. Focus your attention on those budget allocation decisions that are crucial to moving desired strategies forward.

The corollary of the principle of careful selection of budget fights is that governments that are taking strategy seriously will seek to organize things so that strategic planning can generally easily influence budgetary decisions.

Research, which was published just after Bryson's (2004) book, surveyed local authorities in the USA, and the survey questions included some probing how budgets and strategic plans were linked. Based on their findings it might be said that the local authorities engaged in strategic planning seemed to have often got some degree of linkage in place (Poister and Streib 2005, 53):

> More than 80 percent indicated the annual budget prepared by their chief administrators strongly supported their strategic goals and objectives, that their capital budgets reflected these goals, and that "new money" in particular was targeted to achieving strategic goals and objectives ... . Slightly fewer of these respondents, on the order of 75 percent, reported the strategic plan had a strong influence on the budget requests submitted by department heads and other managers, and that their city councils considered strategic goals and objectives when reviewing annual budgets.

A noteworthy finding of the analysis was that targeting "new money in the budget... to achieving your strategic goals and objectives" correlated with beneficial impacts of strategic planning (Poister and Streib 2005, 54). This might suggest that government having separate dedicated budgets for strategic planning might be a way of ensuring government strategies can be implemented and are not held up by lack of money.

His discussion of approaches to implementation frequently acknowledges the political difficulties for implementation that arise because of plural interests and the presence of significant possibilities of resistance to change. One example of this is the recommendation he made about using a coalition of implementers, advocates, and interest groups. This coalition may help with making the implementation of strategies effective. The coalition may defend the implementation process. He extolled the importance of courage in the face of resistance. As well as advocating the building of coalitions to support implementation processes, he suggested the taking of various actions to reduce resistance (including training, problem-solving groups, and ceremonies).

Bryson also addressed the realities of dealing with people during an implementation process (Bryson 2004, 258): "Give special attention to the problem of easing out, working around, or avoiding people who not likely to help the change effort for whatever reason".

In discussing the choice of direct and staged implementation approaches in situations where strategic changes are being implemented in multiple sites, Bryson mostly dwelt on technical difficulties and political difficulties in implementation. (Another parallel set of concepts might be difficulties caused by a lack of knowledge and difficulties caused by resistance to proposals for change.) For example, Bryson suggested that if neither the technical nor the political difficulties were too much, then direct implementation in all relevant sites at the same time might be best.

If technical difficulties are considerable but political difficulties are not an issue, then begin with a pilot project to enable more knowledge to be gained. When facing considerable political difficulties but negligible technical difficulties, he suggests beginning implementation with a demonstration project, which is, as the name suggests, an approach which can show all interested parties that the proposed strategic changes do in fact work.

Going deeper?

In this chapter up to this point, the concern has been mostly to understand the steps and choices to be made by government practitioners during a strategic implementation process. In the remainder of this chapter the concern changes. It is now to isolate the factors that really matter in the case of governments trying to deliver long-term strategic visions. What are the factors that create strategic effectiveness as measured by national performance, meaning a combination of the Human Development Index and the Environmental Performance Index? Any government situation in which long-term strategic visions and government strategies are being delivered, there will be an infinity of conditions (factors) present, but can we isolate a small number that make a big difference to national performance? This will mean getting to a position where we can ignore an infinity of them that have negligible effects.

First, we look at long-term strategic visions for specific policy sectors, and how these relate, if at all, to national performance. Then, second, we turn our attention to strategic delivery capabilities.

Long-term strategic visions for policy sectors

We can make what are probably obvious points that a strategic vision can create a sense of direction and enable more alignment and integration of activities. Less obviously, governments can use the preparation of a long-term strategic vision as an opportunity to engage stakeholders in the process and therefore build support and legitimacy for their attempts to develop a country. The OECD, which mainly has member countries with a high GDP per capita, recently reported that nearly all of them had some sort of strategic vision document (OECD 2020, 46–47). Looking more generally at a wide range of countries, we can note the existence of well-publicized long-term strategic visions, such as those published by Saudi Arabia and the United Arab Emirates. It is also possible to find long-term strategic visions for basic public services such as health and education or the environment or other specific policy sectors.

As might be expected, governments with long-term strategic visions in place, as reported by business executives in the survey carried out for the World Economic Forum's Competitiveness Index, were also governments that expert data for 2016 suggested had strong long-term strategic visions in specific policy sectors. This was a moderately strong association. These policy sectors were human capital (education, health, etc.), territorial and urban planning, protection of the environment, and international and regional integration. Governments that had weak strategic visions in the policy sectors tended not to have a government long-term vision in place (as perceived by respondents to the survey of business executives). These governments included Brazil, Paraguay, Peru, Greece, Romania, and Tunisia. Governments with strong strategic visions in policy sectors and long-term visions in place were to be found among the Gulf States (Bahrain, Qatar, Saudi Arabia, and UAE). Even though they did not have government long-term visions in place to the same extent (as perceived by business executives) as most of the Gulf States, the governments of Canada, China, Germany, and the Netherlands were notable for their strong strategic visions in policy sectors.

There was a slight correlation between governments having relatively strong long-term strategic visions for policy sectors and higher values of performance on national development (HDI and EPI). Governments with high values on both included Canada, Belgium, Germany, and the Netherlands. We can contrast these governments with those of Cambodia, Egypt, Indonesia, Pakistan, and Vietnam, which were rated as having weak long-term strategic visions in policy sectors and low values for their national performance (HDI and EPI). In this matter, the Government of China was rather unusual: it had been rated by experts as having very strong long-term visions for policy sectors, but it was among the governments with a relatively low value for national performance. Another similarly positioned government was Qatar; its national performance was slightly better than that of China and the long-term strategic visions in policy sectors were rated as slightly weaker than in the case of China. In contrast, the government of Greece was relatively unusual in a different way: it had a moderately good record in terms of national performance, but its long-term strategic visions in policy sectors were rated by experts as being relatively very weak.

The finding that the strength of long-term strategic visions in policy sectors is slightly correlated with national performance (as measured by HDI and EPI) is a promising finding. It suggests that governments that strengthen their long-term strategic visions in policy sectors might find that their national development gets better. It also suggests that steering a country's governance using long-term strategic visions for policy sectors is only part of the explanation for variations in national performance. The political will that compels civil servants to take the idea of strategic government seriously is probably essential. Another factor that might matter for governmental performance is the strength of the strategic policy process, in which key delivery capabilities are lodged.

Political will

It is no longer unusual or particularly controversial to say that sound governance requires government leaders to have a commitment to delivering a long-term strategic vision for a better national future. In other words, there is a need for political will. It is useful to see some evidence of what this political will might look like. The example here is the case of the Russian Federation and its planning for long-term economic development in 2012 and 2013.

In May 2012, the Russian President Vladimir Putin signed the Executive Order on Long-Term State Economic Policy. This ordered the Federal Government to deliver five targets:

1   25 million new jobs by 2020
2   Increased investment
3   Increased share of GDP for high-technology and science sectors by 2018
4   Increased labour productivity by 2018
5   A higher ranking for Russia in the ease of doing business index (World Bank) by 2018

Each of the targets was specified to give more precision about what was expected of government, about what was to be achieved and, presumably, to facilitate the process of monitoring. For example, the new jobs were to be "modern" and "highly-productive" jobs, and the increased investment was to be increased by at least 25% of GDP by 2015 and by 27% of GDP by 2018. The very fact that some effort was being made to be precise and to ensure that progress towards the targets was measurable suggested that the Russian president was serious about the targets being delivered.

Incidentally, this same Executive Order instructed the government to "approve a draft federal law on state strategic planning, coordinating strategic management and budget planning measures, and submit it to the State Duma by October 1, 2012" (Federal Government of Russia 2012).

The existence of political will to take strategic goals and planning seriously was also suggested by the publication of discussions at meetings the Russian president held on the action plans federal executive agencies had prepared to ensure his national social and economic development targets were met. At one of the meetings, held in the Kremlin on 7 June 2013, the president began by reminding those present of a review conducted a month earlier and the reason for the planning (Federal Government of Russia 2013a):

> Exactly a month ago now, we reviewed the results of this first year of work to implement the presidential executive orders of May 7, 2012. Our discussion was concrete and got straight to the substance. We also identified the problems that have come up in our work together.

Let me repeat that implementing these orders is a top priority for all of our work, for the Government and all the ministries, and for the authorities at every level. The imperative is to produce real results and work not for the sake of reports and documents, but in the interests of our people.

We agreed at that meeting that the ministries and agencies would present updated action plans for the coming five years, with a year-by-year breakdown of work. We agreed on a deadline of one month for getting these action plans ready.

He had looked through the documentation of the action plans just prior to the meeting and remarked that this planning was essential if the quality of public administration was to improve. Arguably, his next remarks were bound to have sent a clear signal to the government that he was determined that the plans would deliver results:

> Unfortunately, the content and quality of these documents still does not meet the required standards. I therefore propose giving the ministries another 2–3 weeks to revise them, and I ask you to get more actively involved in this work.

His critique of the documents was that they were vague, did not properly address the targets he set, did not contain clear actions, did not include performance indicators, and did not assign responsibility for the delivery of actions. He said (Federal Government of Russia 2013a):

> First, these documents contain too much vague and general wording. ... Second, I sometimes get the impression that some agencies live entirely in their own little world, look solely to their own narrow problems ... For example, the sector-based agencies have all but ignored one of the orders' key objectives, which was to create modern jobs ... Third, we agreed that the action plans would set out the specific measures the ministries will take. Let me stress that by 'measures' I mean real action: laws that take effect and actually work, new plants, hospitals, schools, perinatal centres, cultural facilities, housing for large families. This is what I mean by 'measures', not reports, meetings and working groups. Those things are the routine and are of no interest to our people. To give an example: the Culture Ministry's action plan in many cases (not always, but often) is vague and contains no specific targets or result measurements in all of the different organizational and methodological areas. Other ministries have similar problems. I will not list them all now. Fourth, a number of documents do not support the set objectives with specific indicators. This means that no one can ultimately objectively measure and check the results achieved. ... Fifth,

it has to be absolutely clear who bears personal responsibility for specific results achieved, or for disruptions to work, so that we know who to hold accountable later and so that we do not end up with people looking for excuses to explain why things went wrong. Specific officials either have to be ready to take responsibility for the results, or should start thinking right now about changing their careers. We need the actual names, specific personal responsibility, ...

It is interesting that he stressed that government agencies were living "entirely in their own little world, look solely to their own narrow problems". This is, of course, the accusation that government effectiveness is damaged if parts of the government machinery and civil service are working in "silos". If the government agencies do this, and if they only pay attention to their "own narrow problems", then of course there can be little co-operation and co-ordination occurring within the system of public administration.

The president also promised public accountability of ministers for results and required disclosure of the plans to the public. This was saying that accountability and transparency were important ingredients in how this process was to take place (Federal Government of Russia 2013a):

Let me repeat that when the year is up, I will meet with each minister and hold a public hearing of the reports on the results achieved. Also, we agreed that the action plans on implementing the executive orders would be open and public. I'm forced to bring it to your attention that this is still not yet the case. I therefore ask you to revise the plans and immediately make them public.

In a meeting the president held a few days later with several ministers (Interior Minister; Justice Minister; Civil Defence, Emergencies and Disaster Relief Minister; and the Defence Minister) and various senior officials, he again gave some tough feedback on the quality of the action planning documents (Federal Government of Russia 2013b):

What I have seen in your plans disappoints me, to be honest, but at the same time, I am pleased that I launched this whole process because it's only when you start looking at what and how we plan that you become more aware of the way we work and the way we formulate our objectives. Ultimately, this will help us to make the changes required so as to achieve practical results in our work.

He wanted action plans that had "concrete objectives, the simpler the better". He wanted plans that made clear what results could be expected for each year. He wanted the plans to concentrate on things of "real public importance". He wanted them to plan in line with the framework of the budget that had been approved. And while recognizing the special issues facing some of the ministries in terms of what they could make public, he wanted them to be as open to the public, as transparent, as possible (Federal Government of Russia 2013b):

> … your ministries are in a specific situation in which many of the areas you cover are confidential in nature and in some cases are classified as state secrets. We therefore agreed that, regarding publicity, some specific conditions would apply to your action plans. But let me stress that your work must be open for the public as much as possible, especially as concerns the strategic decisions that will guarantee our national interests and strengthen social guarantees for military servicemen and other groups of people working in your ministries.

The final comment worth making here is that over the period 2010–2019 the Russian Government was outstanding in a comparison of improvements in estimates of government effectiveness published by the World Bank as part of its set of Worldwide Governance Indicators (Chapter 6). If the president's commitment to strategic effectiveness, evident in these two meetings in June 2013, was sustained then part of the explanation might be hypothesized as being the strength of political will at the top of the public governance system. It seems likely that political will would need to underpin the strength of every stage of the strategic policy process.

Strategic policy process

In recent years, the OECD has formulated principles and suggestions for improving public governance. It has explored how this might be done through surveys, and meetings of ministers and public officials. This has led to its view that a whole-of-government approach is good, and it has advocated the role of the "centre of government" in creating and sustaining a whole-of-government approach. It summarized the strategic role of the centre of government as follows (OECD 2020, 46):

> The strategic role of Centre of Government (CoG) has been expanding over the course of the last decade due to the increasing complexity of policy-making and the emergence of whole-of-government strategy-setting and implementation, strategic monitoring of government performance over the medium term, and strategic issues management.

It would be wrong to presume that the OECD thought that an effective centre of government necessitates a centralized and command-and-control style of government. They did stress the benefits of a coordinated response but considered that change management could take the form of co-ordination to achieve integration that is both bottom-up and top-down.

Of course, a whole-of-government approach becomes more and more necessary if the problems of the public become more complex and require cross-ministerial policymaking. The OECD has also publicized the concept of "strategic agility" and has recently linked this to the ability of governments to manage change and innovation (OECD 2020, 56):

> Public-sector innovation is about introducing and implementing new ideas whose impact help promote and improve sound public governance by reinforcing the strategic agility and forward-looking nature of the state.

It might be commented that strategic agility is regarded as a good thing and as requiring, for example, the ability to reallocate and re-use resources and capabilities very swiftly. Strategic agility can be useful for keeping up with a dynamic environment which creates a fast-changing context for strategy, but also can be vital in responding to events calling for strategic crisis management (as was the case when the coronavirus pandemic struck the world in 2020).

The extent of the delivery capabilities of any government, then, can be expected to vary according to its capability for coordinating and creating collaboration within and across government departments, and up and down levels of government, as well as its capability for trying out new policies and learning from delivery experience. A government's strategic delivery capabilities may be defined as capabilities it has learnt during the strategic policy process and used to execute strategic visions and plans. These capabilities matter in aligning the actions and activities of civil servants, government departments, government agencies, and all other government entities with long-term strategic visions of government.

Good management can be used to strengthen and reinforce strategic delivery capabilities. For example, ministers can agree with their senior civil servants a suitably small number of top strategic priorities for management attention so that there can be a clear focus on management attention. Strategic planning can be used to transform the strategic intent contained in long-term strategic visions into proposed courses of action by civil servants and government departments. Systems for allocating and managing budgets and performance management can make it more likely that proposals contained in strategic plans are implemented. Monitoring and evaluation systems linked to performance management can increase the likelihood that learning takes place and improves the results of planned change and innovation. This learning may relate to how different government departments coordinate and collaborate in a delivery chain. Monitoring and evaluation can also deliver the information that policymakers need to revise their commitments and adjust policies.

These remarks have implications for the design and conduct of strategic planning in countries where whole-of-government approaches are being used and strategic agility is practiced. Strategic planning needs to be well-supported by use of data to identify population needs, by effective budgetary governance, by digital strategies and systems (to handle the need for speedy communications and analysis), and by strong monitoring and evaluation systems (which create feedback loops for learning during the implementation and delivery process).

A composite index for the concept of a "strategic policy process" was created using six variables drawn from the IPD (2016). It was created as a simple, additive, and unweighted index. The variables are shown in Table 4.1. There were many moderate and a couple of high correlations between the six variables.

Table 4.1 National performance (HDI and EPI) by strategic policy process (normalized values)

National performance (HDI and EPI)	Government's strategic policy process		
	Weak(−2.5 to −0.51)(N = 17)	Medium(−0.5 to 0.49)(N = 25)	Strong(0.50–1.5) (N = 21)
Good (0.5–1.5)	USA	Denmark, Estonia, Greece, Ireland, Spain	Australia, Austria, Belgium, Canada, Czech Republic, Finland, France, Germany, Italy, Japan, South Korea, the Netherlands, New Zealand, Norway, Portugal, Singapore, Slovenia, Sweden, UK
Modest (−0.5 to 0.49)	Chile, Saudi Arabia	Argentina, Bahrain, Brazil, Colombia, Costa Rica, Hungary, Kuwait, Malaysia, Mexico, Poland, Qatar, Romania, Russian Federation, Turkey, Ukraine, UAE	Lithuania
Poor (−2.5 to −0.51)	Algeria, Cambodia, Egypt, Georgia, Ghana, India, Indonesia, Mozambique, Pakistan, Paraguay, Peru, South Africa, Tunisia, Venezuela	Bangladesh, Nigeria, Oman, Venezuela	China

1　Degree of coordination/collaboration between ministries
2　Degree of coordination/collaboration within administrations
3　Is public policy experimentation prior to its general implementation a common practice?
4　Is the evaluation of public policies a common practice?
5　Authorities' capacity to adapt policies to changes in the economic and social contexts
6　Are the actions of the public authorities in line with a long-term strategic vision?

It is to be expected that these factors are correlated with each other. For example, presuming that there is a clear long-term strategic vision, the existence of extensive and robust monitoring and evaluation of the policies that have been formulated to deliver the vision would seem to be obviously required to ensure that the civil service is acting in line with the vision. Likewise, extensive and robust monitoring and evaluation could be very important in stimulating coordination and collaboration among civil servants and across government departments. Public policy experimentation could be valuable in enabling the civil service to refine and adjust actions so that viable delivery chains are improved and made more fit for the purpose of delivering the long-term strategic visions. If the civil service is to persist in action to deliver a long-term strategic vision it may need to be good at adapting policies as circumstances change so that the revised policies continue to serve as suitable means for delivering the vision. Adapting to changes of circumstances would be a major factor in attributing agility to the government. Such adaptability ought to be assisted by frequent and robust evaluation practices. In aggregate, these variables ought to go a long way towards explaining what is needed for a strong strategic policy process.

It is interesting to note that surveys have shown that centres of government are much more likely to be involved in strategic planning than they are in the monitoring and implementation of government policy. If monitoring and implementation can be deployed to include public policy experimentation and public policy evaluation, then learning and strategic agility can, potentially, be boosted. It is possible that the governments of the world need to give centres of government more responsibility for monitoring and implementation and thus to make a whole-of-government approach to learning and strategic agility more feasible.

Do strategic delivery capabilities make a difference?

The composite index of the strategic policy process, which develops and requires strategic delivery capabilities, is very strongly correlated with both the Human Development Index of the United Nations and the Environmental Performance Index. It is also strongly correlated with national performance (i.e., a composite index comprising HDI and EPI) (Table 4.1).

One of the many possible alternative interpretations of the pattern of multiple correlations between the six variables in the strategic policy process index is that good national performance is produced as follows. First, good national performance is more likely where the actions of civil servants are aligned to the long-term strategic vision of government and where there is a strong capacity for adaptability to changing economic and social contexts. Second, frequent and robust evaluations allow learning to take place so that alignment and adaptability can be increased and improved. Third, evaluation allows coordination and collaboration to be improved and this enhances alignment with long-term strategic vision of government. Fourth, an experimental orientation increases the need for, and use of, evaluation and feeds into a government's capacity for adaptability. In fact, if this interpretation is along the right lines, then frequent and robust evaluation, combined with a clear and strong long-term strategic vision, are the essential underpinnings of a high-performing government (Figure 4.2).

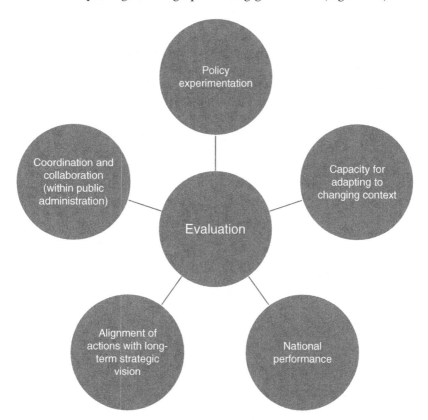

Figure 4.2 A conceptualization of a strong strategic policy process.

Note: Bivariate analysis found correlations between many pairs of variables but in the figure only correlations between policy evaluation and the rest are shown. Two strong correlations were found. The first was a correlation between alignment of actions with strategic vision and coordination and collaboration (within public administration) (r = 0.86). The second was a correlation between alignment of actions with strategic vision and evaluation (r = 0.70).

The performance results of some countries may be affected by special factors. For example, Ireland was one of a group of countries that achieved a relatively high economic growth rate between 2005 and 2018 and higher than might have been expected on the grounds of public investment alone. The special factor in the case of Ireland might have been an inflow of foreign direct investment, which surged to about 80% of GDP in 2015 (Figure 4.3). This was accompanied by a massive increase in gross national income in 2015. This would have impacted on the calculation of the Human Development Index because it included gross national income per capita as an indicator of a decent standard of living.

Strategic agility

There have been several references to agility already in this chapter. At the outset of the analysis conducted for this book, it might have been speculated that some governments are strategic by virtue of clear long-term intentions (by having, for example, a long-term strategic vision and long-term strategic goals), by being good at aligning and coordinating actions though strategic plans, and by being good at controlling the delivery of strategic plans. This could be seen as a type of "strategic performance management" focused on long-term performance. It might also be seen as a form of strategic planning suitable for New Public Management (the latter being a concept developed to make sense of the governance reforms began in the 1980s in countries like New Zealand,

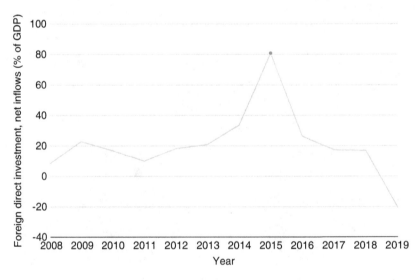

Figure 4.3 Ireland foreign direct investment.

Note: The data for this figure was published by the World Bank as a World Development Indicator. Available at: https://databank.worldbank.org [7 January 2021].

the United Kingdom, and the United States). It might then be conjectured that some governments had moved on from this New Public Management style strategic planning to also become strategically agile, which in some way implies not only being capable of efficiency and effectiveness but also being able to cope with a high pace of change and with sudden change and even crisis.

To some extent, this speculation might be seen as anticipated by debates at an international workshop held by the OECD in Paris in November 2011. Those taking part seem to have believed New Public Management had serious weaknesses. The report of the workshop not only labelled New Public Management a failure but also raised the need to move towards a more "strategic state" which offered long-termism and agility (OECD 2012, 5):

> The failure of New Public Management. With NPM, policy making and its execution were separated. This has not worked; a new model is required. Do we move away from NPM and toward leadership and a more strategic state? It is important to discard what has not worked. But if there is to be a new approach, there is a need to overcome the trends of past decades which stand in the way of new approaches, such as management at the expense of policy.

It was envisaged that strategic agility could be the answer to governance in a time of uncertainty and ambiguity and would require changes in management systems and a move towards engaging citizens, businesses, and communities. For this to be possible, public governance would have to address the legacy of New Public Management, which had fostered decentralization, specialization, and autonomy. (In effect, New Public Management had created fragmentation of public governance and strategic agility needed this fragmentation to be reversed.)

Among the questions identified for further debate were (OECD 2012, 9):

- Resource flexibility is fundamental to strategic agility – how can it be achieved?
- Leadership unity is also fundamental – how can that be achieved?
- How to sustain a long-term vision across political cycles?
- … Can strategic agility be applied in different country settings?

The idea of resource flexibility can be fitted into Philip Heymann's model of strategic management in government. He pointed out that government organizations need legislative support to get resources and authority and whenever the organization needed a change of strategic direction it would need a plan to change organizational structures and resources, as well as gain or change external support from stakeholders, accordingly. This reflected his definition of strategy as being a set of desirable goals plus a plan to achieve them, and his definition of a plan as (i) actions to ensure organizational capacity existed, (ii) actions to ensure support of external stakeholders, and (iii) the sequence of actions to achieve the goals. Based on this thinking we might define strategic agility as being where government quickly and easily changes its organizational capacity (and resources) and its external support (provided) by stakeholders either to take advantage of new opportunities and deal with threats or to adjust to new strategic goals.

Indeed, strategic management might be seen as intrinsically agile compared to older management systems because it explicitly required attention to be paid to events and developments as part of situational analysis and entailed planning of resources to deliver strategic goals. If the goals were changed, a new plan would be needed, and resources would be replanned. This might involve switching resources from one activity to another.

But it is one thing to conceptualize strategic management in this way and another to deliver strategic agility. In practice, as some public organizations found when using the EFQM Excellence Model (Chapter 7), the most difficult changes to make are those in resources and partnerships ("enabler" factors) and society results (what the organization achieves in relation to local, national, and international society as appropriate).

How, then, is agility to be achieved? Maybe there are many different "management tools" that can be used to promote and many variables that can favour or inhibit agility. For example, some budgetary systems in government may reinforce rigidity or incrementalism, rather than agility. As we saw above, the OECD workshop seemed to identify the strategic state with a capacity for agility in public governance, and we might therefore suggest that three of the factors used in this study to define a strategic state are also sources of agility in strategic policymaking:

1   An experimental approach to policy implementation (a management tool)
2   Evaluation of public policies (a management tool)
3   Adapting policies to changes in the economic and social contexts (capacity to adapt)

Using the Institutional Profile Database and examining its 2016 data for 63 countries in the book's usual sample, it was found that all three of the factors were intercorrelated. For example, governments that commonly introduced polices using experimentation in advance of full implementation tended to be ones that commonly evaluated public policies.

And strong capacity to adapt polices to economic and social changes was correlated with a public policy evaluation being done commonly.

An agility index was constructed for 2016 using these three factors, each being weighted equally. Countries that scored highly on this agility index were Singapore, Norway, Sweden, and the UK. In contrast, Nigeria, Paraguay, Venezuela, Algeria, Tunisia, and Kuwait were scored as lowest in agility. The agility of governments with strategic state characteristics will be considered further in Chapter 6.

Back to practice guidance

If the six variables are grouped thematically, the strategic delivery capabilities of the strategic policy process can be presented as in Figure 4.4.

A government with highly developed strategic delivery capabilities could be described as highly capable in aligning actions and activities with long-term strategic visions, in operating a whole-of-government approach based on cooperation and collaboration, in learning from delivery, and in being adaptable.

The guidance on implementation given by Bryson and others arguably has more meaning when linked to these capabilities. Implementation planning by managers that allocates actionable elements of a strategy to individuals who are made accountable for their delivery and the setting of deadlines and performance reporting arrangements could be seen as

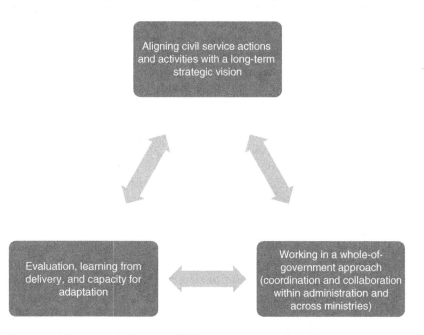

Figure 4.4 Strategic delivery capabilities in the strategic policy process.

contributing to a government capability in aligning actions and activities with long-term strategic visions. The use of monitoring, formative and summative evaluation processes, and reviews at the end of implementation could contribute to a capability in learning from delivery. The use of maintenance actions, as described by Bryson, could be important in keeping civil servants aligned to the long-term strategic visions of government.

Organizational changes to stabilize strategic changes might also improve the functioning of delivery chains and thus make sure the actions of people are aligned with the long-term strategic vision of the government. In other words, the advice given about implementation actions may be helpfully understood as important for their consequences for specific strategic delivery capabilities. Budgetary allocations are evidently very important for the alignment of actions and activities with the long-term strategic vision. Finally, the choices made about people and implementation approaches can be tactically astute or tactically foolish and have obvious consequences for the degree of cooperation and collaboration within government's administrative structures.

Conclusions

In a strategic state, the long-term strategic visions of policy sectors would be providing the direction for the work of the civil service. In order to be effective in delivering the strategic visions the key strategic delivery capabilities of the civil service would be: (1) aligning actions and activities, (2) organizational integration based on cooperation and collaboration, and (3) the ability to operate in an agile manner by means of evaluation and learning from delivery experiences and experiments.

In this chapter, government purpose was investigated through the concept of strong long-term strategic visions in policy sectors. These visions were expected to require strong strategic policy processes (i.e., strong delivery capability). In fact, both long-term strategic visions and strategic policy processes were statistically associated with good national performances, with strategic policy processes having a strong correlation with national performance. It may also be worth repeating here the observation made by Michael Barber and quoted in Chapter 3, delivery needs strategy otherwise delivery is incoherent. If we define strategy as strategic goals and a plan for achieving them, then strategy contains purpose. So, we can deduce from Michael Barber's observation that long-term strategic visions provide the basis for purposeful steering of government actions and ensure their coherence. The visions also provide a clear point of reference for evaluations that are part of the execution of strategic visions.

The chapter reported that there were multiple correlations between the variables used to construct an index of the strategic policy process. It was admitted that these multiple correlations could be interpreted in many ways. The way chosen here placed evaluation at the heart of the strategic policy process. Moreover, evaluation was assumed to support learning. Not only might evaluation and learning tighten up alignment of actions with visions. Evaluation could also feed into government's capacity for adaptability faced by changing economic and social contexts. Interestingly, management consultants advise businesses and businesspeople to be adaptable, which may be defined as an ability to learn (Brassey et al. 2021). People in businesses are recommended to connect their learning to a framework provided by a "strong sense of purpose". The implication is that without clear purpose people find it difficult to separate the urgent and the important. This difficulty may well also be present in governments that have no clear long-term strategic vision – civil servants are unclear as to what is important and what is not. Learning needs to focus on what is important.

Creating a "safe" learning environment for civil servants may take place alongside efforts to ensure more transparency and accountability. These efforts may be at their strongest where there is a political commitment to open government and responsiveness to the public. Presumably, civil servants need to accept responsibility for delivering the long-term strategic visions of government and this may be problematic if there is a culture of "compliance", or a culture of fear created by a political "blame game". We can hypothesize that the political leadership in a government can have a major influence on the creation of a safe learning environment, and that the rise of populist politicians, and populist governments, may have negatively affected the readiness of civil servants to take responsibility for delivery of strategic visions and policies.

References

Brassey, J., De Smet, A., Kothari, A., Lavoie, J., Mugayar-Baldocchi, M., & Zolley, S. (2021) *Future proof: Solving the 'adaptability paradox' for the long term*. August 2021. McKinsey & Company. Available at: https://www.mckinsey.com [4 September 2021].

Bryson, J.M. (2004) *Strategic planning for public and nonprofit organizations: A guide to strengthening and sustaining organizational achievement*, 3rd edition. San Francisco: Jossey-Bass.

Federal Government of Russia (2012) Executive order on long-term state economic policy: Vladimir Putin signed Executive Order on Long-Term State Economic Policy. 7 May 2012. Available at: http://en.kremlin.ru/catalog/keywords/125/events/15232 [20 September 2021].

Federal Government of Russia (2013a) Federal ministries presented to the President their action plans for implementing the May 2012 executive orders. 7 June 2013. The Kremlin. Available at: http://en.kremlin.ru/events/president/news/18277 [11 March 2018].

Federal Government of Russia (2013b) Meeting on ministries' plans to reach the social and economic development targets set by the president. 10 June 2013. The Kremlin. Available at: http://eng.kremlin.ru/news/5553 [11 March 2018].

Heymann, P. (1987) *The politics of public management*. New Haven and London: Yale University Press.

IPD (2016) Institutional Profiles Database. Available at: http://www.cepii.fr/institutions/en/ipd.asp [28 August 2018].

OECD (2012) *International workshop "strategic agility for strong societies and economies": Summary and issues for further debate*. Paris: OECD Publishing.

OECD (2020) *Policy framework on sound public governance: Baseline features of governments that work well*. Paris: OECD Publishing.

Poister, T.H. & Streib, G. (2005) Elements of strategic planning and management in municipal government: Status after two decades. *Public Administration Review*, 65(1), 45–56.

5 The Whole-of-Society Approach

Introduction

Ideas of bringing the public and stakeholders in civil society into processes of government planning and engaging them in the implementation processes have become widely espoused. When "Pakistan Vision 2025" was published in 2014, the Planning Commission of Pakistan reported that a wide range of stakeholders had been consulted. In November 2013, the government had held a national consultative conference, which had been chaired by Pakistan's prime minister. This had been followed up through consultative workshops in the provinces of Pakistan. The resultant vision document endorsed participative planning and citizen empowerment (Government of Pakistan 2014, 2–3):

> The reality is that the quality of planning is one of the key determinants of the speed of action and desired outcomes. Over time, the nature and role of planning has undergone a major transformation. Today the national planning process is more participatory, collaborative, people and market oriented. Plans succeed when they manifest the aspirations of a nation, empower the citizens, and especially the private sector, to play their respective roles, provide equal equitable opportunities to all and assign a very well-defined role to government as a supporter, facilitator, regulator and performance driven service provider.

The best practice is now a partnership of government and society, which we might call a whole-of-society approach. The Singapore Government referred to this as a whole-of-nation approach in a recent long-term low-emissions development strategy (Government of Singapore 2020, 3): "The Government, individuals, households and businesses must work together in a whole-of-nation effort".

Government may take the initiative to create a whole-of-society approach, by reaching out to the public and businesses and non-governmental associations and organizations. It does this, ideally, to

DOI: 10.4324/9781351045797-5

address public purposes in the interests of all. The government may ask citizens and organizations to align what they do with the government's long-term strategic visions and its strategies. The government may seek practical external support in terms of resources and capabilities to supplement those possessed by government (World Bank 1997).

In this chapter, we focus on the support government hopes to get for its long-term strategic visions from the public and from its partners in national development. The first part of the chapter looks at government and society. It then reviews some research into the nature of the public. This is followed by examples of governments that have tried to get the public to participate in the development of long-term strategic visions and plans. The concluding section is an analysis of the extent of whole-of-society approaches and the conditions and potential implications of a strong or weak approach.

What does society want from government?

In thinking about how governments use a whole-of-society approach, we need a realistic understanding of what society expects of government. It would be very easy to assume this relationship between government and society is obvious and unproblematic. At the very least, we should acknowledge the variety of conceptions of government. In the following quote, the state (government) is presented from four perspectives (Dewey 1927, 4–5):

> According to one tradition, which claims to derive from Aristotle, the state is associated and harmonized life lifted to its highest potency ... According to another view, it is just one of many social institutions, having a narrow but an important function, that of arbiter in the conflict of other social units. Every group springs out of and realizes a positive human interest; the church, religious values; guilds, unions and corporations material economic interests, and so on. The state, however, has no concern of its own; its purpose is formal, like that of the leader of the orchestra who plays no instrument and makes no music, but who serves to keep other players who do produce music in unison with one another. Still a third view has it that the state is organized oppression, at once a social excrescence, a parasite and a tyrant. A fourth is that it is an instrument more or less clumsy for keeping individuals from quarrelling too much with one another.

The last of the four could easily be a concise expression of the ideas of Thomas Hobbes.

To paraphrase his ideas, people want and use power to get, and to hang on to, riches and status. He saw the use of power for personal advantage as a threat to others. He claimed the existence of a desire by competitors "to kill, subdue, supplant, or repel the other" (Hobbes 1962, 123). Some people might want a peaceful life and protection, but not everybody was the same. Some people were said to be "needy" and "hardy"; that presumably meant that violence and conflict were tamed but not entirely suppressed (Hobbes 1962, 124):

> On the contrary needy men, and hardy, not contented with their present condition, as also, all men that are ambitious of military command, are inclined to continue the causes of war; and to stir up trouble and sedition: for there is no honour military but by war; nor any such hope to mend an ill game, as by causing a new shuffle.

Taking any society in existence today, we can probably find people who have fears and anxieties about disorder and violence and want to feel more secure and safer than they do. We can probably always find others who have strong aspirations to get on in life and want to have a better life. No doubt, there are many people who want both safety and security and opportunities. Ordinary members of the public might, therefore, have two criteria for judging any government's effectiveness – whether it ensures safety and security and whether it ensures opportunities for a better life.

The security of an individual is not only threatened by poverty due to economic forces and by violence between nations or within communities but also increasingly threatened by the climate crisis. And individualistic ideas of wanting a better life can also be complemented in modern times by the utopian idea of better lives for all – "leaving no one behind" – which was recently articulated and endorsed in relation to the 2030 Agenda of the United Nations.

Serving the public, supporting the government

Governments should serve the public. This perspective was articulated by the United Nation's Secretary-General Kofi Annan in an address to the opening meeting of the United Nations General Assembly in 1999 (Annan 1999):

> The State is now widely understood to be the servant of its people, and not vice versa. At the same time, individual sovereignty – and by this I mean the human rights and fundamental freedoms of each and every individual as enshrined in our Charter – has been enhanced by a renewed consciousness of the right of every individual to control his or her own destiny.

Related sentiments about putting citizens first and working to make their lives better are to be found in the speeches of many country leaders.

Here is one example, from the Prime Minister of Cambodia in 2008, speaking at a Cabinet Meeting (Hun 2008, 41):

> There is no goal more sacred than improving the lives of our people and no other task more rewarding. It is not for our rhetoric but for our record of good and progressive work that we will be remembered. Good, selfless work in the cause of upliftment of our people is its own reward and will surely earn merits for our lives. Therefore, I once again urge you to take up the tasks ahead of us with utmost earnestness, sincerity, devotion and to the best of your abilities.

To serve people well, a modern government is arguably to some degree, a "populist" government. A populist government can be defined as one which seeks to serve people so that they achieve their aspirations. Some would go further and say a populist government seeks to deliver the will of the people on the basis that the public is sovereign. Both these definitions mean government must listen to the people's concerns and aspirations. It must promise to work on the public's main problems, main concerns. Obviously, not everyone in the public has the same concerns and aspirations nor can government do everything that is wanted (Heymann 1987). Government needs to set priorities to be effective. What priorities? Some governments may prioritize a protective function in governance, providing help and assistance to those who are struggling to maintain themselves or are in danger; other governments may prioritize guaranteeing conditions in which some individuals may be richer than others and in which private enterprise and personal initiative is relatively unconstrained. Of course, governments may try to pursue several priorities simultaneously and may set about balancing them and even reconciling them.

One of the challenges for public governance noted by the World Bank is how to ensure all voices in the public are listened to when government decides priorities and policies (World Bank 1997, 110):

> In nearly all societies the needs and preferences of the wealthy and powerful are well reflected in official policy goals and priorities. But this is rarely true of the poor and the marginalized, who struggle to get their voices heard in the corridors of power. As a result, these and other less vocal groups tend to be ill served by public policies and services, even those that should benefit them most.

Governments need the support of the public. It is a major task for any government to maintain public confidence and support for its actions. And, of course, public support will not be total. Heymann made this clear long ago when discussing the strategic role of government managers (Heymann 1987, 14):

The manager cannot attempt to satisfy all those who can exercise influence over the [government] organization. That would be futile and also costly in terms of both coherence and his own vision of what is needed. The manager's task is rather to articulate and then to execute desirable goals, the support for which will provide the money and physical resources, the popular approval and cooperation, the recruits and collaborators, and the authority the organization needs to carry out those goals.

The existence of some critical or disaffected citizens may be unavoidable, but if the numbers of such citizens increase a tipping point may be reached. Large falls in public trust and confidence in government usually mean that public disapproval of existing political leaders rises. For example, in the decade after the financial crisis of 2008 and 2009, there was a loss of public confidence in many governments and in many countries, there was a rise in populist politicians who criticized the failings of "establishment" politicians and civil servants. The public presumably lost confidence in their governments because they thought the crisis should not have come as such a surprise and should not have been allowed to do so much damage. It was also said by some commentators that incumbent governments at the time of the crisis were culpable for the suffering of the public because of failures to regulate markets properly. The OECD (2020b, 22) recently reported that "only an OECD average of 43% of people still trust their governments …".

It is also clear in the case of Europe that disenchantment with incumbent governments included a feeling by some parts of the public that government had failed to halt immigration trends. Large numbers of people in some countries believed that their access to public services and even jobs were threatened by immigration, and some claimed that the social and cultural traditions of their communities, the existing culture, were also under threat. Some observers linked the rise of support for populist leaders with the consequences of pressures on societies stemming from global economic forces. It seemed, therefore, that populations feeling fearful and alienated were switching support to politicians who seemed to understand and champion their fears. In several countries, some extreme forms of democratic populism or even authoritarian populism appeared to grow in significance. One response to such developments was the speculation that citizens who feel "weak and defeated" give their support to authoritarian politicians (Hague 2018).

If such developments occur, the conditions in which public administration takes place also change (Bauer and Becker 2020). Populist politicians who win elections based on their promise to be an instrument of the "will of the people" and then turn the power of government against the "establishment" may use their new executive power to change public administration and the civil service. This may not have the same nature everywhere; the precise intent and the measures used may vary from country to country making it difficult to generalize.

Who are the public?

This section presents a selection of studies on the public, chosen because they represent a thread of studies that attempt to understand the types of people that are to be found among the citizens of a country.

The first is an old but still intriguing study of public social attitudes that was based on a series of national surveys carried out in the UK. The results were said to have a wider significance than the UK: similar changes in social attitudes were said to have been found for Europe and North America. This series of surveys was referred to as the Monitor programme of surveys, with the first survey being conducted in 1973 (MacNulty 1985).

The key findings were produced by factor analysis and were said to reveal the existence of seven Social Value Groups. These seven groups were said to aggregate into three overall major types of people in the UK – sustenance driven, outer directed, and inner directed (Figure 5.1). MacNulty guessed that over the five years from 1984 to 1989, the numbers of sustenance driven people would decline and the numbers of inner-directed people would increase.

The sustenance driven people were said to be motivated by the need for security. This group was said to include people who were economically disadvantaged and people who were comfortably off. MacNulty (1985, 332) remarked:

> Members of these groups are motivated by the need for security. Although they are frequently economically disadvantaged, in which case they are concerned about survival, that is by no means always the case. Many Sustenance Driven people are comfortably well off, and for them survival means clinging to an existing lifestyle.

The outer directed people were said to be generally materialistic and aspired to improve their position. Some of the outer directed people were said to be in one of the seven groups – a group known as "belongers". This group also had members who were identified as sustenance driven. In other words, this was a group that straddled two of the three major types. People in the belongers' group sought a "quiet, undisturbed family life" and tended to be "worried" and "rule following". Perhaps underlining the link to the sustenance driven groups of people, the belongers included individuals whose "interest in the future is to ensure his family's security there" (MacNulty 1985, 333).

The group named "conspicuous consumers" was entirely associated with the outer directed type of people. The conspicuous consumers (MacNulty 1985, 333):

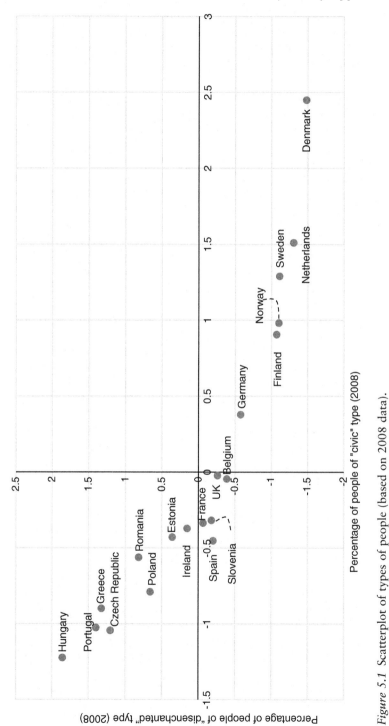

Figure 5.1 Scatterplot of types of people (based on 2008 data).

Note: The data in this figure was obtained from Denk et al. (2015) and the original figures were percentages that were turned into normalised values.

... are motivated by acquisition, competition, and getting ahead. They are traditional, pro-authority, and support law and order. They are also materialistic, pushy, and concerned for their appearance and position.

So far, the analysis of the Monitor surveys contained lots of echoes of the Hobbes perspective, in which there are references both to people wanting security and wanting to be quiet and undisturbed (peace) and people who are pushy (competitive) and materialistic (wanting to get the means to live well). But the third major type of person to emerge from the analysis of the survey data offers something new beyond the Hobbes perspective. These are people that often have societal and ecological concerns. The "social resisters" group were motivated, said MacNulty, by fairness and a good quality of life at the societal level. They were altruistic and concerned about inclusive democratic processes. Presumably, therefore, they saw democracy as a tool of social change. The "self-explorers" favoured progressive social change through changed awareness. They were (MacNulty 1985, 334):

... motivated by self-expression and self-realization. The Self Explorer shares the societal and ecological concerns of the Social Resister, but he is more likely to reject doctrinaire solutions in favour of the more holistic view that change is an organic process that must occur throughout society by means of a growing individual awareness.

It is tempting to deduce from these comments by MacNulty that many of the inner directed people were keen to see life get better at a whole-of-society level in contrast to the more competitive conspicuous consumers who were pushy and wanted to get ahead on a more personal basis (Table 5.1).

Some 25 years later in a follow-up article, the idea of doing cross-country comparisons using the three major types was discussed. It was reported that people in the Middle East were largely sustenance driven, the United States had an unusually small percentage of sustenance driven people compared to other countries in the West, and that the UK and the Netherlands had relatively high percentages of people who were inner directed (MacNulty 2010). Based on this, all we can presume is that public policies and even public governance systems might vary a great deal according to the nature of the public's common social values. Of course, it is possible that public policies and public governance systems influence the social values that are found in a society.

Another line of social science investigation has not taken general social values as the subject but some of the specific attitudes of the public towards political systems. It too has revealed variety rather than uniformity.

Table 5.1 Three major types of people based on analysis of their attitudes (MacNulty 1985)

Sustenance driven	Outer directed	Inner directed
• "Members of these groups are motivated by the need for security". • "Although they are frequently economically disadvantaged, in which case they are concerned about survival, that is by no means always the case. Many Sustenance Driven people are comfortably well off, and for them survival means clinging to an existing lifestyle. As one might expect, Sustenance Driven people tend to be clannish, set in their ways and resistant to change".	• "Outer Directed people are motivated by the search for esteem and status". • "The criteria by which they measure their success are external to themselves. They want to marry the 'right boy or girl', to be seen to live in the 'right part of town', drive the 'right car', etc. They are interested in their family's appearance and behaviour; and particularly that their children should be a 'credit to the family'. As a whole, Outer Directed people are materialistic, and they seek to improve their position in financial and social terms".	• "Inner Directed people are motivated by self-actualization". • "They are largely unconcerned about the opinion of them held by the world at large; their criteria for success and the standards of their behaviour are within themselves. This does not imply withdrawn or reclusive behaviour. Indeed, the Inner Directed individual usually has a broad horizon, a good understanding of world events and a high tolerance of other people's positions".

Note: The quotations in this table were from pages 332–334 of MacNulty (1985).

A recent example was a study that analysed data from nearly 50,000 individuals in 25 European countries (Denk et al. 2015). Using statistical techniques to analyse political attitudes the researchers found four types of citizens. They named the citizens as "civic" citizens if:

• they were interested in politics,
• they did not think politics were too complicated,
• they did not think it was difficult to make up their mind about political matters,
• they had trust in national parliaments, politicians, and political parties, and
• they were satisfied with the democratic system at the national level.

In other words, the civic types were people engaged with political debates and confident in the political system. Since the study was focused on attitudes, we do not know what these attitudes meant for their behaviour; in particular, we do not know if they were more likely to respond to government calls for support and cooperation or to government invitations to participate in strategic decision-making.

The other three types of citizens were variants of civic citizens. "Critical" citizens lacked trust in parliament, politicians, and political parties and had relatively low satisfaction with democracy at a national level. But they were, like the civic citizens, interested in politics and did not find politics too complicated; and nor did they find it difficult to make up their mind on political matters. "Stealth" citizens were the opposite of critical citizens. They had trust in politics (politicians etc.) and they had relatively high levels of satisfaction with national democracy, but they lacked political interest, they found politics complicated, and they reported difficulty in making up their mind on political matters. The "disenchanted" citizens had low political trust and low satisfaction with national democracy, and they were also not interested in politics, found politics too complicated, and found it difficult to make up their minds on political matters.

Based on this analysis of four types of people, none of the 25 countries only had a single type of citizen and the composition of the public in terms of the four types varied massively. For example, Denmark had many civic citizens (69%); Bulgaria had many critical citizens (47%); Spain, Finland, and Norway had many "stealth" citizens (48%, 38%, and 38%, respectively); and Latvia, Hungary, Croatia, and Bulgaria had many "disenchanted" citizens (48%, 46%, 45%, and 43%, respectively) (Table 5.2).

We should refrain from jumping to conclusions, but we can propose a hypothesis about the implications of these findings for a government's prospects if, and when, it attempts to follow a whole-of-society approach. If the public's political attitudes were to translate into a disposition to cooperate with government strategies to deliver long-term visions for a society, it might be hypothesized that in 2008 both Denmark and the Netherlands offered very favourable conditions for a whole-of-society approach. On the other hand, countries like Hungary and Poland might be seen as not only posing more challenging conditions

Table 5.2 Four types of citizens

Interested in politics, don't find politics too complicated, and don't find it difficult to make up mind about political matters	*Trust parliaments, politicians, and political parties; and relatively high satisfaction with national democratic system*	
	Low	*High*
Agree	"Critical"	"Civic"
Disagree	"Disenchanted"	"Stealth"

Note: The four types of citizens were identified in a study by Denk et al. (2015).

for the creation of a whole-of-society approach but might also provide fertile ground for populism.

In fact, some reanalysis of the data presented by Denk et al. for 19 of the European countries suggests two observations. First, the percentage of people of the civic type was strongly negatively correlated with the percentage of people of the disenchanted type (Figure 5.1). It looks as though the conditions that create more of one type diminishes the percentages of the other type. In conceptual terms, of course, they are polar opposites.

A second observation is based on analysing this 2008 data together with the findings of The Global Party Survey (Norris 2019) on vote shares of populist political parties. It seems that for this small sample of 19 European countries both the percentage of people of a civic type and the percentage of people of a disenchanted type are slightly correlated with the strength of populist parties in elections up to a decade later. The percentage of civic type people is negatively correlated, and the percentage of disenchanted people is, as would be expected, positively correlated. So, we might speculate that having large percentages of people who do not trust their parliaments and politicians, who feel uninterested in politics, who find politics too complicated, and find it difficult to judge political matters make it more likely that populist parties will thrive.

The positive correlation of populist party share of the vote with the percentage of people of a disenchanted type would have been very strong but for the presence of Greece, Portugal, Estonia, Ireland, and France in the sample. For these countries, the electoral strength of populist parties simply did not match what might have been expected given the relatively high percentages of people of the disenchanted type in these countries. Why they were not more affected by a rise in populist parties is not clear.

One final point, this small sample showed a very strong geographical pattern: Northern European countries had high percentages of the civic type of people and, subsequently, had relatively low strength populist parties; these countries included Denmark, Finland, the Netherlands, Norway, and Sweden. The countries that had high percentages of the disenchanted type of people and subsequently had flourishing populist parties were Hungary, the Czech Republic, Poland, and Romania. Poland and the Czech Republic are neighbouring countries, as are Hungary and Romania. All are in Eastern Europe. The relevance of all this is that it suggests that whole-of-society approaches encounter quite different conditions in different countries, although neighbouring countries may resemble each other in important ways.

One possible implication of the findings of a large-scale international survey of trust, the 2017 Edelman Trust Barometer, was that the disenchanted citizens of Denk et al.'s study made the transition to supporters of populist political leaders because of a growth of multiple fears.

Ries (2017) commented on the trust survey and connected the belief in a broken system, the presence of a set of fears, and provided this interpretation of the evidence:

> The 2017 Trust Barometer found a significant relationship between those who held fears – fear of corruption, globalization, immigration, the pace of change and innovation, and changing social values – and those who believe the system is broken....
>
> If you look at the list of 10 countries where a majority of the population believe the system is failing them, and where an above-average percentage of the population hold multiple fears, the list reads like a "who's who" of countries where the people have taken action against established systems. The list includes the U.K. (Brexit), the U.S. (the election of Trump), Italy (the rejection of reforms and a change in government), Brazil (an impeached president), and Colombia (the rejection of the government's peace treaty). The loss of belief in the system provides the context in which a variety of fears can spur people to act.

In the case of Europe, populist leaders often capitalized on concerns about immigration. Populist politicians in the UK, for example, in 2016 campaigned for Brexit by saying it was necessary to get back control of national borders (and other things) and the implication was that the flow of immigrants from Europe would be stemmed.

The system described as failing in the analysis of the 2017 Trust Barometer survey data included government, business, media, and NGOs. It was not just a loss of trust in government. Individuals who thought the system was failing:

1   saw society's elites as using the system for their own advantage,
2   were pessimistic about their own and their family's future,
3   did not have confidence that leaders would solve the problems of the country, and
4   wanted to see "forceful reformers" in power to make specific changes happen.

Public participation

Various rationales may be offered for increasing public participation in government. The World Bank championed participation as a means of making the state more effective (World Bank 1997, 129):

> Where appropriate, states should work to ensure broad based public discussion and evaluation of key policy directions and

priorities. At a minimum this means making available information in the public interest and establishing consultative mechanisms such as deliberation councils and citizen committees to gather the views and preferences of affected groups.

Public participation may be aimed specifically at improving policy-making. In early 2004, the Premier of China told the National People's Congress that public participation was a key element in improving policymaking (Wen 2004):

> We need to improve the policy-making process by integrating public participation, expert evaluation and government decision-making to ensure that our policies are scientific and correct. We need to speed up the formation and improvement of systems for making collective decisions on major issues, for soliciting opinions from experts, for keeping the public informed and holding public hearings, and for accountability in policy-making. All major policies must be decided collectively on the basis of in-depth research, widely solicited opinions, and full evaluation by experts. These procedures must be closely followed as one of the long-term basic systems for government work.

Policymaking may be improved by government gathering information and opinions from the public, especially on the matters that are of concern to citizens. For at least a quarter of a century, governments have also experimented with forms of participation that might help policymaking by creating opportunities for members of the public to engage in deliberations on issues and policy topics. Citizens' Juries, Citizens' Assemblies, Citizens' Councils, and Citizens' Dialogues are forms of public participation used to engender more in-depth consideration of matters of public concern and have been used in many countries. There are many examples of representative deliberative processes from Germany, Australia, Canada, and Denmark. They have been tried out at local government level as well as at national level. In Ireland, a Citizens Assembly was approved by the Irish Parliament (the Houses of the Oireachtas) in 2016. This, the first, Assembly held its deliberations in the period of 2016–2018. One of five matters identified for its deliberations was "How the state can make Ireland a leader in tackling climate change". The Assembly reported back to the Irish parliament (OECD 2020a, 38):

> The Irish Citizens' Assembly involved 100 randomly selected citizen members who considered five important legal & policy issues ... [which included the issue of] climate change. The Assembly's recommendations were submitted to parliament for further debate. Based on its recommendations, the government ... declared a climate emergency.

Another rationale for participation is that it may also increase legitimacy of government decision-making and decisions. The OECD (2020b, 66) mentions this specific argument for the utility of inclusiveness:

> Recent experiences in OECD Member countries show that when the planning process is open and includes stakeholder engagement, such as citizen-driven approaches through citizen participation mechanisms, strategic planning can enhance the legitimacy of policy making and increase the sustainability of policies beyond the electoral cycle. (OECD, 2016, 23)

There is also a rationale that says participation can be used to rebuild civic cultures. This can be illustrated using an example of public participation in local government strategic planning. During 1995 and 1996 in Orange County in Florida (United States), there was an initiative to involve citizens in governmental strategic planning. The result was a set of strategic goals for the county government of Orange County (Denhardt et al. 2000, 718):

> These strategic goals take into account the needs and interests of the citizens involved in the survey, the focus groups, the retreat sessions, and other involvement efforts.

The philosophy that spurred the efforts was promoted as "Citizens First!"; in this philosophy public participation was framed in terms of the responsibilities of citizens rather than the needs of consumers of public services (Denhardt et al. 2000, 719):

> In the view of … Orange County officials, government must not just stand by, watching civic interest erode. Instead, public officials, citizens in neighbourhood and community groups, the business community, and average citizens must come together to restore a connection between citizenship and government. After all, a responsive and committed citizenry is a prerequisite to both the quality of community life and the effectiveness of government. Government must be ready to listen and to respond in a way that helps people meet their needs. Citizens First! suggests a strengthening of the responsibility, by both citizens and their government, to make Orange County the best community possible and to restore the link between citizens and their government.

Public participation in governance comes in many different forms. In many countries, the public participates in governance through elections and referenda. Just how much power these participation channels gives the public has long been disputed, but it is generally understood that in populous countries involvement in political decisions is likely to be through elected representatives. That is, in big countries government decision-making is done for the people and not by the people, with decisions being taken by elected representatives. In the 1990s onwards, many governments at central and local levels were experimenting with additional forms of public participation, using a range of tools and channels (e.g., town hall meetings, neighbourhood forums, service user panels, opinion surveys, focus groups, citizen's juries, and e-democracy).

It seems that participation by the public through non-election channels (IPD 2016) tended to be more prevalent in countries scoring highly on a variety of indicators of political participation and capacity for participation. For example, *The Economist* published data on political participation in 2016, and using this we can identify as indicators variables such as voter turnout, adult literacy, public interest in political news, the extent of public membership of political parties, government encouragement of political participation, women being strongly represented in parliaments, and ethnic, religious, and minority groups having a reasonable degree of voice in the political process (EIU 2016). Countries judged to have a high extent of political participation and capacity for participation in 2016 included Australia, Canada, Finland, Germany, Norway, South Africa, Sweden, the United Kingdom, and the United States. At the opposite end of this participation spectrum are countries such as Bahrain, Cambodia, China, Egypt, Oman, Pakistan, Qatar, Saudi Arabia, and United Arab Emirates. And expert judgements about the extent of public participation in political decision-making at central and local government levels of participation seems to correlate strongly (IPD 2016).

Interesting initiatives in public participation have occurred over many years. The first example is from Botswana. In 1996 at Botswana's National Business Conference, the President of the country responded positively to the private sector's idea that there should be a long-term vision for Botswana. A task force to work on the vision was set up. Next, a public consultation process was undertaken (World Bank 2005, 66):

> A consultation process was carried out through public meetings and submissions, and visits were made to villages throughout the country to collect opinions and establish consensus regarding the aspirations of the people of Botswana for our nation in the year 2016, when we will have been independent for 50 years. The decision was made to focus on very broad parameters, and thus make the issue less political.

The vision which emerged had seven priority areas: "we seek to be an educated and informed nation; a prosperous, productive, and innovative nation; a compassionate, just, and caring nation; a safe and secure nation; an open, democratic, and accountable nation; a moral and tolerant nation, and a united and proud nation" (World Bank 2005, 66–67). The vision was carried forward into national development plans and backed by an annual budget. A headline target was set for the country's per capita GDP to be achieved by 2016.

Mahomed Iqbal Ebrahim, who was Vice President of the Botswana Confederation, Industry and Manpower (BOCCIM), made the observation that the effort to formulate a vision had to be underpinned by consensus (World Bank 2005, 67):

> Consensus building is an important part of the process of developing a national vision, because while two political parties may well share a broad goal, say to become a fully educated nation, they will not necessarily agree on the strategies by which to achieve such a goal.

Large-scale public participation was a feature of work to develop strategic planning by Mexico's Presidency. The context for this was described in 2005 by Mohammad Azarang Esfandiari, who had been head of the Presidency's Strategic Planning Unit. He summarized what the President of Mexico was trying to do as follows (World Bank 2005, 117):

> ... when his administration took office, President Fox proposed a series of goals, referring to his administration as the Strategic Government, or the Government of Change. According to these goals, it was our job to be a government with clear direction, objectives, strategies, and goals, capable of analyzing, measuring, and continually improving its performance, making decisions based on the facts.

Apparently, some 140,000 Mexican citizens participated in the creation of plans and made over 340 proposals. Presumably, these proposals were incorporated into the preparation of a vision for the next six-year period, the six-year National Development Plan, and the 40 programmes to deliver the Plan. Mexico's President, through his cabinet, then drafted a 25-year vision to sit alongside the six-year vision.

The initiative then ran into severe difficulties in the Mexican Congress, which would not allow specific reforms to be progressed, even though most of what the President put forward was approved. One commentator expressed the view that however good the approach to strategic planning was, progress through Congress had proved difficult (World Bank 2005, 126):

> Four years ago, President Vicente Fox introduced a very ambitious plan describing how to project a country vision, first over a six-year

period and then over a 25-year period, but this approach, which was so well designed in the practical terms of strategic planning, suffers from an essential gap. Because the executive branch does not have a majority in the Congress, it has failed to pass three substantial reforms: fiscal reform, labor reform, and energy reform. I am not saying that this is the fault of President Fox, but rather that Mexico has stood still politically for the last four years in an institutional deadlock. It cannot move forward without first resolving fundamental matters from the political perspective.

Mohammad Azarang Esfandiari did not actually disagree with this commentary on Mexico's experience of creating visions and development planning (United Nations 2005, 132):

> When Mexico's National Development Plan was devised, the plan and the vision were shared by parliament, arriving at it through consensus.... parliament no longer allows the passage of reforms. I believe that this is because each [political] party concerns itself with its own priorities instead of those of the country. President Fox acknowledges that his hands are tied and cannot make good on his promises. No excuse is being offered here; this is just the situation as it stands right now.... I do not blame the original vision for not working out or being implemented on a lack of agreement on planning but, rather, on political disagreement.

So, civil servants may think they have done the strategic planning job very well technically, but political difficulties must also be managed; and even large-scale citizen participation in preparing visions and strategies does not guarantee a consensus among legislators. Another commentator seemed to suggest that the President's cabinet consisted of people well suited to management, "who surely were very competent administrators, but poorly versed in politics" (United Nations 2005, 133). Perhaps, this suggested that they did not understand the management of politics that was required to get the reforms through Congress (Heymann 1987). This commentator on the Mexican experience also seemed to consider it to be a misunderstanding of reality to say that problems were occurring because issues had become politicized (United Nations, 133):

> Moreover, we constantly hear the so-called politicians who run government departments complain, "Issues are being politicized". Well, these are political issues; how can you avoid politicizing them? They are already politicized even before they can be discussed. Politicization is understood as something negative, which causes confusion among politicians, the press, and civil society.

While there has been interest in the idea of public participation for many years, it continues to be seen as relevant for the years ahead. Especially where commentators note reduced public trust in government, and are concerned about a weakening relationship between citizens and their governments, consultation and participation mechanisms may be seen as offering ways of repairing weaknesses in the governance situation (OECD 2019, 9):

> Public institutions have tools at their disposal that allow them to reconnect with citizens and improve the effectiveness of public policy. Key among these are people-centred approaches to policy-making and delivering services. Such approaches allow governments to consult citizens about their needs, encouraging direct participation in designing and implementing policies.

For conceptual clarification, it can be noted that public participation can be variously described as an element of a whole-of-society approach to governance, a "people-centred" approach to governance, and part of an "open government strategy". A whole-of-society approach – as defined in this book – includes public participation as one strand and government mobilizing external stakeholders beyond government as another. And one way in which stakeholders may be mobilized is through intelligent outsourcing, which allows government to use public funding to incentivise stakeholders to work towards government's strategic goals. A people-centred approach puts the public first and listens to them and consults them. One definition of open government is that it is "a culture of governance that promotes the principles of transparency, integrity, accountability and stakeholder participation in support of democracy and inclusive growth" (OECD 2017b). A strategy of increasing openness and transparency can have the consequence of "improving the capability and effectiveness of the state" (World Bank 1997, 129). Clearly, whole-of-society approaches, people-centred governance, and open government are related and overlapping concepts and can be purposefully combined in practice.

Valuable partners in economic and social development

Governments may seek to enlist the cooperation of social partners (business, trade unions), religious organizations, and various types of nongovernmental organizations (NGOs) in its strategic planning. If a government succeeds in mobilizing the public and stakeholders to support long-term strategic visions and strategies, and this support translates into greater success in delivering desirable outcomes for society generally, then this could feed back into public trust in government. With greater trust in the government, the level of support for long-term strategic visions and strategies might ratchet up further, creating an upward spiral in public governance.

The World Bank identified NGOs as potentially very important in providing a channel through which the state might hear the voice of citizens (World Bank 1997, 116):

> Yet given the many obstacles facing ordinary citizens, especially the poor, in articulating and pressing their needs, these associations play a vital role in channeling their voice and in building capacity for participation in public affairs.

However, the World Bank was aware of the limitations in relying on the NGOs to advocate on behalf of individual citizens (World Bank 1997, 114, 116):

> ... not all NGOs are involved in the delivery of services. Many others are research and civic education groups, advocacy organizations, and professional and business associations that represent particular interests or seek to educate the public about issues in their collective interest.... Unlike the electoral process, however, where all votes are counted equally, not all these organizations are equally representative, either of their clients' interests or of the public interest more broadly.... Some NGOs are created opportunistically, to advance the interests of narrow and privileged constituencies, often at the expense of the less vocal and less powerful.

The last point in this quotation is worth stressing; NGOs cannot be assumed to in every case work in the public interest – they may pressurize or work on behalf of special interest groups or on one side of an issue.

In early 2005, Brazil's Council for Economic and Social Development was working on a vision for the country and other development related matters. It was intended the vision for Brazil would cover three periods: until 2007, from 2007 to 2015, and from then until 2022. This body was reported to include representatives of civil society (United Nations 2005, 49–50):

> The Council comprises 90 individuals from civil society, including business people, union leaders, religious organizations, and cultural and academic non-governmental organizations. These 90 individuals plus 12 state ministers occupy seats on the Council, which was created by presidential decision and decree. Participating members were invited by the President of Brazil, who by presidential decree appointed them to two-year terms on the Council.

Chile's government had, by 2017, achieved a good reputation for its efforts to carry though governance reforms and for its concern to provide better public services. According to the OECD (OECD 2017a, 9),

> Chile is among the approximately 50% of overall OECD countries endowed with a strategy or law on citizen participation in the policy cycle, as well as a well-developed strategy on access to information, digital governance and implementation of the Open Government Partnership. (OECD 2016)

Despite these positive remarks, the OECD referred to Chile as facing a deficit in participative governance and noted low voting rates in the country's 2013 elections. It was commented (OECD 2017a, 6), "This low participation could also be related to frequent corruption scandals, as well as voter disenchantment and apathy, seemingly the country's greatest challenges".

Nevertheless, in the years after 1990, Chile had made efforts to enlist public participation for the work of national development. In 2002, there was public debate about the need for a development vision and the importance of moving away from short-termism. It seems that neither business nor trade unions, nor politicians, were able to produce a credible long-term vision, but a project beginning in 2003 based on civil society participation did develop long-term visions. This was judged by Gastón L'Huillier, President of the Chilean College of Engineers, to be a successful initiative (World Bank 2005, 90–91):

> ... a group of professionals [were inspired] to generate a development vision within an environment free of special, union, and political interests and to assign priority to attracting the community with a positive, challenging long-term development vision. Work began in January 2003 by calling the commissions to meet, bringing together experts on 34 subjects, all of them excellent communicators, and outstanding majority leaders from the public and private sectors. These commissions gather 250 participants, who consult with another 2,500 specialists in the hopes of covering all of the valid opinions on these matters on the national level. It was a very participatory project, which received a wide variety of opinions. Using business sector methodologies, such as balanced scorecards and strategic maps, to define development plans, the project was structured as a central commission, generating visions for these 34 sectors and a national development vision that was widely accepted in all sectors.

A whole-of-society approach

A simple, additive, and unweighted index for a whole-of-society approach was created using the 2016 data published in the Institutional Profiles Database. The published data, comprising expert ratings, was turned into normalized values for the calculation of index values. The resultant figures in the index were then transformed into normalized values (Table 5.3).

Among the sample of 63 countries used for this book, the governments with a strong whole-of-society approach and those with a weak approach are shown in Table 5.4.

Some of the governments listed in the strong group and in the weak group were not a complete surprise. For example, among the governments with a strong approach were several from Northern Europe that had become social democratic in their cultures several decades ago and which had, consequently, sought to institutionalize industrial conflict by creating cooperation between government, business leaders, and trade unions.

Among the group that had weak approaches were three that were Gulf State governments. In this part of the world, public finances have been very dependent on the oil industry and the countries are

Table 5.3 Whole-of-society approach (IPD 2016)

1 Do national public authorities and local stakeholders (local authorities, private sector, NGOs, etc.) work together to develop and improve public policy effectiveness?
2 Do the public authorities have the capacity to encourage public and private stakeholders to work towards long-term strategic vision (though tax and financial incentives, etc.)
3 Degree of cooperation between public and private sectors
4 Degree of involvement of the state's highest authorities in the cooperation between public and private stakeholders
5 Public participation in political decisions (excluding elections) at national level (e.g., surveys, commissions, public debates, etc.)
6 Public participation in political decisions (excluding elections) at local level (e.g., surveys, commissions, public debates, etc.)

Table 5.4 Strong and weak whole-of-society approaches (2016)

Strong whole-of-society approaches	*Weak whole-of-society approaches*
Belgium, Canada, Denmark, Germany, Lithuania, Netherlands, Norway, Slovenia, Singapore, Sweden, the UK, and the USA	Algeria, Bahrain, Cambodia, Greece, Pakistan, Peru, Qatar, Romania, Saudi Arabia, and Venezuela

sometimes said to have rentier state characteristics. One possible interpretation of the implications of a rentier state is that government is left to do all the "heavy lifting" of strategic transformations and stakeholders may be a little passive. In fact, an interesting point about the Gulf States is the degree to which they have embraced the ideas of strategic planning and the value of well-publicized long-term strategic visions for the economy and society (Joyce and Al Rasheed 2017). In the context of the weakness of their whole-of-society approaches, it might be deduced that the governments of Bahrain, Qatar, and Saudi Arabia must find, or must have found so far, that these long-term strategic visions have not encouraged much practical support by stakeholders. The long-term strategic visions then become fundamentally important for the civil services of these countries as they carry out reforms and transformation projects. Logically, this combination of strong long-term strategic visions and relatively weak whole-of-society approaches makes them outliers in relation to international patterns.

It is tempting to conclude that a strong strategic policy process makes a strong whole-of-society approach possible. This is based on the observation that governments that were strong in terms of their strategic policy process also often had a strong whole-of-society approach, whereas a weak strategic policy process was often associated with a weak whole-of-society approach. It does not take much imagination to think that a civil service that cannot cooperate and collaborate internally is not going to be very good at cooperating and collaborating with stakeholders and the public. Further, if stakeholders and the public have little confidence that the civil servants will themselves be acting in alignment with visions and strategies, why would they be encouraged to help deliver the same visions and strategies. Finally, any ambitious long-term strategic visions that are set for the country will make big demands on the implementers to evaluate, learn, and evolve what they are doing. If stakeholders and the public embark on a whole-of-society approach and, while working with government on the delivery of visions and strategies, discover that government and the civil service are inflexible, rigid, slow to learn lessons, and not open-minded and experimental in their attitudes, won't they become discouraged and disenchanted?

Before we finish this brief look at a whole-of-society approach, it can be noted that there was some slight evidence that a strong approach seems less likely to be found in societies where there is a lot of internal conflict and, also, seems less likely where populist parties had flourished in recent years.

By internal conflict in society is meant conflicts of an ethnic, religious, regional, or social nature or conflicts connected with land-related issues. Countries such as Sweden and Norway had little of this internal conflict in 2016 and had a strong whole-of-society approach, whereas other countries such as Egypt, Pakistan, and Peru were rated as having high levels of internal conflict. Of course, establishing that this is a pertinent factor let alone how conflict in society relates to the strength of a whole-of-society approach is bound to be difficult. It may seem intuitive that a whole-of-society approach may be more difficult to bring about in a society where there is a lot of internal conflict. Of course, the level of internal conflict may be the effect of governance capabilities and achievements.

There are similar challenges in understanding the slight covariation between the strength of populism in electoral terms and the weakness of a whole-of-society approach. Countries such as the Czech Republic, Hungary, Italy, Poland, and the Russian Federation not only had high vote shares for populist parties in recent years but also had weak whole-of-government approaches. The Netherlands, Sweden, Norway, Canada, Lithuania, and Germany had strong whole-of-society approaches and very low shares of the vote for populist parties. While this was only a slight correlation, it would seem to make sense in terms of the nature of populist politics. According to populism, populist leaders seek to win elections so that they can deliver the "will of the people" in the face of the resistance of the "establishment". The democratic populist government sees itself as exercising governmental power on behalf of an electorate that has been ignored. Such a narrative does not seem to lend itself to the idea of a whole-of-society approach – it is about using the power of the state to impose the will of the majority on the situation, not about everybody coming together cooperatively and collaboratively.

If conflict has a strong grip on the life of a society, turning this around to get a whole-of-society approach is a tall challenge. According to the Executive Director of the International Institute for Governance in Catalonia, many societies are in difficult situations in terms of governance (World Bank 2005, 37):

> Going from a conflict to consensus is extraordinarily difficult when the actors are weakened by internal factionalism or feeble representation, and when some of them articulate their interests in a very short-term fashion and are incapable of subsuming them into a national project or national development vision. In these situations of low institutional development and lack of actor capacity for processing conflict and building consensus, it is normal for acute social polarization or acute social erosion to occur. I estimate that close to 70 states could now be classified as failures, incapable of guaranteeing minimal governance to their societies, or at risk of getting into such a situation.

Conclusions

This chapter has focused on whole-of-society approaches, which may be defined in various ways, including defining it as government getting support from the public and stakeholders to deliver its long-term strategic visions and strategies. Another way to define is to say that it exists when government engages the public and stakeholders at all key stages of the strategic policy process.

The conceptualization of the whole-of-society approach here included public participation in political decisions at central and local levels of government (but not including elections). Examples of large-scale public participation in developing government visions and plans were noted. As pointed out by the World Bank, some sections of populations do not have their voice heard much in public governance processes; these sections include poor people. If their voices are not adequately heard, then public policies and services are not as suitable as they might be. Governments have been advised for many years now to work harder at maintaining public confidence and support for government actions. On the basis that more needs to be done to give the public a voice, some argue that NGOs could be useful in creating additional channels for members of the public to have a voice, despite the acknowledged limitations of such channels in terms of representativeness.

In this chapter, also, some effort was made to underline the complexity of the public, whether the public was analysed in terms of social values (MacNulty 1985), or whether citizen orientations to politics were being analysed (Denk et al. 2015). What became apparent is that although there is much variation from country to country, some account must be taken of geography as a factor, becausevery often neighbouring countries resemble each other in terms of the social and political attitudes of their populations. We also mentioned at one point that in the decade following the financial crisis of 2008 and 2009 there was a big reduction in public confidence in many governments and that in recent years, in many countries, there had been growing public support for populist politicians who criticized the failings of "establishment" politicians and civil servants. It was interesting to find that for a small sample of European countries that the percentage of people with specific political orientations in 2008, referred to as civic and disenchanted types, were correlated (in one case negatively and in the other case positively) with the strength of populist parties in elections up to a decade later. So, the complexity of the public has a comparative dimension but also a temporal dimension.

Data from the Institutional Profiles Database for 2016 was used to assess the extent of a whole-of-society approach in a sample of 63 countries. Analysis of this sample was the basis of a number of observations including the following:

Countries such as Sweden and Norway had little internal conflict in and had a strong whole-of-society approach, whereas other countries, such as Egypt, Pakistan, and Peru, were rated as having high levels of internal conflict and a weak whole-of-society approach.

Some countries that had weak whole-of-society approaches nevertheless had very strong long-term strategic visions in place, which seems to imply that their long-term visions have more practical significance for the strategic planning of transformation projects by the government sector rather than for actions by the public and stakeholders.

A strong whole-of-society approach was less likely to be found in societies where populist parties had flourished in recent years.

The strength of a whole-of-society approach covaried with the national development performance of a country in terms of human development and environmental performance.

The last observation suggested that a strong whole-of-society approach is important for national social and economic development, and in the next chapter we see how the approach fits into a model of the strategic state.

References

Annan, K. (1999) Secretary-General presents his annual report to General Assembly. Available at: https://www.un.org/press/en/1999/19990920.sgsm7136.htm [1 July 2019].

Bauer, M.W. & Becker, S. (2020) Democratic backsliding, populism, and public administration. *Perspectives on Public Management and Governance*, 2020, 19–31.

Denhardt, R.B., Denhardt, K.G., & Glaser, M.A. (2000) Citizen-driven strategic planning in local government: The case of Orange County, Florida. In Rabin, J., Miller, G.J. & Hildreth, W.B. (Eds.) *Handbook of strategic management*, 2nd edition. New York and Basel: Marcel Dekker, pp. 709–720.

Denk, T., Christensen, H.S., & Bergh, D. (2015) The composition of political culture—A study of 25 European democracies. *Studies in Comparative International Development*, 50, 358–377.

Department of the Taoiseach (2017) *National risk assessment 2017: Overview of strategic risks*. Dublin.

Dewey, J. (1927) *The public and its problems*. Athens: Swallow Press, Ohio University Press.

EIU (2016) EIU Democracy Index. Available at: www.eiu.com [2 June 2021].

Government of Pakistan (2014) Pakistan 2025: One nation – One vision. Available at: https://www.pc.gov.pk/uploads/vision2025/Pakistan-Vision-2025.pdf [7 October 2021].

Government of Singapore (2020) *Charting Singapore's low-carbon and climate resilient future*. Singapore: National Climate Change Secretariat Strategy Group, Prime Minister's Office. Available at: www.nccs.gov.sg [24 November 2020].

Hague, U. (2018) Beating authoritarianism isn't as simple as you think. *It's even simpler*. Available at: https://eand.co/beating-authoritarianism-isnt-as-simple-as-you-think-it-s-even-simpler-6800b8dfc119 [19 June 2018].

Heymann, P. (1987) *The politics of public management*. New Haven and London: Yale University Press.

Hobbes, T. (1962) *Leviathan*. London: Collins.

Hun, S. (2008) "Rectangular strategy" for growth, employment, equity and efficiency phase II. First Cabinet Meeting of the Fourth Legislature of the National Assembly. https://www.ilo.org/wcmsp5/groups/public/–asia/–ro-bangkok/–sro-bangkok/documents/genericdocument/wcms_112939.pdf [15 September 2021].

IPD (2016) Institutional Profiles Database. Available at: http://www.cepii.fr/institutions/en/ipd.asp [28 August 2018].

Joyce, P. & Al Rasheed, T.F. (2017) *Public governance and strategic management capabilities: Public governance in the Gulf States*. London: Routledge.

MacNulty, C.A.R. (2010) The value of values for IO, SC, Intel. *IO Journal*, August, 2(3), 29–34.

MacNulty, W.K. (1985) UK social change through a wide-angle lens. *Futures*, 17(4), 331–347.

Norris, P. (2019) The global party survey. Available at: www.GlobalPartySurvey.org [16 July 2021].

OECD (2016) *Open government: The global context and the way forward*. Paris: OECD Publishing.

OECD (2017a) *Chile: Scan report on the citizen participation in the constitutional process*. Paris: OECD Publishing. Available at: http://www.oecd.org/gov/public-governance-review-chile-2017.pdf [15 January 2020].

OECD (2017b) Government at a Glance 2017. Available at: https://www.oecd-ilibrary.org/governance/government-at-a-glance-2017_gov_glance-2017-en. [17 September 2021].

OECD (2019) *Government at a Glance 2019*. Paris: OECD Publishing.

OECD (2020a) *Innovative citizen participation and new democratic institutions: Catching the deliberative wave*. Paris: OECD Publishing.

OECD (2020b) *Policy framework on sound public governance: Baseline features of governments that work well*. Paris: OECD Publishing.

Ries, T. (2017) The fall of trust, the rise of populist action. *Edelman*. 15 January 2017. Available at: https://www.edelman.com/post/fall-of-trust-rise-of-populist-action [21 October 2021].

Wen, J. (2004) Report on the work of the government. Speech delivered at the second session of the tenth National People's Congress on March 5, 2004. Available at: http://english.gov.cn/official/2005-07/29/content_18349.htm [24 March 2014].

World Bank (1997) *World development report 1997: The state in a changing world*. New York: Oxford University Press.

World Bank (2005) National visions matter: Lessons of success. Available at: http://siteresources.worldbank.org/CDFINTRANET/Resources/nationalvisionsmatter.pdf.Downloaded [14 March 2019].

6 Intelligent Government Acting in and for Society

Introduction

In the 1960s influential thinking on the management of the corporate business sector suggested that intelligent management could be based on strategic planning. Later, in the 1970s, strategic management was being advocated as an advance on strategic planning. Intelligent management meant, first, acting with a purpose in mind. This could be based on setting strategic goals. It did not mean acting based on habit or acting spontaneously. Intelligent management tried to avoid nasty surprises. So, attention was paid to identifying threats, weaknesses, and future risks. Third, intelligent management was smart in the sense of appraising circumstances, options, and resources. The situation was not to be taken for granted; it needed to be carefully analysed and understood. Being intelligent meant taking the time to identify a range of options in pursuing the goals that had been set and then picking options that were most likely to result in their achievement. It meant taking stock of existing skills, technological capabilities, and resources in the broadest sense and considering how these could be most effectively used. Fourth, intelligent management was sensitive to the time dimension in decision-making, including being sensitive to the way decisions made now would have consequences in the future, and being sensitive to time as a factor when planning implementation. That is, thinking about the time required for acquiring the necessary means, acting, and achieving the goals.

Alan Budd, an economist who had worked for a while in the UK Government's Treasury, introduced the idea of government making use of strategic planning in a book published towards the end of the 1970s. Budd mentioned that the political and parliamentary system had given too much attention to immediate issues and neglected long-term implications. He also said that it could be argued that the present system did not pay enough attention to strategy but was preoccupied with tactics. He positioned strategic planning as the best solution for the future of government, neither leaving everything to the market to decide nor trying to plan everything from the top of a centralized state. He

DOI: 10.4324/9781351045797-6

based his ideas about strategic planning on the ideas of a sociologist – Lindblom (1975). He summed up Lindblom's view of strategic planning in these words (Budd 1978, 153): "… 'strategic planning' … is cautious in selecting its tasks and makes much use of interaction: 'A conventional planner would be willing directly to tackle the task of resource allocation for an entire economy: a strategic planner would not'". Strategic planning's chief virtue, it seemed, was recognizing that the ability to control the environment was limited. So, strategic planning does not aim to control everything. From these suggestions of the appropriateness of strategic planning for government, we can make two propositions: strategic planning works best when it is selective and when it is inclusive, with decision-making drawing strength from government interactions with society, rather than top-down expert decision-making.

In the 1980s and 1990s, sub-national governments provided many examples of pioneering uses of strategic planning by governments. There was also a growing realization that strategic analysis was not enough to ensure success. Planning implementation and the capable execution of strategic plans were also needed for success. In other words, practical capabilities were also needed to ensure strategic effectiveness. Over the previous two chapters, we have been exploring some of these possible strategic capabilities that are essential for successful strategy. It is now time to put together the insights from the preceding chapters to formulate a model of what we will refer to here as the "strategic state".

This chapter covers the following ground. First, we introduce some concepts and how they relate to each other to form the concept of the strategic state. Second, we examine a case study of Lithuania to explore one example of the path a government may take towards becoming a strategic state. Third, we make use of the Institutional Profiles Database again – this time to analyse the links between a strategic state and national social and economic development. Fourth, recognizing that the strategic state is one component of a "sound" public governance system, we consider two other structures that sit alongside the strategic state component. And finally, we carry out some rudimentary investigations of the conditions which exist in society and may be pertinent to explaining the existence of a strategic state and sound public governance.

The concept of the strategic state

It is possible to see the idea of a strategic state as presented here as a synthesis of many different theoretical contributions and policy statements over four or more decades. However, a major inspiration for the conceptualization of the strategic state in this book was the thinking of Philip Heymann, which was based on his professional experience of working in government agencies and his analysis of case studies.

He provided basic definitions of his key terms in relation to strategic planning by government agencies (Heymann 1987, 12):

> Goals is as good a word as any to describe decisions – visions – about what is to be accomplished, what and who is important and why, and what alliances will form the broader political networks of the agency. Strategy is the broader concept that includes both goals and the plans designed to bring them to reality.

Three important concepts are threaded through all his analysis and arguments: goals, capacity, and outside support. The goals should relate to social needs. The government organization's capacity must be sufficient, and this capacity will rest on capabilities and values. The outside support should be mobilized through the promises implicit in the goals and be understood as necessary alliances. Writing about appointed officials in the American system of public governance, he defined their responsibilities using these concepts (Heymann 1987, 14–15):

> The appointed manager, then, has a basic responsibility to discover, define, and effectuate goals that meet the social needs that he, his superiors, and sometimes the president see in the area and satisfy two additional criteria. First, the goals must be within the present or achievable capacity of the organization and consistent with the values that mobilize its energies. Second, at the same time, the goals must say things about the values of the manager and the organization, promise things about what it will do, and give indications of its likely alliances which, together, will bring it whatever outside support it needs in practical terms to carry out its goals.

These three concepts are explained and applied in a series of case studies occupying the first part of his 1987 book. His analysis of the case studies builds up to quite a distinctive perspective about what things deserve close attention in the formulation of strategy for government organizations. His perspective is condensed into Figure 6.1, which may be used as a way of testing the soundness of a particular strategy.

One aspect of Heymann's distinctive perspective was the idea that goals, capacity, and outside support must fit together. He specified this as a requirement for "congruence" (Heymann 1987, 22):

> Only certain combinations of goals, outside support, and organizational capabilities are stable....

> Beyond a sense of alternative equilibria, then, an organizational strategy requires a notion of whether (and how) it is possible to move to, and maintain, a new balance among goals, outside support, and organizational capabilities.

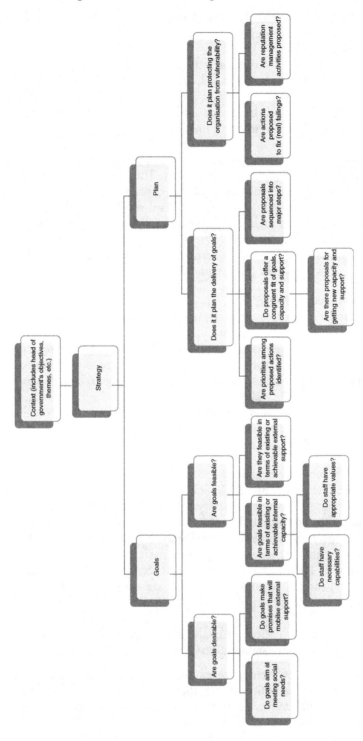

Figure 6.1 Testing for the soundness of a strategic plan prepared by a government entity.

Note: Based on the ideas of Philip Heymann (1987).

As Heymann pointed out in relation to the federal government of the United States, two very different vantage points are possible when looking at any government. We can look at government as a coalition of organizations and we can zoom in on the strategy of the individual organizations. Or we can look at the executive branch of government as a whole and analyse strategy from the point of view of the centre of government. Heymann's own approach was the former, the analysis of strategy for each government organization. The approach in this book is to look at the government as the unit of analysis.

In Figure 6.2 are to be found three factors that are versions of the same three concepts at the heart of Heymann's analysis and arguments. For goals, there are "long-term strategic visions in policy sectors". The concept of capacity is represented by "strategic policy process", which is seen here as containing some of the most vital factors for the strategic capacity of government. And the outside support is addressed through the idea of a "whole-of-society approach".

No specific assumption is being made that the three factors in the strategic state concept must be congruent, although it is suggested that the three factors may tend to develop in tandem. So, for example, strong long-term strategic visions in policy sectors may be associated with a strong strategic policy process, and a strong whole-of-society approach may be associated with a strong strategic policy process. Why they would develop in tandem is not known. Perhaps, it is

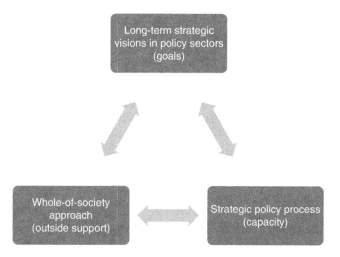

Figure 6.2 The three factors of the strategic state.

difficult to create capacity through a strategic policy process unless there are existent and strong long-term strategic visions to be delivered? And perhaps it is difficult to persuade the public and stakeholders to provide outside support to government if the government itself does not have credibility – with the credibility resting on the government's real capacity for strategic policymaking?

The shift to strategic government

The years 2002 to 2005 witnessed significant developments in governmental planning at a national level in a number of countries. These countries included the Russian Federation, China, Indonesia, Cambodia, Saudi Arabia, Vietnam, and Lithuania.

In 2003, the Russian Federation having been engaged in solving major problems besetting the national situation for three years announced that a more long-term and strategic course was now to be charted. The President defined the country's strategic objective for national development as follows: "Russia will take its recognised place among the ranks of the truly strong, economically advanced and influential nations" (Putin 2003, 1). This was followed in late 2005 by the federal government's deployment of national projects as the basis of Russia's long-term strategic policy.

China's Strategic Planning Department (SPD) of the National Development and Reform Commission (NDRC) carried out a mid-term review of the Tenth Five-Year Plan in 2003. Based on this review, it was decided to develop a monitoring and evaluation framework for future five-year plans. The Director-General of the NDRC described China as moving its five-year planning towards results-based strategic planning (Wang and Lin 2007).

In 2004, Indonesia passed the State Planning Law that set out a national development planning process and the role of the National Development Planning Agency (Blöndal et al. 2009). The 2005–2025 Long-Term National Development Plan, which was contained in an Act of 2007, was required by the 2004 Act to be a "visionary" plan. The vision in the plan was for: a self-reliant nation; an advanced nation in economic, social, and political terms; and a nation that was just and prosperous. The plan aspired to development that was people-centred (President of Indonesia 2007, 47):

As the actors and movers of development and also as the object of development, the people has the right to participate in the planning and implementation of development, as well as in benefiting from the fruits of development. Development must be implemented from the people, by the people, and for the people. Therefore, the aspect of justice is also an important dimension of national development.

According to one report, Cambodia had "little cohesive national-level planning" before 1996 (Thornton et al. 2009, 13). The first development plan covered the period between 1996 and 2000 and the second five-year development plan was drafted in 2001. But it looks like the 2003 Rectangular Strategy was a real turning point. It was then that the government started to pull together its development planning and its national poverty reduction strategy. Subsequently, the government recognized the need for consistency between the Rectangular Strategy, the National Strategic Development Plan, and Sectoral Development Strategies. The theme of this period from 2003 onwards seemed to be integration of goals and plans (Royal Government of Cambodia 2010, 2):

> Following the 3rd General elections on 27 July 2003, the newly elected Government made public its "Rectangular Strategy" as the successor of the Triangular Strategy of the Royal Government in the Second Legislature of the National Assembly. It outlined the economic policy agenda to support the policy platform of the Royal Government in the Third Legislature of the National Assembly (2003–2008). The Rectangular Strategy synthesised the key elements from the Cambodia Millennium Development Goals, the Socio-Economic Development Plan 2001–2005 (SEDP II), the Cambodia National Poverty Reduction Strategy 2003–2005 (NPRS), and various important policies, strategies, plans and other reform programmes, all of which had been formulated through broad consultations with all national and international stakeholders. The main aim of the Rectangular Strategy for Growth, Employment, Equity, and Efficiency was to promote economic growth, generate employment for Cambodian workers, ensure equity and social justice, and enhance efficiency of the public sector through the implementation of the Governance Action Plan and in-depth reforms that are coordinated and consistent across all levels and sectors.

Saudi Arabia was another country with a five-year planning system that began to think that it was time to evolve it towards a strategic planning model. In 2002, the Saudi Ministry of Economy and Planning organized a national symposium on a vision for the Saudi economy. The Long-Term Strategy 2025 setting the direction for the economy was then developed. This strategy then provided the context for the Eighth Development Plan, covering the years 2005–2009, which was seen by government officials as enacting a change in the development planning process (Ministry of Economy and Planning 2005, 678):

> The strategic planning approach has significantly influenced the Eighth Development Plan, which, in fact, represents the first building

block of a strategic edifice outlined by the Long-Term Strategy. The planning methodology should, therefore, accommodate this development by ensuring consistency between the sectoral strategies and the national strategy, as well as by ensuring closer integration and synchronization between the preparation of the five-year plans and the reviewing and updating the long-term strategy.

The Vietnamese government developed a ten-year socio-economic development strategy for the period 2001–2010. During the early part of this period, there seems to have been a major evolution in how the country approached planning (Turk, 44):

> The adoption of a Comprehensive Poverty Reduction and Growth Strategy in 2002 marked a major turning point in the country's planning processes. Vietnam's planning has enhanced the country's poverty-oriented results focus as well as its implementation of a Harmonization Action Plan. Previously, Vietnamese planning and development strategies reflected a command view of the economy. By contrast, the Comprehensive Poverty Reduction and Growth Strategy relies on decentralization, broadened social participation in planning, and attainment of Millennium Development Goals adapted to Vietnam's national vision.

These countries were not the only ones making changes in how they planned at this time. Other examples include the UK which developed five-year strategies for its policy sectors in the period 2003–2004 and Turkey which passed a new law in 2003, the Public Financial Management Law No. 5018, that made strategic planning a requirement for ministries and other government entities. Nor were they the first countries to develop strategic planning at a national level; they were preceded by the United States and Ireland in the 1990s. But looking at these six examples above it is suggestive of a hypothesis that something was happening in the public governance world in the period 2002–2005. We have one example from the six of a government emerging from a number of years of crisis and short-termism saying it wanted to act more strategically, thinking about strategic objectives, and using strategic projects to act long term. We have two governments adjusting five-year planning systems to make them more like strategic planning. There is another government in the six synthesizing different plans and strategies into a more unified and integrated approach to planning. And we have a government making its approach to strategy more inclusive and participative. It seems, therefore, to have been a time for governments to reconsider how they did planning. It seems to have been a time for trying out new ways of planning. And it was a time for adopting strategic planning ideas and methods. These years from 2002 to 2005 were ones in which some governments were experimenting in how to be more strategic.

Lithuania – a strategic state in the making

Lithuania's government is reported to have begun strategic planning at the national level in the year 2000 (Nakrosis et al. 2020). It then published a resolution on strategic planning methodology in June 2002 (National Audit Office 2018). According to the resolution, this "establish[ed] the system of strategic planning, the principles of strategic planning and budget formation based on programmes, as well as the procedure for the drafting of the strategy of development of a branch (sector) of the economy" (Government of the Republic of Lithuania 2002). In this resolution, strategic planning was not differentiated as a process from strategic management. It was understood to involve the monitoring and reporting of results and required making efficient use of resources to complete the mission and achieve the strategic goals. It also seemed to promise that government would be focused and selective by saying the government had "priority strategic goals", which were defined as the "major activity trends or main objectives" for a period of time. Several techniques were specifically mentioned: environment analysis, resource analysis, and SWOT analysis.

In May 2012, the Lithuanian parliament approved the National Progress Strategy – Lithuania 2030. It was said to have been prepared in a consultative and inclusive way. The active support of the public was considered essential (Government of the Republic of Lithuania 2012, 4):

> The Strategy will require public approval, commitment to change, mutual trust, respect and pro-activeness. If the public is but a passive observer, the initiatives will be doomed to failure, and we will be unable to address the issues of social exclusion, public reticence, community solidarity, gender equality, and other key areas. We have to overcome inertia and contrasts, and set clear goals to be consistently pursued. The citizens should know that their rights will be properly protected, social tensions reduced, and safe environment ensured enabling everyone to pursue their favourite activities, get a reasonable remuneration, and ensure personal and family well-being, while at the same time contributing to the national success.

Originally published to cover the twenty years to 2030, in recent years there were plans to revise it and incorporate the Sustainable Development Goals of the United Nations.

It contained a vision statement and a slogan (Government of the Republic of Lithuania 2012, 7):

We aim at a creative empowerment of each and every member of the society, focusing on ideas that would help Lithuania to become a modern, energetic country, embracing differences, and with a strong sense of national identity.

LITHUANIA IS A SMART COUNTRY: A GOOD PLACE TO LIVE AND WORK

The idea of Lithuania as a smart country was elaborated to mean a smart society (and a happy society), a smart economy (based on social responsibility and green growth), and smart governance. The last of these – smart governance – was defined as open and participatory, responsive to public demands, ensured high-quality services, competent, and "able to take targeted strategic decisions" (Government of the Republic of Lithuania 2012, 8).

Recent evaluations of strategic planning in the Lithuanian Government suggest two main developmental challenges:

1 Improving the strength of monitoring and evaluation
2 Alignment of the actions of civil servants with the government's political priorities

Even after many years of developing strategic planning, there was still scope for further improvement in its evaluation capabilities. This was the implication of an audit carried out during the period 2015–2018 by the Lithuanian National Audit Office. The audit looked at the implementation of policy objectives, state budgeting, and management of the state's real estate. It was reported that the government was very close to being a classic rule-based bureaucracy (National Audit Office 2018, 11), which could be taken to mean very poor at evaluation and learning:

> It means that we have the procedures required by the law regulating budget shaping and implementation, strategic planning, performance evaluation and monitoring as well as other results-based management tools, however, difficulties still emerge when implementing them, especially in performance evaluation stage: when determining priorities, developing strategies and planning activities for their implementation, allocating responsibilities and determining evaluation criteria, especially qualitative, monitoring and evaluating the implementation process.

The National Audit Office of Lithuania found deficiencies in the setting of criteria to evaluate strategic activity plans of ministries. It found that the "data important for the evaluation of performance results that is gathered is of poor quality (incomplete, inaccurate, untimely) or it is not gathered all; means for data collection are not created, etc" (National Audit Office 2018, 14). Apparently (National Audit Office 2018, 14),

> About 20% of data on ministries' performance results present in the Monitoring Information System (implementation of strategic activity plans' programmes) are still not credible and incomplete, therefore, they are not appropriate for the monitoring of performance results and reporting. In the Monitoring Information System in 2016 80% of data on evaluation criteria results of the Government Programme implementation are not present.

Evidently, in terms of the strategic policy process, monitoring and evaluation is a weak link and it is hard to see how learning and experimentation can occur without robust evaluation being undertaken.

Before 2018, there was a concern that the government's political priorities were not sufficiently steering strategies. A revision was made in the system of strategic planning in 2018 to ensure that financial resources could be better focused on the implementation of government priorities. This revision was known as the introduction of "change baskets": the government was to define annually a set of priorities that would "be incorporated in the strategic plans and budget programmes of budgetary institutions" (Nakrosis et al. 2020, 301). Based on survey findings, Nakrosis et al. concluded that the planning process was very focused on political priorities and budgeting was more influenced by them. However, they quoted the views of an advisor who said that the implementation of the plans was problematic (Nakrosis et al. 2020, 301):

> Political leadership has recently been strengthened, and senior managers now focus more on political priorities. However, the rank and file of the civil service are still resistant to change and tend to address all policy issues ... instead of focusing on the most pressing challenges.

So, it seems that the introduction of change baskets led to changes in top-level strategic plans and budgets, but the weak link was further down the delivery chain.

It is possible that there is much more work that could be done to improve strategic planning in Lithuania. The National Audit Office of Lithuania carried out audits on budgetary governance and strategic planning in 2016–2017. It was reported that (National Audit Office 2019, 3):

> ... we analysed the design of strategic plans, the monitoring of their implementation and performance reporting, and the management of the State Investment Programme (SIP). We have submitted

recommendations to the Office of the Government and the Ministry of Finance to improve budgetary governance: link the budget allocations to expected results, establish clear links between planning documents, optimise the number of strategic planning documents, review budgetary programming practices, take decisions on the calculation and reporting of management costs, ensure the quality of the data provided to the Monitoring Information System, improve the Government's reporting on results, etc.

These National Audit Office reports and the evaluation by Nakrosis and colleagues may help us to appreciate just how fundamental and far-reaching is the transformation of a government and its civil service from a classic rule-based bureaucracy to a strategic government. It is difficult to ensure that public governance makes full use of strategic planning and to make the delivery chain between long-term strategic vision and outcomes for the public work in approximately the way it is intended. This transition from bureaucratic government to strategic government is not for the faint hearted.

Judging the effectiveness of a strategic state

On the back of the sobering words about the scale of the challenge to transition from a bureaucracy to a government reformed around the concept of strategic planning, we turn now to one of the most important parts of the analysis offered in this book. Using the data from the 2016 Institutional Profiles Database, a strategic state index was constructed. This was then used in a scatterplot with national performance and a bivariate correlation calculated.

As shown in Figure 6.3, the countries with the highest scores on the strategic state index were all in a group of countries that were top rated for their performance in respect of the Human Development Index and the Environmental Performance Index. A big proportion of the countries with governments that had low scores on the strategic state index were also countries that were scoring relatively poorly in terms of national performance. The correlation between the two variables is evident from looking at the scatterplot but was also confirmed on the basis of the bivariate correlation (correlation 0.59). In summary, strategic states perform better than the rest.

In Chapter 4 a discussion at an international workshop organized by the OECD in 2011 referred to the possible relationship between strategic state characteristics and agility. Three factors used in measuring strategic policymaking were used to construct an agility index. These referred to experimentation in policy implementation, evaluation of public policies as a common practice, and a capacity to adapt public policies when social and economic contexts change.

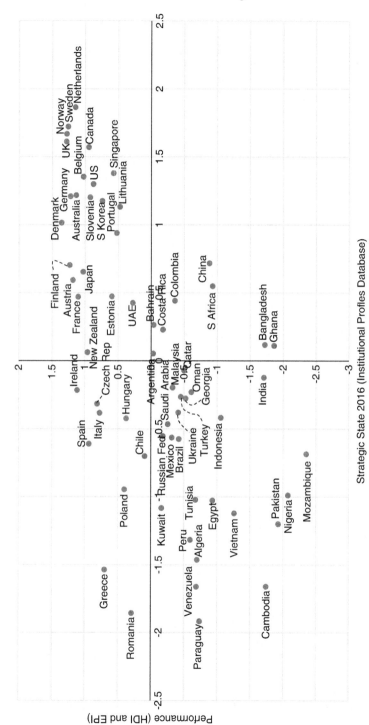

Figure 6.3 The strategic state and national performance.

Since the three factors composing the agility index were drawn from a set of factors used in the strategic state index, some correlation between the two indexes is to be expected. In fact, using the 2016 IPD data, the correlation was high at 0.86 for the sample of 63 countries. This is, of course, a very strong positive correlation. In this case, the argument is not that they are correlated because of a cause-and-effect relationship. Instead, the argument made here is that the high degree of association of the two indexes permits the conclusion that a strategic state (as defined here) is also an agile state (as defined here). So, an initial speculation that a strategic state can be a strategic performance state, but need not be agile, is rejected based on the analysis of the 2016 data used here.

Although the correlation between the strategic state index and the agility index was very strong, a few countries were more agile than might be expected based on their strategic state score. These included Singapore, Georgia, Chile, Poland, and Romania. There were some that had less agility than might be expected based on their strategic state score: Netherlands, Canada, Belgium, New Zealand, and Nigeria. There were also variations between them. Singapore and Georgia had been especially highly rated for their use of experimentation to implement public policies. Chile's ratings suggested that despite weakness in experimentation and evaluation it nevertheless was considered to have a good capacity for adapting policies to changing contexts. Nigeria had poor ratings for experimentation, evaluation, and adaptability of policies to changing contexts, whereas Belgium was weakest on evaluation of policies.

Finally, the presence of New Zealand and the Netherlands in the group appearing to have weaknesses in agility was curious. These two countries were also reputed to have been serious implementers of New Public Management. There have been reports not only of the strength of New Zealand's application of New Public Management but also its deleterious effects on governance. There had been problems of "fragmentation" and issues about taking a whole-of-government approach (Croissant and Miller 2019, 34):

> The core executive in New Zealand is organized according to new public-management approaches and methods. Most importantly, contracts are negotiated between ministers and chief executives. With the large number of government departments and ministers (26, with a further three undersecretaries), most of whom are responsible for several portfolios, taking a whole-of-government approach to policy development can be complex and time-consuming. Recent governments have reacted to concerns about fragmentation by recentralizing the steering capacity of the core executive.

In the case of the Netherlands, it has been suggested that New Public Management had created problems of coordination and cooperation (Hoppe et al. 2019, 53):

> Since the 2006 elections, politicians have demanded a reduction in the number of civil servants. This has resulted in a loss of substantive expertise, with civil servants essentially becoming process managers. Moreover, it has undermined the traditional relations of loyalty and trust between (deputy) ministers and top-level officers. The former have broken the monopoly formerly held by senior staff on the provision advice and information by turning increasingly to outside sources such as consultants. Top-level officers have responded with risk-averse and defensive behavior exemplified by professionally driven organizational communication and process management. They have embraced some Dutch variation of New Public Management thinking and practices. The upshot is that ministerial compartmentalization in the preparation of Council of Ministers meetings has increased. Especially in the Ministry of Justice and Safety, the quality of bureaucratic policy and legislation preparation has become a reason for serious concern.

Based on these reports, it looks as though participants at an OECD international workshop, held in 2011, might have had a point when it was suggested the legacy of New Public Management's reforms might create problems for developing agility and a strategic state approach to public governance (OECD 2012). But it might also be suggested that if a government does not develop agility adequately this may be diagnosed as problems of steering and difficulties in getting whole-of-government working. So, agility could be a multi-dimensional phenomenon: involving organizational cooperation, management tools (experimental implementation, evaluation), and capabilities; agility is not just about an ability to speedily flex resources and partnerships to achieve goals and solve problems.

Public governance

When the Russian President referred to the health of public governance in the Russian Federation in a speech to the Federal Assembly in May 2003, he mentioned both progress and continuing concerns (Putin 2003):

> Over these last three years not only have we worked hard to clear the mountain of problems that life itself forces us to tackle practically on a daily basis, we have also achieved some positive results. Now we

must take the next step and focus all our decisions and all our action on ensuring that in a not too far off future, Russia will take its recognised place among the ranks of the truly strong, economically advanced and influential nations....

Russia must become and will become a country with a flourishing civil society and stable democracy, a country that fully guarantees human rights and civil and political freedoms.

... Through all of this, we will create the conditions for people to enjoy a decent life and enable Russia to take its place as an equal in the community of most developed nations.... The adoption of the third part of the Russian Civil Code marked an important stage in our work on codifying our laws.... We have made great strides towards creating a genuinely independent court system.... We have improved the electoral system. We now have the conditions we need for the development of a real civil society, and also for the establishment of genuinely strong political parties.... But the Russian bureaucracy has proved itself poorly prepared to develop and implement the decisions our country needs today.

Within this wide-ranging speech can be seen references to three important elements of the set of institutions that together form public governance: these are the court system, the electoral system, and the "bureaucracy". It is clear that the President was setting out a strategic project for renewing the government of the Russian Federation, which he suggested would be important for delivering both decent lives for citizens and an improvement in the standing of the Federation in the world.

We can find references to three elements of public governance in Aristotle's "The Politics" written more than 2,000 years ago. He defined a state as an association of citizens in a constitution. Aristotle thought the state came into existence in part to prevent injustices by citizens, against each other, but he said a state was more than that. He strongly argued that it existed to secure the good life for its citizens. Indeed, in this quote from "The Politics", Aristotle seemed to be saying that the state commences as a means of providing safety and security to people but was sustained because it helps to bring about the good life (Aristotle 1981, 59): "... while the state came about as a means of securing life itself, it continues to secure the good life".

Aristotle was a strong advocate of laws as a part of the governance system. Public governance needed not only courts and judges to make decisions but also laws to guide the decisions made by judges (wherever possible). He clearly preferred the rule of law rather than rule by a single person making decrees. He wanted intelligent decision-making and not "angry" decision-making (Aristotle 1981, 226):

... he who asks the law to rule is asking God and intelligence and no others to rule; while he who asks for the rule of a human being is importing a wild beast too; for desire is like a wild beast, and anger perverts rulers and best of men. Hence law is intelligence without appetition.

He advocated the rule of law even where there was a single person in the ruling role (Aristotle 1981, 226): "even if it is better that certain persons rule, these persons should be appointed as guardians of the laws and as their servants".

Aristotle put alongside the rule of law the need for deliberative decision-making (Aristotle 1981, 228):

Among the matters which cannot be included in laws are those which are the subjects of deliberation. Yet they do not deny the inevitability of such decisions being taken by a man; they merely say that there should be not one man only but many.

The deliberative element had sovereignty over decisions on the following: "war and peace, the making and dissolving of alliances, legislation, the penalties of death, exile and confiscation of goods, the choosing of officials, and the scrutiny of their conduct on expiry of tenure" (Aristotle 1981, 277). The assembly to carry out such deliberations would nowadays include parliaments of elected representatives. Since such parliaments pass laws, they may be referred to as legislatures.

It brings us to how Aristotle conceived the overall architecture of governance. He parcelled the governance of a society into three sovereign elements as follows (Aristotle 1981, 277):

There are three elements in each constitution in respect of which every serious lawgiver must look for what is advantageous to it; if these are well arranged, the constitution is bound to be well arranged, and the differences in constitutions are bound to correspond to the differences between each of these elements. The three are, first, the deliberative, which discusses everything of common importance; second, the officials ...; and third, the judicial element.

Aristotle's three components of the governance system were the inspiration for the concept of public governance used in this book and as depicted in Figure 6.4.

The representative system index constructed here is to some extent a measure of the development of institutions of representative democracy. It is based on three factors:

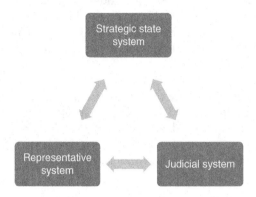

Figure 6.4 The public governance system.

1   Is there freedom of elections at national level?
2   Are electoral processes flawed?
3   Do the representative political institutions (e.g., Parliament) operate in accordance with the formal rules in force (e.g., Constitution)?

To achieve a high score on this index, a country would have free elections at national level, no irregularities in electoral processes, and its representative institutions would operate in line with constitutional rules.

The judicial system index was also based on three factors:

1   Degree of enforcement of judicial decisions
2   Timeliness of judicial decisions
3   Equal treatment of citizens before the law

For a high score on this index, the judicial system would have to deliver strong enforcement of decisions, fast decisions, and equality of treatment for citizens.

The strategic state index was based on the three factors identified earlier in this chapter: strong long-term strategic visions in four policy sectors, a strong strategic policy process, and a strong whole-of-society approach.

An analysis using the data from the 2016 Institutional Profiles Database showed that all three factors in the public governance system correlated with each other. There was a moderate correlations between the judicial system and the representative system and between the strategic state and the representative system. There was a strong correlation between the strategic state and the judicial system (correlation of 0.74). One implication of this is that the strategic state had a tendency in 2016 to be linked to strong judicial systems and to strong representative systems. Further analysis suggested a strong correlation between the public governance system and the national performance of a country (correlation of 0.74) (Table 6.1).

As the tabular presentation shows, some countries such as Bangladesh, India, Ghana, and South Africa seemed to be underperforming based on their public governance system. Others – such as Greece, Ireland, Italy, Spain, and Romania – seemed to be slightly overperforming based on their public governance system score. But in overall terms the fact is that there was a strong covariation of public governance system and national performance, and this yielded a stronger correlation than the strategic state index by itself.

Arguably the most important and interesting finding in the analysis above was the strong correlation between the public governance index

Table 6.1 National performance by public governance system

National performance (HDI and EPI)	Public governance index (based on Institutional Profiles Database 2016)		
	Low score	*Medium*	*High*
High	Greece	Czech Republic, Ireland, Italy, Spain	Australia, Austria, Belgium, Canada, Denmark, Estonia, Finland, France, Germany, Japan, South Korea, Lithuania, Netherlands, New Zealand, Norway, Portugal, Singapore, Slovenia, Sweden, the UK, United States
Medium	Romania, Russian Federation, Saudi Arabia, Turkey, Ukraine	Argentina, Bahrain, Brazil, Chile, Colombia, Costa Rica, Hungary, Kuwait, Malaysia, Mexico, Poland	
Low	Algeria, Cambodia, Egypt, Mozambique, Nigeria, Pakistan, Paraguay, Peru, Tunisia, Venezuela, Vietnam	Bangladesh, Georgia, Ghana, India, Indonesia, Oman, South Africa	

and the national performance variable (as computed using HDI and EPI). This outcome data were taken from sources other than the Institutional Database and the data were arguably very robust and very valid as measures of national social, economic, and environmental performance. As a subsidiary check on the meaningfulness of the public governance index, it was correlated with the Worldwide Governance Indicator of government effectiveness published online by the World Bank. The correlation between the public governance index and the indicator of government effectiveness was an astonishing 0.88, which is a very strong correlation. The countries with the strongest public governance systems and the most effective governments included the Netherlands, Norway, Denmark, Finland, and Singapore. It is important to recognize that the public governance index was not simply about management matters such as visions, strategies, policy, organizational co-operation and coordination, but also incorporated indexes for the judicial system and the system of representation. All these things appeared to be implicated in the estimates of government effectiveness being high.

Governance conditions

The question now arises as to the conditions in which strong public governance systems arise? One possible answer emerged from correlational analysis: there was a moderate tending towards a strong negative correlation of 0.64 between the extent of internal conflict in a society and the strength of the public governance system. This would be as expected on the basis that establishing effective governments is thought to involve the government getting a grip on violence and conflict within national borders. Levi (2006), as we have already noted earlier in the book, considered that effective government had to be established by addressing and subduing the violence, the ethnic violence, and violent criminality that was occurring within the borders of country while building a national identity.

> In virtually every state - or government - building project, it is necessary to "tame the violence" within the country's borders, to stop the "roving bandits", to halt ethnic violence and build a national identity, ...

It is interesting to note that whereas public governance systems get stronger as internal conflict diminishes and is replaced by peace, internal conflict has a non-linear relationship with the extent of democracy of a country. Internal conflicts – ethnic, religious, social, and land conflicts – are at their maximum for intermediate levels of democratic development. For example, countries such as Nigeria, Turkey, Ukraine, Georgia, Bangladesh, and Tunisia had relatively high levels of internal conflict and were at intermediate levels of democratic character; whereas the Gulf States and the Russian Federation had little internal conflict but were very low in their extent of democratic structures and practices. It was evident from this analysis that internal conflict can be reduced under two very different public governance systems. But it seems, that whatever the public governance system the extent of sound governance (as defined here) is linked to internal peace. This analysis also suggests that a Hobbesian understanding of society, or some theory derived from a Hobbesian perspective, is worth serious consideration.

Furthermore, looking at a sample of European countries, it appears that internal conflict in a society in 2016 was slightly correlated with a large percentage of disenchanted individuals in society in 2008. If we assume that large percentages of disenchanted citizens can persist over periods of eight or nine years, then it is possible that internal conflict can be caused, in part, by disenchanted populations, and this means having a society with many who are disinterested in politics and lack trust in politicians and parliaments. This would presumably make it more difficult to create "whole-of-society" approaches. As noted towards the end of the previous chapter, there was some evidence that a weak whole-of-society approach was likely to be found in societies where there was a lot of internal conflict.

This does not establish by itself the conclusion that internal conflict and peace are pertinent conditions for the development of strategic state systems and sound public governance. But it seems enough to say that this possibility should be taken seriously.

Model patterns

If we consider the decade from 2010 to 2019, it is evident that some countries that were estimated to have low or middling levels of government effectiveness, as shown by the data published as Worldwide Governance Indicators, increased their effectiveness much faster than the rest of the countries. In this book's sample of 63 countries, eleven of them stand out because of their big improvements in government effectiveness during the decade to 2019. These countries were the Russian Federation, Georgia, Ukraine, UAE, China, Paraguay, Indonesia, Cambodia, Saudi Arabia, Vietnam, and Lithuania. Except for Lithuania, these were not countries appearing in the top group of countries for sound public governance in 2016. What this means for the future of public governance is not yet clear. If these countries continued to grow in government effectiveness faster than others, they could trigger changes in our perceptions of the factors important for effectiveness. It is also possible that the governments of these countries could continue to become more effective and at the same time they could make changes in the characteristics of their public governance so that they resemble more closely those currently identified as the most effective governments.

The assumption made here is that history shows us that nothing political or social in nature persists forever. Things keep on changing, which includes public governance institutions (Dewey 1927, 33–34):

> In concrete fact, in actual and concrete organization and structure, there is no form of state which can be said to be the best: not at least till history is ended, and one can survey all its varied forms. The formation of states must be an experimental process. The trial process may go on with diverse degrees of blindness and accident, and at the cost of unregulated procedures of cut and try, of fumbling and groping, without insight into what men are after or clear knowledge of a good state even when it is achieved. Or it may proceed more intelligently, because guided by knowledge of the conditions which must be fulfilled. But it is still experimental. And since conditions of action and of inquiry and knowledge are always changing, the experiment must always be retried; the State must always be rediscovered ... It is not the business of political philosophy and science to determine what the state in general should or must be. What they may do is to aid in creation of methods such that experimentation may go on less blindly, less at the mercy of accident, more intelligently, so that men may learn from their errors and profit by their successes. The belief in political fixity, of the sanctity of some form of state consecrated by the efforts of our fathers and hallowed by tradition, is one of the stumbling-blocks in the way of orderly and directed change ...

As can be seen, John Dewey thought that changes in government should be through intelligent experimentation. He also warned against what we might call "model pattern" thinking (Dewey 1927, 45–46):

> The idea that there is a model pattern which makes a state a good or true state has affected practice as well as theory. It, more than anything else, is responsible for the effort to form constitutions offhand and impose them ready-made on peoples. Unfortunately, when the falsity of this view was perceived, it was replaced by the idea that states "grow" or develop instead of being made. This "growth" did not mean simply that states alter. Growth signified an evolution through regular stages to a predetermined end because of some intrinsic nisus or principle. This theory discouraged recourse to the only method by which alterations of political forms might be directed: namely, the use of intelligence to judge consequences. Equally with the theory which it displaced, it presumed the existence of a single standard form which defines the state as the essential and true article ... Incidentally, the theory flattered the conceit of those nations which, being politically

"advanced", assumed that they were so near the apex of evolution as to wear the crown of statehood.

It seems quite easy to slip into thinking that there is a hierarchy of states, graded from primitive or backwards through to "advanced". It would seem also quite likely that country leaders would notice the economic and political characteristics of "advanced countries" at the top of the hierarchy and set these as ideals, or principles to follow, in making decisions about how to speed up their national development. In 2007, the government of Indonesia included the following remarks in their vision for the country's development over the long term (President of Indonesia 2007, 46–47):

> From the standpoint of economic growth, the progress of a nation is measured by its standard of living, as reflected in its level of income and the distribution thereof. The high per capita income level and the more equitable distribution of income make the relevant nation to be more prosperous and more advanced…. In addition to having better social and economic indicators, an advanced nation also has an established political system, established political institutions, including an established law system. The political and social institutions are already functioning on the basis of basic rules, namely on the constitution that has been determined by its people. An advanced nation is also characterized by having the concrete and effective participation of the people in all aspects of life, encompassing economic, social, political aspects, as well as in defence and security matters. With regard to the political aspect, history has shown that there is close link between the level of prosperity of a nation and the political system it applies. An advanced nation generally applies the democratic system, that is in line with its culture and historical background. An advanced nation is a nation that respects the rights of its citizens, assures their security and social stability.

In fact, a model pattern can also be found in the World Bank Worldwide Governance Indicators (WGIs). Using these indicators all governments can be listed in percentile rankings. It is important to be clear about this, the rankings are based on judgements based on definition of each indicator and are not based on outcomes data. An example of the definition underlying this ranking process is that government effectiveness is estimated using judgements that include one on the independence of the civil service. Hypothetically speaking, a country that wants to move up the percentile rankings of government effectiveness could try reforming its civil service to make it even more independent. So, in this case, the evaluation of government effectiveness is based on a model pattern (a template) of what effective governments look like in conceptual terms, that is, by definition, and not on data showing the consequences of government.

We can contrast this with John Dewey's view which was not in favour of imposing a model pattern. As stated earlier, he thought that the state is formed through experimental action and has to be reformed over time through experimental action. This means reform is guided by learning from the consequences that occur when experimental action is taken. The experimental process rests on judging the goodness of government not according to its correspondence with a model pattern, but according to whether it produces good consequences.

The risk of evaluations of government based on model patterns is that they may for a time be true in the sense that they are empirically verified by producing good outcomes, but governments may continue to apply the model patterns through their decisions even when conditions have changed, and the model pattern has become out of date. So, to sum up, as history moves on, as conditions change, existing models of governance that are successful may be called into question. We need, therefore, to be sensitive to the durability of conclusions about public governance and our conclusions about how the strategic state fits into it.

And in practice we need an openness to being experimental. The need for experimental processes in relation to steering the evolution of government was recently given a modern gloss by the Government of Finland, which as we have seen has been among the group of the world's most strategic and effective governments. A section of the Prime Minister's Office in Finland made a case for experimentation in the introduction to a guide for the support of experiments in the public sector (Experimental Finland 2019, 6):

> In a world full of complex challenges, solutions born on the designer's table alone will not work. That is why we increasingly need to take swift action – developing by experimenting. The more complex the problem, the more crucial it is to experiment. One of the policies in the Government Programme of Prime Minister Sipilä is to introduce an experimenting culture. The aim has been to create innovative solutions for developing our society and various services, encourage proactivity and entrepreneurship, strengthen regional and local cooperation and promote citizen-driven ways of working. An experimental culture as an aim included in the Government Programme has been a unique feature on a global scale. The wider aim is to make Finland the world's best environment for innovating and experimenting by 2025.

Summary

Philip Heymann's ideas of strategic management in government were an important inspiration for the conceptualization of the strategic state in this book. It must be stressed that his ideas were just an inspiration and so there was not an immediate identity between his major concepts and those used in this book to define the strategic state. Heymann's emphasis on goals correlates with this book's "long-term strategic visions in policy sectors". His concept of capacity correlated with this book's concept of "strategic policy process", seen as consisting of key factors in the strategic capacity of government. And for his idea of outside support, the strategic state has the concept of a "whole-of-society approach".

It is not entirely clear how the three factors in the strategic state concept interrelate. We can speculate. It seems unlikely that a strong strategic policy process can exist in the absence of strong long-term strategic visions to be delivered. And it seems unlikely that the public and stakeholders will be mobilized to support government if the government lacks the credibility that comes from strong strategic policymaking. So, maybe the interrelation emerges as a processual development from long-term visions through strategic policy making and ending with support by public and stakeholder.

We have noted the developments that occurred in planning in the early 2000s in several countries. They included the changes that the Director-General of the National Development and Reform Commission on China considered amounted to a movement of the five-year planning system towards results-based strategic planning. They included the government of Indonesia passing the State Planning Law setting out a national development planning process and the role of the National Development Planning Agency. They included the evolution in Saudi Arabia's development planning systems, also towards strategic planning.

We also noted in the cases of Cambodia and Lithuania, the philosophy of these developments was people centred. The citizens were considered as not only beneficiaries of strategic planning by government but also essential active partners. Through the case of Lithuania, the point was also made that for a government to move from a classic rule-based bureaucracy to a strategic government was a fundamental and massive transition.

The transition of government from a bureaucracy to a government built around a strategic capability is not to be underestimated. It is a fundamental and radical transformation and probably not achievable in a short space of time. But, and this is one of the most important insights of this book, countries with the most developed strategic state characteristics were all in a group of countries that scored high for their national development performance (as measured by the Human Development Index and the Environmental Performance Index). Most of those with the least developed strategic state characteristics were poor performers in terms of national development. The strategic states perform better than the rest.

The chapter then moved on to look at public governance as a totality, with evidence that the strategic state governments had a tendency in

2016 to be linked to strong judicial systems and to strong representative systems. There was a strong correlation between the public governance system as a whole and the national performance of a country. As a check on the meaningfulness of the findings, the public governance index was correlated with the Worldwide Governance Indicator of government effectiveness published online by the World Bank. The correlation was astonishingly high. Governance and government effectiveness are much more than an issue of public sector management.

In effect, this chapter acknowledged that strategic states are about governance and not markets or quasi-markets. Consequently, the issues of conflict and peace in society were examined to see if there was a connection with public governance within which the strategic state is lodged. It was discovered that whereas public governance systems get stronger as internal conflict diminishes and is replaced by peace, internal conflict has a non-linear relationship with variations in the democracy of a country.

We finished with a consideration of Dewey's remarks about "model patterns" and set this against the findings that in the decade from 2010 to 2019 it was evident that some countries that were estimated to have low or middling levels of government effectiveness, as shown by the data published as Worldwide Governance Indicators, had increased their effectiveness much faster than the rest of the countries. We speculated that if these countries continued to grow in government effectiveness faster than others, they could trigger changes in our perceptions of the factors important for government effectiveness.

The argument was made that the risk in relying on model patterns was that they may for a time be true in the sense that they are empirically verified by producing good outcomes, but governments may continue to believe in the truth of model patterns even when the model pattern has become out of date. This was the basis, in the end, for arguing the need for experimental processes in relation to steering the evolution of government. The recent advocacy of experimentation by the Government of Finland was noted, a government which as we have seen is one of the most strategic and effective governments in the world.

References

Aristotle (1981) *The politics*. London: Penguin Books.

Blöndal, J.R., Hawkesworth, I., & Choi, H.-D. (2009) Budgeting in Indonesia. *OECD Journal on Budgeting*, 2009/2, 1–31.

Budd, A. (1978) *The politics of economic planning*. London: Fontana.

Croissant, A. & Miller, R. (2019) *New Zealand report: Sustainable governance indicators*. Gutersloh: Bertelsmann Stiftung.

Dewey, J. (1927) *The public and its problems*. Athens: Swallow Press, Ohio University Press.

Experimental Finland (2019) *How to support experiments: A guide for the mentors*. Helsinki: Prime Minister's Office. Available at: https://kokeilevasuomi.fi/en/frontpage [14 September 2021].

Government of the Republic of Lithuania (2002) Resolution no 827. On the approval of the strategic planning methodology. 6 June 2002. Vilnius. Available at: https://e-seimas.lrs.lt/portal/legalAct/lt/TAD/966edb0080a711e6a0f68fd135 e6f40c?jfwid=q8i88m8py [15 September 2021].

Government of the Republic of Lithuania (2012) Lithuania's progress strategy "Lithuania 2030". Available at: https://lrv.lt/uploads/main/documents/files/EN_version/Useful_information/lithuania2030.pdf. [16 September 2021].

Heymann, P. (1987) *The politics of public management*. New Haven and London: Yale University Press.

Hoppe, R., Krouwel, A., & Bandelow, N.C. (2019) *Netherlands report: Sustainable governance indicators*. Gutersloh: Bertelsmann Stiftung.

Levi, M. (2006) Why we need a new theory of government. *Perspectives on Politics*, 4(1), 5–19.

Lindblom, C.E. (1975) *The sociology of planning: Thought and social interaction*. In M. Bornstein. Cambridge, MA: Ballinger.

Ministry of Economy and Planning (2005) *Eighth Development Plan, 2005–9*. Riyadh: Ministry of Planning Kingdom of Saudi Arabia.

Nakrošis, V., Šiugždinienė, J., & Antanaitė, I. (2020) New development: Between politics and strategic planning—the management of government priorities in Lithuania. *Public Money & Management*, 40(4), 299–303. 10.1080/09540962. 2020.1715096

National Audit Office (2018) *Assessment of maturity of budgetary governance*. 10 October 2018. Vilnius. National Audit Office.

National Audit Office (2019) *Assessment of changes in strategic planning and budgeting*. 10 December 2019. Vilnius. National Audit Office.

OECD (2012) *International workshop "strategic agility for strong societies and economies": Summary and issues for further debate*. Paris: OECD Publishing.

President of the Republic of Indonesia (2007) Law of the Republic of Indonesia, number 17 of 2007 on long-term national development plan of 2005–2025. Available at: https://www.bappenas.go.id/files/6715/3173/4665/RPJPN_2005–2025.pdf [15 September 2021].

Putin, V. (2003) Annual address to the Federal Assembly of the Russian Federation. Available at: http://en.kremlin.ru/events/president/transcripts/21998 [9 July 2019].

Royal Government of Cambodia (2010) National strategic development plan update 2009–2013. Available at: https://www.ilo.org/wcmsp5/groups/public/–asia/---ro-bangkok/documents/publication/wcms_145085.pdf [15 September 2021].

Teramoto, M. (2002) Section 5. Development plans of Cambodia. In *Japan International Cooperation Agency (2002) The Kingdom of Cambodia: From Reconstruction to Sustainable Development*. Tokyo: Japan International Cooperation Agency. Available at: http://www.jica.go.jp/english/publication/studyreport/index.html [15 September 2021].

Thornton, P., Rogers, D., Sophal, C., & Vickery, C. (2009) Evaluation of DFID country programmes: Cambodia. Evaluation Report EV703.

May 2009. Available at: https://assets.publishing.service.gov.uk/government/uploads/system/uploads/attachment_data/file/67733/cambodia-evaluation.pdf [15 September 2021].

Turk, C. (2006) Vietnam: A comprehensive strategy for growth and poverty reduction. In OECD *and World Bank. Emerging good practice in managing for development results. First issue.* Paris: OECD, pp. 44–50.

Wang, M. & Lin, X. (2007) China: Towards results-based strategic planning. In *Emerging good practice in managing for development results*, 2nd edition. Available at: http://www.mfdr.org/Sourcebook [4 April 2019].

7 Quality Public Services

Introduction

Can the strategic management process of government be directly related to the quality of public services? In other words, are public services of a better quality when there are long-term strategic visions, capabilities for strategic management, and a whole-of-society approach? The answer from the analysis presented in this chapter is that there is a strong alignment of high-quality public services and these factors.

Taking inspiration from the World Bank's 1997 view of public services and national development, this chapter probes how quality public services link to national development. This means looking at how quality public services link to strong strategic policy processes, the strategic state, public governance systems, national outcomes, and public happiness. During the analysis, we will also look at one of the generic strategies for a public governance system: to outsource or not to outsource public services? We will also encounter two unusual national cases that we will probe a little deeper: the United States and South Africa. Using data from the Institutional Profiles Database for 2016, our analysis reveals that they appear to have performed badly in the delivery of quality public services compared to many other countries, especially when account is taken of estimates of their government effectiveness. The explanation for each case seems to be different and helps us to appreciate in a little more depth how the system of public governance has been working in different countries in recent times.

Policy perspectives and strategic options

The advice of World Bank policy specialists in the second half of the 1990s was that government had a "central role in ensuring the provision of basic services – education, health, infrastructure" (World Bank 1997, 27). Governments with the lowest institutional capability were advised to concentrate on "providing the pure public goods and services that markets cannot provide ... as well as goods and services with large

DOI: 10.4324/9781351045797-7

positive externalities, such as property rights, safe water, roads, and basic education" (World Bank 1997, 40).

Using the 1997 views of the World Bank as our springboard, we might expect that the world then and now had governments of varying amounts of capability and, consequently, of effectiveness. The governments that had least capability and least effectiveness were presumably ones that had the lowest availability of quality public services. In consequence of this framing of the issue of government effectiveness, and assuming operational definitions of government effectiveness can encompass causes and consequences, we can see the logic of a definition of government effectiveness that included the quality of public services, as well as the quality of policy formulation and implementation and the capabilities of the civil service. Just to complete this framing of the issue of quality public services, a reasonable hypothesis based on this thinking would be that the extent of the availability of quality public services would be a good predictor of public confidence in government. If true, we would expect some governments to manage public services partly with the aim of maintaining or improving public confidence. It is noteworthy, therefore, that the Government of Canada (2019) recently stated: "The effective management of government services contributes to value for money, produces high levels of client satisfaction, and promotes confidence in government".

We can also highlight the World Bank's judgment in 1997 that citizens needed to be empowered and given a voice to create a pressure on governments to deliver quality public services (World Bank 1997, 54):

> Perhaps the most important change in the incentive environment [of government] is to empower users themselves with "voice" not only to work in partnership with providers where localized information is key to efficient delivery, but also to monitor providers' performance and to enforce, through the political process, a commitment to quality.

The rhetoric of reforms of government in the 1980s had stressed efficiency and competition between service providers. In the 1990s, the rhetoric had evolved to include quality and partnerships with stakeholders. All these themes found their way into this quote.

If citizens and service users reported being dissatisfied with the availability and quality of public services, the implication is that their needs and expectations were not being met. Conversely, if they were satisfied, we can infer that their needs and expectations were being met. Just to labour the point, in judging their satisfaction or dissatisfaction with public services, they are making a valuation, and this valuation tells us about the quality of the public services from their point of view. This leads us to stress a particular definition of the quality of public services: if a public service is of low quality, it can be defined as being of low quality because it is failing to meet citizen's needs and expectations. If public services meet the needs and expectations of citizens very well, then the public services are high quality. Such a citizen-centric definition can sit alongside other definitions (e.g., politician-centric, professional-centric). The fact of these different definitions should convey the possibility that different valuations will be made of the quality of a public service by the public, the politicians, and the professional civil servants, who have related but different interests in public services.

The citizen-centric definition of quality has some affinity with the concept of "public value" as made popular in the public administration literature by Moore (1995). His view is not identical to the citizen-centric view because, rightly, he also recognizes the role of politicians representing the public in determining public value. His formulation is that individual preferences do establish the value of what the government spends money on and does, but this valuation is subject to a political test. This is the authorization process conducted by representative institutions. But, of course, if the politicians are making decisions about what public money is spent on and what government does, and make these decisions as members of representative institutions, they should be representing the citizens when they make these decisions. Recognizing the role of both the public and their representatives in valuing public services is a necessary addition to the complexity of our understanding of public value.

The responsiveness of the politicians to public preferences when authorizing spending and actions is often a complex process requiring much judgment. Societies have varying amounts of internal conflicts (along cleavage lines that could be ethnic, religious, regional, social, or land-related). The "will of the public" is not self-evident in a society where there is a substantial level of internal conflict. In such circumstances, there is a clear necessity for the politicians to develop a point of view: should they back a majority view, a minority view, seek a compromise between various preferences, or, more ambitiously, try to foster a discussion involving the public to form a genuine consensus (or more of a consensus). All these are theoretically possible as the politicians make their minds up.

The pursuit of quality public services might be treated as one option in a set of generic strategies. But arguably, the best-known generic strategy approaches were developed for private business leaders wanting to know how to beat their competitors in the same industry. But is beating competitors the top requirement for government strategy? By 1997, the World Bank was really saying that governments to be effective needed to be citizen centric. This means placing at the top of the list of requirements for a government strategy a focus on the needs and expectations of the citizens. In fact, it is not clearly the case that even individual public sector organizations should put all their eggs in the basket of strategy dominated by a desire to beat competitors. If the whole public governance system is trying to improve the well-being of citizens and protect and improve the natural environment, then this governance system will be trying to mobilize individual public sector organizations, or organizations operating under public authority, to place citizen well-being and the natural environment first.

Strategic choices of organizations and the quality of public services

One much-discussed approach in the academic literature of public sector strategic management is the idea that there are a small number of generic strategies and the trick for leaders doing strategic thinking is to work out which of the generic strategies is optimum in the situation faced by the public sector organization. When this type of thinking prevails in academic research, it can motivate a search for which of the generic strategies is most successful. It is worth initially exploring the generic strategy concept as it developed for private sector businesses. It is these ideas that are taken and tested in the public sector context.

In the private sector, a business facing tough competition in their industry from other businesses with lower costs that are selling products or services of equal quality at lower prices should think about a strategic response. One option is that it could try to reduce its costs and then lower its prices. Another option is to try to raise the quality of its products or services enabling it to charge higher prices (Ohmae 1991). This thinking suggests that the two basic defensive strategies are either to cut costs and prices or to increase quality so that prices can be raised. Related but not identical strategic choices were suggested by the Defender and Prospector archetypes of Miles and Snow (1978) and the Cost Leadership and Differentiation strategic choices of Porter (1980).

While choosing between competing on price and competing on quality explicitly deals with the issue of quality, Miles and Snow and Michael Porter were largely opaque in how their strategic choices related to quality. That does not stop us from speculating on what their theories might mean for quality of products and services. For example, the Prospector's archetype of Miles and Snow, with its focus on product and market innovation, might have a connection with quality. It is possible that innovation could be seen as meeting hitherto latent needs, offering increased productivity to the business, and producing better quality in the eyes of customers. But to be clear, Miles and Snow do not suggest better quality is integral to innovation. Turning to Michael Porter's Differentiation strategy, this focused on value engineering by delivering higher value to customers providing the differentiation allowed higher prices to be charged. This differentiation could be offering more quality based on new or additional qualities built into the products or services.

In appraising such theories, some realism is needed about the extent to which government organizations choose strategies and then manage their implementation. A recent example of research into generic strategies in government organizations is the investigation by Jacobsen and Johnsen (2020). They were interested in the Miles and Snow typology of prospectors, defenders, and reactors in Norwegian local government. In their research, they suggested that earlier studies had not investigated the alignment of structure with strategy. This is a serious criticism if the point of the earlier studies was to verify the archetypes presented by Miles and Snow. Figure 7.1 is (more or less) based on Miles and Snow's conceptual model and shows the importance of alignment of structure with strategy in it. So, what did Jacobson and Johnsen discover? They analysed 2016 data on 173 municipalities and looked for evidence that changes in strategy were followed by changes in structure. The link was present in the data, but it was there only to a modest degree. The researchers comment on this suggesting the weakness of alignment of structure when strategy changes may explain why the relationship between strategy and performance has been weak (low) in studies of public sector organizations in some countries.

But, as interesting as these findings of Jacobsen and Johnsen are, perhaps the more important judgment to be made is that theoretical ideas developed to help private sector businesses beat competitors in markets and industries are not as useful as they might seem at first sight.

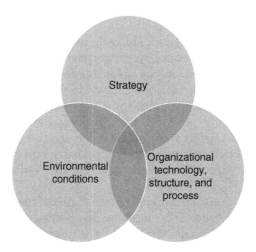

Figure 7.1 Miles and Snow (1978): pertinent conditions for successful strategy.

Notes: Key questions are: Is there a clear strategy? Is the strategy right for environmental conditions? Are technology, structure, and process linked to strategy properly?

So, we now turn to strategies that are pertinent to public governance systems as a whole: outsourcing and open government. To improve quality, it is necessary to focus on effectiveness, fitness for purpose, and it leads to changing and aligning services to get a better fit with public needs. Alignment ranges in impact; it can mean services are adjusted and refined to improve quality, or more radically services are redesigned and changed, and most radical of all innovations in public service systems are made. Outsourcing can be used to reform public services systems. Public participation is more open-ended in its impacts on quality.

Outsourcing as a strategy

One of the basic strategic choices to be made about public services is whether the government should be providing most public services using ministries and government agencies or whether it should use substantial amounts of public money to fund contracts with private and voluntary sector organizations to provide public services on behalf of government. In the 1980s in some countries, there was a big shift to the second of these options – "outsourcing". The World Bank backed a pragmatic selection of providers of public services (World Bank 1997, 27):

> Although the state still has a central role in ensuring the provision of basic services – education, health, infrastructure – it is not obvious that the state must be the only provider, or a provider at all. The state's choices about provision, financing, and regulation of these services must build on the relative strengths of markets, civil society, and state agencies.

This makes it clear that in the World Bank's judgment the responsibility for the public services would remain with government, but public sector organizations would not have a monopoly of public service provision.

This outsourcing option had been heavily promoted in the highly influential book by Osborne and Gaebler, which was published in 1992. While mostly concerned with experiences and developments in the United States, Osborne and Gaebler's list of ideas for creating high-performing and flexible government organizations included the proposal to move towards what they called "competitive government" (Osborne and Gaebler 1992).

Their arguments began with the memorable phrase that governments should be "steering" and not "rowing" – meaning being strategic and not (always) being a provider of public services. In a way, their book's arguments reflected the historical moment when they could reflect on a decade of governments that had outsourced provision in a bid to reduce government's production costs and just as quality management was emerging as a new concern, focused on effectiveness and not just efficiency. Their understanding and arguments seem to straddle two different phases of government modernization and reform.

It is important to note that they were not suggesting government should be abdicating responsibility for public services (Osborne and Gaebler 1992, 45, 47):

> Services can be contracted out or turned over to the private sector. But governance cannot. We can privatise discrete steering functions, but not the overall process of governance. ... "It makes sense to put the delivery of many public services in private hands (whether for-profit or nonprofit), if by doing so a government can get more effectiveness, efficiency, equity, or accountability. But we should not mistake this for some grand ideology of privatizing government. When governments contract with private businesses ... they are shifting the delivery of services, not the responsibility for services".

A second point worth noting is that governments that commission services from the private sector can choose to maintain or even enhance the quality standards of public services, as the following argument suggested (Osborne and Gaebler 1992, 35):

> Freeing policy managers to shop around for the most effective and efficient service providers helps them squeeze more bang out of every buck. It allows them to use competition between service providers. It preserves maximum flexibility to respond to changing circumstances. And it helps them insist on accountability to a quality performance: contractors know they can be let go if their quality sags; civil servants know they cannot.

In fact, Osborne and Gaebler seemed to be saying that outsourcing had the potential to enable governments to achieve higher quality public services than if delivery was kept "in-house". A few years later, the World Bank also took the view that outsourcing could raise quality (World Bank 1997, 97): "Using the market to deliver contestable services – too many of which are now the sole domain of government - can lower costs and improve service quality". Over the many years since the Osborne and Gaebler book was published, there have been many critics of outsourcing that have asserted that it had led to reductions in the quality of public services, and to the extent that standards of quality fell, this might be the result of governments choosing lower costs even if quality fell. However, it must be said that outsourcing can provoke ideological attitudes both for it and against it. It is critical from a public governance perspective that outsourcing is pragmatic in the best sense of the word, that is, with outsourcing being used where government is getting the effectiveness, efficiency, and accountability that are the ideal or desired results of an out-sourcing strategy.

By becoming more focused on a strategic role (steering) and by commissioning voluntary and private sector organizations to take on public services provider roles, it is possible that governments were transitioning to both competitive government and enabling government. In a later book, Osborne and Plastrik (1997) explained their idea of "steering" (which was, in effect, their preferred way of talking about strategic planning) as follows (Osborne and Plastrik, 106–107):

> Steering is about setting goals, choosing strategies to achieve them, choosing organisations to carry out those strategies, measuring how well the strategies and organisations do in achieving the goals, and making adjustments. (106–107)

In the Osborne and Gaebler's book, there is an approving reference to the city government of St Paul Minnesota in the 1970s which not only used volunteers' time in a range of areas and used voluntary organizations to operate recycling programmes but also outsourced garbage collection and youth services to the private sector. They say that the city government was doing more with less (Osborne and Gaebler 1992, 26):

> By constantly catalysing solutions outside the public sector, Latimer was able to increase his government impact while trimming its staff by 12 per cent, keeping budget and property tax growth below the rate of inflation, and reducing the city's debt. Without massive layoffs-in fact, while enriching the lives of public employees-he gave voters what they wanted: a government that did more but spent less.

Obviously, the capabilities government needs to outsource public services successfully will not be identical to the capabilities needed to directly deliver public services. Also obviously, the use of an outsourcing strategy must be done competently. So, as governments transition from a traditional model to a new model in which there is an outsourcing strategy they need to learn and develop the appropriate capabilities. Osborne and Gaebler could give examples of where such learning and development had occurred (Osborne and Gaebler 1992, 87–88):

> Cities like Phoenix have learned a great deal about how to manage their competitive contracts. Phoenix ties reimbursement closely to performance and puts withholding clauses in its contracts, so contractors who do not perform are not paid. It tracks citizen complaints by area and incidence, so managers can tell a contractor exactly where the problem is and defer payment until it is solved. And it uses inspectors to compare contracted areas and areas served by public agencies.

Table 7.1 Performance management: in-house and competitive contracts

	In-house performance management	*Management of competitive contracts*
Monitoring results/ performance	Use performance targets	Track citizen complaints
Ensuring consequences of performance	Link targets to individual goals of top managers	Include withholding clauses in contracts
Evaluation	Track results over time	Inspectors compare areas contracted and areas served by public agencies

This example of Phoenix, the capital of Arizona in the United States, suggests a comparison with a standard model of the management of in-house performance of public services (Table 7.1).

Osborne and Gaebler's prescriptions meant changes for both providers and consumers of public services: they argued that there could be better results by introducing competition between public service providers, involving private sector providers, and empowering consumers of public services by offering them choices between providers. Right at the start of the book, they made this claim (Osborne and Gaebler 1992, 2):

> ... new kinds of public institutions are emerging. They are lean, decentralised, and innovative. They are flexible, adaptable, quick to learn new ways when conditions change. They use competition, customer choice, and other nonbureaucratic mechanisms to get things done as creatively and effectively as possible. And they are our future.

So, Osborne and Gaebler argued that governments should be redesigning public services to offer consumers a choice of providers and to create effective competition by using funding mechanisms that ensured consumer choices had income consequences for providers. In other words, the competition between providers of public services had to be competition to be chosen by consumers and competition for government funding. They provided examples of this working very well in public education. They summed up this reform package as follows (Osborne and Gaebler 1992, 169):

> ... governments have begun to transform themselves. They have begun to listen carefully to their customers, through customer surveys, focus groups, and a wide variety of other methods. They have begun to offer their customers choices-of schools, of recreation facilities, even of police services. And they have begun to put their customers in the driver's seat, by putting resources directly in their hands and letting them choose their service providers.

It is interesting to note that in this quote reforming governments were described as not only redesigning services to give consumers a choice of provider, and to create competition between public service providers, but also as engaging with the public through consultation and other means (e.g., test marketing). We might infer government was being told to find out what consumers of public services wanted and then deliver more responsiveness by offering users a choice of provider. And it is worth underlining that this was not seen as inevitably a cause of decline in the quality of public services. Osborne and Gaebler thought that consumer choice and provider competition would create pressure on providers to be efficient and to increase the quality of services.

In some countries, the extent of consumer choice of public service provider and competition between public service providers have increased over the last two decades. One example is Sweden where the welfare system went from being based almost entirely on government provision to one where non-government providers deliver significant proportions of child and elderly care and education. Evaluation studies in Sweden sometimes suggested that outsourcing elderly care and schooling had a small or moderate effect on quality and sometimes that there had been no effect on quality (OECD 2020). Studies evaluating user choice in the UK found an unclear picture of its effects on quality (Lewis 2017). An overview of the topic of consumer choice and competition in publicly funded services recently suggested that private sector providers tend to be more efficient but may reduce quality to achieve it. It was also suggested that "In some circumstances, a well-designed consumer-choice system can result in both cost-efficient (private) provision and high quality" (OECD 2020, 2).

The public participation strategy and quality of public services

Public participation was discussed and examples of it were presented in a previous chapter but, in this chapter, we are interested in public participation specifically in relation to the quality of public services, and the examples here show, or suggest, the consequences of public participation for the quality of public services.

The World Bank gave the following example of how participation and improvements in the quality of services were associated (World Bank 1997, 123):

In Teocelo, a town in Mexico's state of Veracruz, decentralization has created opportunities to organize resources for health more efficiently by identifying the population's needs and designing strategies to foster participation through community organization and health education. Coverage increased for both preventive and curative care, the quality of services improved enormously, and infant mortality rates fell. In addition, users of health facilities reported that the attitudes of health personnel and the quality of services had improved greatly.

In this second example, the absence of public participation was associated with poor services. The example is from Mexico again. Two states in Mexico – Oaxaca and Chiapas – were quite similar in a number of respects (World Bank 1997, 122): "The two states have similar resource endowments and development potential, and both have a high percentage of poor and indigenous populations". But whereas Oaxaca had "a long tradition of participatory mechanisms for indigenous populations and the poor" in Chiapas there was "the denial of such options". This denial of participatory mechanism was said to have led to poor services in Chiapas.

How does participation lead to higher quality public services? At least two mechanisms can be suggested. First, public participation may open government to more and better understanding of what service users want and what problems they are having with the services as they are. Public hearings and surveys are two of the tools that can help with getting a better understanding of the public (Denhardt et al. 2000, 714):

> Some local governments continue long-established practices of developing strategic plans and initiatives, then seeking public input and building public support through public hearings. ... Citizen surveys are another instrument for gauging public sentiment and preferences while not requiring massive turnouts for citizen forums. Well designed and implemented surveys are excellent tools for guiding strategic planning initiatives, providing insights into the concerns and priorities of citizens.

Second, public participation may encourage stronger "civic cultures" in which members of the public take more responsibility for the success of their communities and public services. More active citizens, it may be argued, emerge from the experience of active involvement. This was a point made in relation to local government attempts in the United States to involve citizens in setting priorities and deciding on strategies at the local level (Denhardt et al. 2000, 711):

> The guiding philosophy is that face-to-face democracy is most likely to unleash in citizens the sense of personal responsibility for helping to solve problems, a willingness to work for the good of the community instead of selfish interests alone, the opportunity for the type of dialogue necessary to build consensus, and access to the public policy decisions making processes likely to be helpful in solving local problems.

More active citizens in the ranks of the public could be quite critical in many public services where the delivery process is a co-production process. This is certainly the case in health and education where people need to be active and take responsibility in health and educational processes if they are to increase their chances of being healthy and better educated.

Which countries have had good quality public services?

In practice, it seems that there is a great deal of variation between countries in the quality of public services. The first indication of this is the great variation between countries in citizens' satisfaction with public services.

A Eurobarometer survey in the Spring of 2016 asked people in the Member States of the European Union how good they judged the provision of public services in their country (European Union 2016, 37). Looking at only the Member state countries included in this book's core sample of 63 countries, answers ranged from, at the top end, 88% of respondents saying "good" in one country down to a mere 8% in another country. As we have noted before in this book, a geographical pattern was evident. The countries in the north of Europe generally did best. The Netherlands came top, with 88% of Dutch respondents saying public services were good, followed by Finland (79%), Sweden (69%), Denmark (64%), and the UK (62%). Countries with low percentages of respondents saying "good" were to be found in the south of Europe: worst was Greece, where only 8% of Greek respondents said services were good, and with other countries in the south of Europe doing much better: Italy (23%), Portugal (36%), and Spain (31%). Countries in the centre and east of Europe were mostly in the middle range in terms of percentages seeing public services as good: Czech Republic (56%), Hungary (47%), Lithuania (49%), and Poland (39%). The remaining countries had percentages saying the provision of public services was good ranging from just under 50% to a relatively high percentage: Austria (66%), Belgium (60%), Estonia (65%), France (52%), Ireland (45%), and Slovenia (49%).

Data published by the OECD on citizen satisfaction and confidence with named public services in 2016 also highlighted great variations between countries (OECD 2017a). In the data presented here, we concentrate on countries included in this book's core sample of 63 countries. Starting with citizen satisfaction with the availability of quality public services, satisfaction with the health care system was most widespread in Belgium (91% satisfied) and least in the Russian Federation (27% satisfied). Satisfaction with the education system was most widespread in Norway (86% satisfied) and least in the Russian Federation and Greece (both 44% satisfied). Turning now to citizen confidence with the judicial system, Denmark and Norway came joint top (82% of respondents confident) and Chile was bottom (21% of respondents confident). Finally, with respect to citizen confidence with local police, this ranged, at the top end, from Finland (88% confident) down to Mexico (40% confident) at the bottom end.

Expert ratings of quality

There are data on the quality of public services published in the 2016 Institutional Profiles Database. These data are produced by expert ratings. The experts were asked to make judgments about the quality of the public services provided by the public sector in the following: primary and secondary education in urban and rural areas, higher and university education (teaching and research), basic healthcare, and public transport. It is important to note that the experts were asked about the quality of services provided by the public sector. The experts made their judgement using a 5-point scale, with the lowest point being "very low quality" and the highest point being "good quality". These were then averaged to give a single value for the quality of public services provided by the public sector.

The scatterplot in Figure 7.2 is intended to display visually the cross-country variations in the expert ratings of the quality of public services provided by the public sector. It shows countries that were rated as having high-quality public services included Austria, Finland, Germany, Japan, the Netherlands, Norway, Singapore, South Korea, and the UK. Among the countries with the lowest quality ratings were Cambodia, Chile, India, Mozambique, Paraguay, Peru, and South Africa. Also, it should be noted that the United States was judged to provide relatively low-quality public services.

The low quality of the United States' public services stood out especially when it was compared with countries that had governments estimated to be highly effective in terms of international comparisons. The United States seemed to be an outlier in terms of governments considered very effective. Was the expert judgment wrong? It is to some extent corroborated by other expert judgments. Quirk et al. (2018) report that public services in the United States have been largely delivered by local and state levels of government and that there has been no presumption of national standards. That is, the federal level had largely not intervened in public services standards. They suggested that for a long time primary and secondary education had been disappointing. On the health care system, they said (Quirk et al. 2018, 12): "The system has provided significantly inferior care to the large segment without coverage (especially people of relatively low income, ineligible under the means-tested Medicaid program)". In relation to policing services, they reported that violence has been a problem (Quirk et al. 2018, 16):

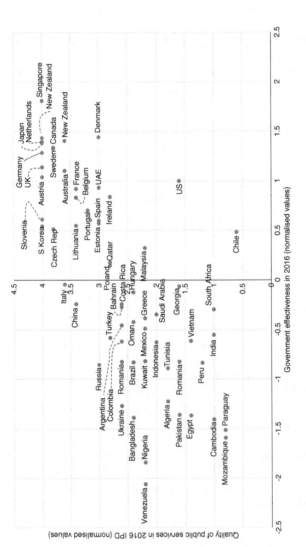

Figure 7.2 Scatterplot of expert ratings of the quality of public services and government effectiveness.

Notes

1 The quality of public services data is from the Institutional Profiles Database for 2016. Expert ratings were made of different public services using a five-point scale. The ratings ranged from the lowest point which was "very low quality" to the highest point which was "good quality". These were then averaged to give a single value for the quality of public services provided by the public sector. The data was obtained from: http://www.cepii.fr/institutions/EN/ipd.asp [28 August 2018] and was normalised for the scatterplot.

2 "Government Effectiveness captures perceptions of the quality of public services, the quality of the civil service and the degree of its independence from political pressures, the quality of policy formulation and implementation, and the credibility of the government's commitment to such policies. Estimate gives the country's score on the aggregate indicator, in units of a standard normal distribution, i.e. ranging from approximately –2.5 to 2.5." The data was downloaded from: https://databank.worldbank.org [4 July 2020]. For this analysis the data was normalised.

First, a number of large cities are plagued by homicides, primarily in inner city black and Latino neighborhoods. New Orleans, St. Louis, Baltimore, Detroit and Chicago all number among the world's 50 cities with the highest homicide rates. Second, there are repeated instances of individuals conducting large-scale violent attacks on civilians in public spaces, killing large numbers of people, often using semi-automatic weapons with large ammunition clips....

In addition, the 2014 fatal shooting of an unarmed black teenager by a police officer in a St. Louis suburb drew attention to a possibly growing phenomenon of excessive police violence, especially against African Americans. The Black Lives Matter protest movement gained momentum during 2015, highlighting the insecurity of racial minorities vulnerable to harassment or violence by local police departments.... In terms of actual casualties and loss of life, the frequency of mostly black-on-black inner-city violence is by far the greatest failure to provide safe living conditions.

Surveys of the public in the United States conducted in 2016 did not paint an overly pessimistic analysis of the basic public services, although public satisfaction with education was very average and the public's confidence in the judicial system was relatively poor. Arguably, the expert judgments of the quality of public services in the Institutional Profiles Database were not completely implausible.

We might expect that the Institutional Profiles Database data on the quality of public services might approximately mirror the data on citizen satisfaction and public confidence in public services. The analysis of the covariation of the expert ratings and citizen satisfaction and confidence data do reveal slight or moderate correlations. Why are they not strong correlations?

One possible explanation is that the public's ratings of their satisfaction may be influenced by their expectations and these expectations may be affected by local conditions and events. They may also be affected by "public discourse" and this may be impacted by political parties and affected by the traditional and social media.

Another possible explanation is that the experts were asked to judge the quality of public services provided by the public sector, whereas the satisfaction and confidence data might be different because citizens might also be reacting to outsourced public services. This will depend on whether the public lump all public services together irrespective of the provider. There are some data on outsourcing in 2016 for 22 countries in the book's core sample. This is shown in Table 7.2. As can be seen, the Netherlands and Germany outsourced a relatively large amount of the provision of goods and services to the public, whereas Denmark

Table 7.2 Government outsourcing in 2016

Country	Government expenditure on outsourcing to non-government sector to deliver goods and services to the public in 2016 (percentage of GDP)	Total government spend on outsourcing in 2016 (percentage of GDP)
Austria	4.1	10.6
Belgium	8.0	12.0
Canada	2.2	9.5
Czech Republic	3.1	9.3
Denmark	1.5	10.5
Estonia	2.0	9.0
Finland	2.8	13.8
France	6.0	11.0
Germany	8.6	13.4
Greece	2.4	7.1
Hungary	2.0	9.0
Ireland	2.0	5.6
Italy	2.7	8.1
Lithuania	2.0	6.8
The Netherlands	10.3	16.1
Norway	2.4	9.4
Poland	1.9	7.7
Portugal	1.8	7.5
Slovenia	2.0	8.5
Spain	2.6	7.6
Sweden	3.8	11.9
United Kingdom	2.2	10.8
Average	3.47	9.78

Notes

(1) Data from OECD (2017a). Data downloaded from StatLink: http://dx.doi.org/10.1787/888933532029 [17 September 2021].

(2) Total government outsourcing is defined as all goods and services used by government, and financed, by the government, in 2016. This includes finance for outsourcing goods and services provided to the public.

and the United Kingdom spent a relatively large sum of public money on goods and services that were used by government.

If outsourcing the provision of services and goods for the public to non-governmental organizations led to lower quality, then we might expect that countries with more such outsourcing (measured as a percentage of GDP) might have lower expert ratings of the quality of public services. Instead of this, the analysis revealed a slight positive correlation (correlation = 0.37): that is, the countries where government outsourced more provision for the public in 2016 tended to have higher expert ratings for the quality of public sector provision of public services.

To illustrate this, Germany and the Netherlands outsourced relatively large amounts of provision for the public and had high ratings for the quality of public services delivered by the public sector, whereas Greece and Hungary did not outsource much provision for the public (measured as a percentage of GDP) and did not have high ratings for the quality of their public services as delivered by the public sector.

There are several possible reasons why the quality of public services delivered by the public sector might covary with the amount of government outsourcing to non-government providers of services and goods to the public. It might be that governments outsourced the public services that were of very poor quality when delivered by the public sector, so the public sector is left with services that were of high quality. Perhaps, the lower costs of an outsourced sector allow more to be spent by government on services provided by the public sector. The reason that is probably most likely is that sound public governance produces both higher quality ratings for public services provided by the public sector (as shown in Figure 7.2) and produces more government outsourcing of non-governmental provision of public services to the public. We will come back to the question of sound public governance in the next section.

Presumably, there are additional factors that might modify the link between the availability and quality of public services and the subjective experience of citizens. For example, people who have greater need for public services, make more use of them, or who find it harder to access them might be more positive or more negative in their opinions of the public services than their fellow citizens. There was some evidence of this in the case of Europe. In the Spring of 2016, older people, unemployed people, and people with less years of education were less likely to say public service provision was good (European Union 2016, 38). And there could be other factors too, as well as the ones we have mentioned.

Some of the variations in the quality of public services could have been caused by the extent of public participation at the national level. But there appeared to be a very slight covariation between service quality and public participation at the national level when the 2016 data from the Institutional Profiles Database were analysed. Cases consistent with the thesis that more public participation at national level is good for the quality of public services were Finland, Germany, the Netherlands, Norway, and the UK (which were all judged to have strong participation in political decisions at the national level excluding elections) and were judged to have good quality public services. Countries with weak public participation at national level and relatively poor-quality public services included Algeria, Cambodia, Mexico, Oman, and Pakistan. But there were cases that contradicted the thesis. These cases included the United States and South Africa, both of which were judged to have poor-quality public services, and the United Arab Emirates and China, both of which had very little public participation at the national level and relatively positive judgments about the quality of public services. Indeed, China was up with the best when it came to the evaluation of the quality of public services.

Budgets and government production costs

Some of the explanation for variations in the quality of public services may reflect budgetary decisions. Countries in the north of Europe were prominent among countries allocating a big proportion of the national income to the funding of public services. For example, Finland, Norway, and Sweden, which had attracted highly positive judgments about the quality of their public services had very high government production costs in 2016, over 30% of GDP in two of the cases. In contrast, Ireland, Poland, and Spain, which were judged to have much lower quality public services had relatively low production costs (14.4%, 20.3%, and 21.0% of GDP, respectively (OECD 2017b)). Of course, we do not know if the governments commit the money to improving the services, and this produces the better quality of services; or whether the services are of good quality, and this creates public trust in the government so that it is supported by the public when it proposes to spend more money on public services. We should keep in mind that both things could be occurring at the same time.

Looking at cost data for 2015 (OECD 2017b) countries with relatively low government production costs included the United States (18.7% of GDP). Referring to the scatterplot in Figure 7.2, perhaps budgetary decisions are therefore a possible factor in explaining the low quality attributed to the public services of the United States in 2016. Budgets are not necessarily the only factor that might have caused low-quality public services – but it is a possible reason. Another surprising feature of the United States situation in 2015 was that only a third of the government production costs of the United States was composed of government outsourcing costs, which was by no means a high share of the total for outsourcing. This suggested that it was closer to a traditional mode of public administration than might have been expected for a country that was the home of Osborne and Gaebler's seminal text on reinventing government.

In contrast to the case of the United States, the government production costs of South Africa were relatively high at 24.5% of GDP in 2015, which was higher than the OECD average of 20.9%. And yet its quality of public services in 2016 was judged to be very low. It is tempting in this case to hypothesize that public funding was not translating into as much quality as might be expected. Why? Perhaps South Africa was suffering from "aftershocks" from the apartheid period, which came to end officially in the period 1991–1994; maybe public administration in 2016 was still learning how to repair the damage done to civil society under apartheid and still trying to create an effective system of public services? What do public administration experts say?

It obviously requires many more facts and much analysis to get to the bottom of the poor quality of public services in South Africa in 2016.

But some indication that it might be worthwhile exploring the legacy of apartheid is to be found in the observations of P.S. Reddy in an article coincidentally published in 2016 (Reddy 2016, 7):

> There have been several government initiatives introduced to address service delivery challenges and the dysfunctionality of municipalities to date, and none of them have really borne any fruition in terms of responding to the local governance crisis. At the same time, residents in local communities have become very agitated and in some cases have even resorted to violence in expressing their frustration at poor service delivery.
>
> The South African local governance system, if judged according to the legislative and policy framework, can be described as 'world class' internationally; however, to complement that framework, there has to be the requisite human and financial resources committed to the municipal structures and ensuring that the system works. Those responsible for the political deployment of municipal functionaries have to take into account the passion, commitment, competence, qualifications and ethical leadership of those in line to be appointed or elected. Having 'struggle credentials' is not good enough as ANC 'deployees' will be playing a pivotal role in formulating and implementing policies relative to service delivery and development.

There is an implication in Reddy's observations that leadership capabilities are critical for the quality of public service.

We have been considering various factors, such as government outsourcing, government production costs, and public participation, and how they might help us to better understand the causes of high (or low) quality public services. In the next section, our analysis considers the possible relevance of strategic state capabilities and public governance in explaining the causes of quality.

The strategic state and the quality of public services

The possibility of linking together strategic planning and quality management to improve public services was explicitly considered in the early 1990s, which was a time when there was some growth of interest in quality management and the total quality management (TQM) movement in the United States. One hypothesis was that TQM could be used to link transformational leadership and strategic management. It was suggested that leaders could encourage and coordinate creativity at all levels of an organization to achieve transformation (Nutt and Backoff 1993).

Another linking of strategy (strategic planning) and quality occurred in the public sector in the late 1990s and onwards when individual European public sector organizations made use of the EFMQ Excellence Model. For example, the Model was used in local government organizations in the UK as a particular framework for self-assessment and improvement planning. This meant that it was used as a diagnostic tool. Managers could identify weaknesses and search for possible cause and effect linkages between areas such as, say, leadership and customer results. It required that data were collected and assessed in relation to nine criteria (Kermally 1997). These criteria were split between "enablers" and "results". Each of the criteria was defined. For example, partnerships and resources were how an organization planned and managed its external partnerships and internal resources to support its policy and strategy and the effective operation of its processes. Resources included finances, buildings, equipment, materials, technology, information, and knowledge. Society results referred to what the organization was achieving in relation to local, national, and international society as appropriate.

The EFQM Model, regarded as a TQM tool, included "strategy" as an enabler of organizational excellence. An early evaluation of the use of this tool in UK local government, based on a survey carried out by the Improvement and Development Agency at the end of the 1990s, suggested that resources and partnerships and society results were the least amenable of factors to the planned improvements sought through the EFQM Excellence Model.

What about other linkages of strategic management and quality in more recent years? We might speculate that strong strategic policy processes, strategic state characteristics, and sound public governance systems directly cause the availability of quality public services and that the public consuming these services react to the availability of good quality services by expressing satisfaction and confidence in the services.

Using the 2016 data from the Institutional Profile Database bivariate analysis was conducted to find the correlates of good quality public services provided by the public sector. It was found that there was:

- A moderate correlation with the strength of long-term strategic visions for selected policy sectors (correlation = 0.64)
- A moderate but approaching a strong correlation with the strength of the strategic policy process (correlation = 0.68)
- A moderate correlation with a whole-of-society approach (correlation = 0.49)
- A strong correlation with the extent of a strategic state (correlation = 0.70)
- A strong correlation with a sound public governance system (correlation = 0.72)

An overall inference from the results of the bivariate analysis is that high-quality public services are woven into the "fabric" of a modern strategic state and of sound public governance. There may be a slight hint in this bivariate analysis that a whole-of-government approach (comprising strong long-term strategic visions and a strong strategic policy process) carried more of the burden of creating high-quality public services than the whole-of-society approach. But none of the three elements of a strategic state should be discounted – all were part of the situation creating high-quality public services.

One possibility that might seem to be suggested by the Osborne and Gaebler thesis that governments should be reinvented by them focusing on strategic functions ("steering") and withdrawing from service delivery functions ("rowing") is that good public services are not important to the social and economic development of a country. Of course, Osborne and Gaebler might not have meant that all direct involvement in public services delivery should be ended. It is also possible that when governments develop more of an enabling posture to address societal problems, they must set up new public services to do the enabling work required to help stakeholders engaged in problem-solving. For example, governments may want to enable markets to work better and therefore set up information services for consumers. As another example, some governments may develop an economic policy on small businesses; they may have a goal of improving a sluggish economy and want small businesses to take a lead in creating new products and services and new jobs. Such a policy may involve the government setting up business support services for small firms.

An analysis of the covariation of the quality of public services and national performance, based on the Human Development Index of the United Nations and the Environmental Performance Index, found a strong correlation between the two variables (correlation = 0.77). An immediate reaction to this finding might be that national social and economic development is greatly helped by high-quality public services. It is worth saying, based on analysis above, that it does not seem likely that governments using a lot of outsourcing were more likely to have poor-quality public services, and so it may be that an effective development of strategic state capabilities supports both good quality public services and the (strategic) use of outsourcing of the provision of services and goods to the public. Further, recalling that sound public governance was strongly correlated with good national performance, we can say that strategic state capabilities and sound public governance were strongly associated with both high-quality public services and good national performance. Disentangling their precise causal interactions is likely to prove a challenging task (Figure 7.3).

If we think that strategic state capabilities and sound public governance might have been strongly associated with both high-quality public

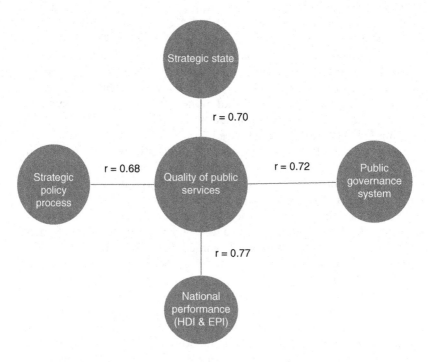

Figure 7.3 The correlates of high-quality public services.

services and good national performance, this may suggest that the national performance of both the United States and South Africa was below what it might have been because of the relatively poor quality of their public services. We should expect to find that their national performance was at the lower end of the range of performances for governments that matched them for government effectiveness. This would suggest, in their two cases, that the benefits of government effectiveness was being compromised by poor-quality public services.

Finally, if good national performance is reflected in high ratings of the average person's subjective well-being, then we can expect the quality of public services to correlate with the average subjective well-being of citizens. In fact, the correlation was 0.68, which is approaching a strong correlation. So, societies with good quality public services tend to have people who are on average reporting high levels of subjective well-being (that is, happiness with their lives).

Summary and conclusions

Different stakeholders judge the quality of public services in different ways. As a result, different valuations will be made of the quality of a public service by the public, the politicians, and the professional civil servants, who have related but different interests in public services.

Rather than going down the route of organizational studies and looking at generic strategies or strategy archetypes, this chapter drew on the public administration literature to highlight strategic choices and developments considered by governments over the last thirty or forty years. Attention was paid to outsourcing of the provision of goods and services to the public and to public participation and how they might impact the quality of the public services.

In relation to outsourcing, it was noted that one of the basic strategic choices to be made about public services is whether the government should be providing most public services using directly employed personnel in ministries and government agencies or whether it should spend money placing contracts with non-governmental organizations – private and voluntary sector organizations – to provide the public with a range of services on behalf of government. The empirical analysis found that the quality of public services delivered by the public sector covaried positively with the amount of government outsourcing to non-government providers of services and goods to the public. To illustrate this, we noted that Germany and the Netherlands had high-quality public services but spent a lot on outsourced provision for the public, whereas Greece and Hungary had much lower quality public services and did not outsource much provision for the public.

Examples of public participation were briefly discussed. They suggested that public participation may increase the quality of public services. Participation may improve the design of public services because it means that there is better knowledge and understanding of the concerns and preferences of the public. It could also encourage stronger "civic cultures" in which members of the public take more responsibility for the success of their communities and their public services.

In fact, empirical analysis suggested that public participation might be beneficial for the quality of public services. Finland, Germany, the Netherlands, Norway, and the UK were judged to have good quality services, and these same countries had high levels of public participation at the national level.

There were also some intriguing exceptions to the rule that better quality public services and more public participation at the national level went together. The United States and South Africa despite high amounts of public participation were judged to have poor-quality public services. In contrast, United Arab Emirates and China, despite low levels of public participation at the national level, had attracted relatively positive judgments about the quality of public services.

The outstanding finding in this chapter was that strategic state capabilities and sound public governance were strongly associated with both high-quality public services and good national development performance. It is possible, therefore, that strong strategic policy processes, strategic state characteristics, and sound public governance systems directly cause the availability of quality public services and that the public consuming these services react by expressing satisfaction and confidence in the services.

The quality of public services in both the United States and South Africa were far below what might have been expected of governments with their reputations for government effectiveness. Future research in this area could usefully investigate if the national performance of both the United States and South Africa are harmed by the relatively poor quality of their public services.

References

Denhardt, R.B., Denhardt, K.G., & Glaser, M.A. (2000) Citizen-driven strategic planning in local government: The case of orange county, Florida. In Rabin, J., Miller, G.J. & Hildreth, W.B. (Eds.) *Handbook of strategic management*, 2nd edition. New York and Basel: Marcel Dekker, pp. 709–720.

European Union (2016) Standard Eurobarometer 85, Spring 2016. Public opinion in the European Union. Report. Available at: https://europa.eu/eurobarometer/surveys/detail/2130 [18 September 2021].

Government of Canada (2019) 2017 to 2018 Management Accountability Framework government-wide report. 10 April 2019. Available at: https://www.canada.ca/en/treasury-board-secretariat/services/management-accountability-framework/2017-18-management-accountability-framework-government-wide-report.html [9 October 2021].

Jacobsen, D.I. & Johnsen, Å. (2020) Alignment of strategy and structure in local government. *Public Money and Management*, 40(4), 276–284.

Kermally, S. (1997) *Management ideas…in brief.* Oxford: Butterworth-Heinemann.

Lewis, P. (2017) Quasi-markets: An overview and analysis. Working paper, Department of Political Economy, King's College London.

Miles, R.E. & Snow, C.C. (1978) *Organisational strategy, structure, and process.* New York: McGraw-Hill Book Company.

Moore, M. (1995) *Creating public value: Strategic management in government.* Cambridge, MA: Harvard University Press.

Nutt, P.C. & Backoff, R.W. (1993) Transforming public organizations with strategic management and strategic leadership. *Journal of Management*, 19(2), 299–347.

OECD (2017a) Government at a Glance 2017. Paris: OECD Publishing. Data on satisfaction and confidence downloaded from https://stats.oecd.org [26 January 2021].

OECD (2017b) Government production costs. Data downloaded from 10.1787/888933531991 [17 September 2021].

OECD (2020) How and when consumer choice drives efficient competition in publicly funded services – Note by Mats. A Bergman. 17 September 2020. Paris: OECD. Available at: https://one.oecd.org/document/DAF/COMP(2019)8/en/pdf [21 September 2021]

OECD (2021) Government at a Glance 2021. Paris: OECD Publishing. Available at: https://www.oecd.org/gov/government-at-a-glance-22214399. htm [19 September 2021].

Ohmae, K. (1991) Getting back to strategy. In Montgomery, C.A., & Porter, M.E. (Eds.) *Strategy: Seeking and securing competitive advantage.* Boston, MA: Harvard Business School Press, pp. 61–74. (First published as an article in 1988.)

Osborne, D. & Gaebler, T. (1992) *Reinventing government: How the entrepreneurial spirit is transforming the public sector.* Reading, MA: Addison Wesley Publishing Company.

Osborne, D. & Plastrik, P. (1997) *Banishing bureaucracy: the five strategies for reinventing government.* New York: Plume.

Porter, M. (1980) *Competitive strategy: Techniques for analyzing industries and competitors.* New York: Free Press.

Quirk, P.J., Lammèrt, C., & Thunert, M. (2018) *United States report: Sustainable governance indicators.* Gutersloh: Bertelsmann Stiftung.

Reddy, P.S. (2016) The politics of service delivery in South Africa: The local government sphere in context. *The Journal for Transdisciplinary Research in Southern Africa*, 12(1), a337. doi:10.4102/td.v12i1.337

World Bank (1997). *World development report 1997: The state in a changing world.* New York: Oxford University Press.

8   Sustainability and the 2030 Agenda

Introduction

This chapter is focused on the United Nation's 2030 Agenda and the efforts of individual governments within their own national borders to deliver it. Its central concern is to judge whether the extent of strategic state capabilities was a factor in the national delivery of sustainable development in the first few years of implementation. It also looks at the strategic autonomy of national governments in delivering the 2030 Agenda and its complexity because of strategic issue tensions in the 17 sustainable development goals.

The President of the European Council, Charles Michel, clearly identified human agency in bringing about the dire state of the world's natural environment. In his speech to the United Nations General Assembly in September 2021, he said (Michel 2021):

> I am talking about the war that humans have waged against nature. We have tortured our planet. Abused our natural resources. We have committed acts of war against our environment. And now ... nature is fighting back. Bringing us back to our senses. Back to humility.
> No one can say: "I didn't know". For decades, scientists have sounded the alarm. But their warnings fell on deaf ears. We turned away, so as not to see. And today, the shock is brutal.
> We are reaping what we have sown.

Studies of extreme weather events confirm some of Michel's observations. Researchers have detected "significant anthropogenic influences" in the occurrence of heatwaves, extreme rainfall, and flooding because of rising sea levels (World Meteorological Organization 2021). These events can be disastrous, and they can turn into crises. Lives have been lost, and economic losses have been considerable. Many different countries have been harmed by the climate crisis, but a third of deaths because of weather, climate, and water extremes over a fifty-year period have been in Africa. Extreme weather seems to be getting worse. For

DOI: 10.4324/9781351045797-8

example, "The United States experienced more than twice the number of billion-dollar weather- and climate-related disasters during the 2010s (119) as compared with the 2000s (59) even after adjusting for inflation (as of January 2020)" (World Meteorological Organization 2021, 46).

Charles Michel also made the case for ending the economic policies that he blamed for social and environmental problems (Michel 2021):

> ... our model of economic development has run its course. Its flaws are increasingly visible: the extreme exploitation of resources and increasing inequality. We must escape this vicious circle.

The 2030 Agenda resolution of the United Nations in 2015 was a "utopian" manifesto – one that was seen as ambitious but achievable. The aim was to improve human wellbeing and the state of the natural environment, while delivering economic growth. The leaders of the world's nations adopted this resolution and showed publicly that they accepted the importance of sustainable development. They showed they accepted the need for action on poverty, on the natural environment, on climate change, and on many other things. There was also an acceptance that this was to be an inclusive strategic agenda – that no one was to be left behind. This was decided by the General Assembly in adopting a United Nations resolution (United Nations 2017, 1/25) which reaffirmed

> the pledge that no one will be left behind in implementing the 2030 Agenda for Sustainable Development, that the 2030 Agenda is people-centred, universal and transformative, that the Sustainable Development Goals and targets are integrated and indivisible and balance the three dimensions of sustainable development – economic, social and environmental ...

Did countries make progress in delivering the sustainable development goals in the early years of the 2030 Agenda? Sachs et al. (2020) produced an SDG Index score for individual countries. The findings they report could be described as paradoxical. While the highest scores on the index were awarded to the high-income OECD countries, these countries were not in the forefront of delivering the sustainable development goals. Poorer countries were given low scores on the index, and yet they were often found to be making progress in delivering the goals (Sachs et al. 2020, 25):

> ... three Nordic countries top the 2020 SDG Index: Sweden, Denmark, and Finland. Most countries in the top 20 are OECD countries ... many high-income countries are not making significant progress on sustainable consumption and production or the protection of biodiversity, particularly in relation to Goal 14 (Life Below

Water), for which most high-income countries are stagnating ... most low-income countries are making progress in ending extreme poverty and in providing access to basic services and infrastructure, particularly under SDG 3 (Good Health and Well-Being) and SDG 8 (Decent Work and Economic Growth), ...

The main issue for this chapter is deciding whether strategic states perform better than other ones in delivering the sustainable development goals of the 2030 Agenda. The chapter begins by looking at the performance of countries on the 2020 SDG Index. It then looks more deeply into the relationship between strategic state characteristics and national responses to the sustainable development goals. The concluding sections look at the strategic autonomy of countries and the complexity of the sustainable development goals as a result of strategic issue tensions.

Sustainability performance measured by the 2020 SDG Index

It might be expected that governments with strategic state capabilities are most likely to be successful in delivering the 2030 Agenda. For, as shown in earlier chapters, countries with strong strategic state capabilities had achieved strong national development (as measured by the Human Development Index and Environmental Performance Index). It was also seen that the strategic state was associated with higher quality public services, which might be very useful in tackling the delivery of sustainable development goals.

Making evaluations of national performance against the goals of the 2030 Agenda is a fraught process. First, evaluations require the availability of good performance data at national level. At the time of the 2015 resolution being adopted, there were gaps in data availability and national variations in the quality of the data. This must make it difficult to track and evaluate delivery of the sustainable development goals over the period 2015 to, say, 2021. Second, countries varied massively in their initial starting point in 2015. Third, countries may plan different trajectories in delivering progress, with some planning to make a slow start but building momentum all the time, whereas others might have intended a strong start on delivery that enabled them to coast at later stages, and so on. Fourth, countries could vary in the profile of their progress on the 17 sustainable development goals. One country may have performed well in cutting poverty but made little progress on cutting greenhouse gas emissions, whereas another might have done the opposite, making great strides in cutting greenhouse gas emissions but not in cutting poverty. So, some caution and tentativeness are warranted when offering judgments of what happened in the immediate aftermath of the adoption of the 2030 Agenda.

In fact, analysis revealed a positive correlation between strategic state characteristics and the score achieved on the 2020 SDG Index. This might have been guessed from the observations made by Jeffrey Sachs and his colleagues above and from knowing that poorer countries tend to have less strategic state capabilities than their richer counterparts. But it is clearly demonstrated in Figure 8.1. (There is some debate over whether it is a good idea to aggregate performance on sustainable development goals in a single index. As will be seen, this chapter uses both the SDG Index and individual indicators.)

Why was there a correlation between the index and strategic state characteristics? One answer would be that countries with governance based on strategic state capabilities could have achieved relevant national social, environment, and economic developments prior to, or by, 2015. This would have shown up as reductions in poverty, improvements in health and life expectancy, improvements in educational provision, better environmental measures, and so on. For example, Statistics Sweden (SCB), a government agency responsible for official and other government statistics, judged that data for 2015 showed that Sweden had already met some of the 2030 Agenda goals.

In fact, national strategies for sustainable policies and futures were in existence prior to 2015. One example is the UK, which had published a Government White Paper on long-term sustainable energy strategy in 2003. This suggested that the UK Government wanted to achieve positive consequences for the environment, ensure reliable energy generation, prevent fuel poverty of the poorest in society, and provide new commercial opportunities. So, the strategy sought to address poverty and sustainability, reliability of energy supply and economic growth. A key idea was to achieve integrated policies (Department of Trade and Industry 2003, 8): "Our new energy policy will ensure that energy, the environment and economic growth are properly and sustainably integrated" (Figure 8.2). Even before 2015, the UK was among the top countries for cutting carbon dioxide emissions per capita.

As a second example, we can consider the Danish Government's "Denmark 2020", which was published in 2010. According to this strategy Denmark was to be made wealthier through "cleverness and hard work". One national goal in the strategy was to become a green and sustainable society. This must have seemed a credible goal, feasible because of the country's recent national achievements (Government of Denmark 2010, 25): "We are among the most energy efficient societies in the world and among the countries that have increased their share of renewable energy the most".

The Danish Government had not only set what must have seemed to be a realistic strategic goal but also made public investment and taxation decisions aligned to this intent to be green (Government of Denmark 2010, 25):

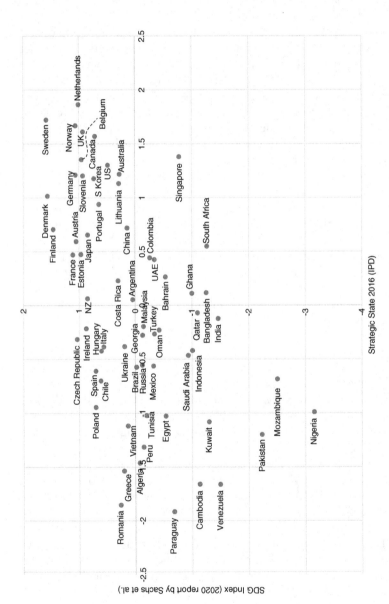

Figure 8.1 Scatterplot of 2020 SDG Index by extent of strategic state characteristics.

Note: SGI Index – see Sachs et al. (2020). The data used by Sachs and his colleagues in the Index was as recent as possible. Correlation r = 0.51.

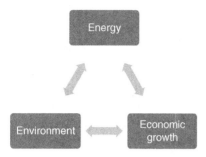

Figure 8.2 Integrated solutions and not trade-offs.

We have established a fund for green restructuring and industrial innovation, designed partly to promote the development of new climate-friendly solutions. In addition, with the tax reform, we have lowered tax on earned income and raised tax on energy and pollution.

In summary, the Danish Government had an ambitious green agenda, was intending to build on existing momentum towards a green future, had made green growth a top priority, and was making public investment decisions and tax decisions aligned to this strategic priority. Along with the UK, Denmark had a record of cutting carbon dioxide emissions prior to 2015.

While countries with strong strategic state capabilities might have been delivering green goals prior to 2015, they were the richer countries of the world and their previous social and economic development had also been damaging to the environment, for example, producing high levels of carbon dioxide emissions per capita. Therefore, the progress made by governments with strong strategic state capabilities prior to 2015 might have been correcting a problematic environmental record.

The diversity of starting points

We can illustrate the diversity of national starting points for the implementation of the 2030 Agenda for four countries: Sweden, Saudi Arabia, South Africa, and Pakistan. This uses indicators and rankings reported by Jeffrey Sachs and his colleagues in their 2016 SDG Index, which they based on a large set of indicators and data (Sachs et al. 2016).

We might have expected Sweden was well placed at the start of the 2030 Agenda to perform well on indicators used to measure sustainable development goals. The Government of Sweden had a reputation for being serious about sustainable development. In relation to ending poverty, the Swedish Government said, absolute poverty had been eliminated, although 15% of the population were relatively poor because they had disposable income lower than 60% of the national median income. The Government reported that carbon dioxide emissions had been decreasing since 2010, measured as an amount per unit of added value, even though the economy had grown. But another report gave Sweden a poor rating for carbon dioxide emissions per capita (Sachs et al. 2016). Sachs et al. (2016) reported a homicide rate for Sweden which suggested it was relatively free of violence. Sweden was ranked first out of 149 countries on the SDG index meaning that at the outset of the 2030 Agenda period, Sweden was the country rated as the most advanced in achieving the sustainable development goals.

In contrast to Sweden, three countries – Saudi Arabia, South Africa, and Pakistan – were starting on the journey to 2030 in the bottom half of the SDG Index rankings.

Saudi Arabia was ranked 85th out of 149 countries in the SDG Index rankings (Sachs et al. 2016). The country scored highly in relation to eliminating poverty with 0% of the population assumed to be living on less than $1.90 per day. It scored very poorly on carbon dioxide emissions from energy. It scored moderately well on people feeling safe walking at night, and very well on its homicide rate (which was very low in international terms).

South Africa was ranked 99th in the 2016 SDG Index. It had poor scores on the following indicators: poverty (measured at $1.90 a day), per capita carbon dioxide emissions from energy, and its homicide rate.

Pakistan was ranked 115th on the 2016 SDG Index. It had a poverty problem; over 8% of people were living on less than $1.90 per day. Other indications of a poverty problem in Pakistan included the incidence of wasting, stunting, and deaths of children under five, which was relatively high. Neonatal and maternal mortality rates were relatively high. Life expectancy was relatively low. Pakistan was rated as having a low per capita amount of carbon dioxide emissions from energy. Finally, Pakistan had a high homicide rate.

The different starting points of the four countries are presented in Table 8.1.

Were strategic state governments outperforming other governments?

Were governments with strategic state capabilities making more progress in delivering the 2030 Agenda in the period 2015–2020 than other governments? It might be objected that this is too short a period for serious evaluation. But it can be argued that it is critical to evaluate this period because the world's governments only had until 2030 to deliver the sustainable development goals and were under great pressure to bring the climate crisis under control.

Table 8.1 Uneven starting points in delivering the 2030 Agenda: ratings for
selected indicators

Sustainable development goal (2030 Agenda)	Indicator	Pakistan	South Africa	Saudi Arabia	Sweden
1	Poverty (%)	intermediate	poor	good	good
13	Carbon dioxide emissions from energy (per capita)	good	poor	poor	poor
16	Homicide rate (per 100,000)	poor	poor	good	good
2016 Ranking on SDG Index		115	99	85	1

Note: The ratings and rankings are from Sachs et al. (2016). There were 149 countries in
the 2016 rankings.

In Table 8.2, selected countries and sustainable development indicators are shown to illustrate the sorts of changes that were occurring
in the period 2015–2020. As can be seen, changes in a positive direction
had occurred:

i   The extent of poverty fell in Bangladesh, Cambodia, China, and
    Vietnam. The falls in Bangladesh and Cambodia were spectacular in
    such a short period.
ii The concentrations of particulate matter in the air fell in Bangladesh,
    China, Qatar, and Vietnam.
iii The percentage of the population using the Internet went up in
    Algeria, Cambodia, Peru, Qatar, Singapore, and Vietnam.

It is also interesting to note some specific developments in public governance. There were both positive and negative changes:

i   The share of parliamentary seats increased for women in Chile,
    Costa Rica, Peru, and Qatar.
ii Corruption (as measured by the Corruption Perception Index)
    declined in China and Vietnam but increased in Qatar.
iii The extent of press freedom declined in Algeria, Bangladesh,
    Cambodia, Chile, and Qatar.

The next finding is of great importance in relation to assessing the significance of strategic state capabilities for delivery of sustainable development goals. This is the finding: the 2016 SDG Index and the 2020
SDG Index created by Sachs and his colleagues were very strongly correlated. Countries performing well on the indicators in their 2016 report
were still performing well in their 2020 report. And vice versa: countries

Table 8.2 Sustainability indicators for selected countries 2015–2020

Country	Sustainable development goals	Indicators	Start of period (2015)	End of period	Direction
Algeria	9	Population using the internet (%)	38.2	49.0 (2018)	Positive
	5	Seats held by women in national parliament (%)	31.6	25.8 (2020)	Negative
	11	Annual mean concentration of particulate matter of less than 2.5 microns in diameter (PM2.5) (μg/m³)	36.1	38.9 (2017)	Negative
Bangladesh	16	Press Freedom Index (best 0–100 worst)	41.7	45.8 (2019)	Negative
	1	Poverty headcount ratio at $1.90/day (%)	17.0	4.3 (2020)	Positive
	1	Poverty headcount ratio at $3.20/day (%)	53.2	31.0 (2020)	Positive
	5	Ratio of female-to-male labour force participation rate (%)	40.3	44.5 (2019)	Positive
	11	Annual mean concentration of particulate matter of less than 2.5 microns in diameter (PM2.5) (μg/m³)	67.0	60.8 (2017)	Positive
Cambodia	16	Press Freedom Index (best 0–100 worst)	45.94	50.7 (2019)	Negative
	1	Poverty headcount ratio at $3.20/day (%)	31.2	12.3 (2019)	Positive
	9	Population using the internet (%)	6.4	40.0 (2018)	Positive
	14	Ocean Health Index: Clean Waters score (worst 0–100 best)	49.6	53.1 (2018)	Positive
	16	Press Freedom Index (best 0–100 worst)	40.7	45.9 (2019)	Negative
Chile	5	Seats held by women in national parliament (%)	15.8	22.6 (2019)	Positive
	9	Population using the internet (%)	76.6	82.3 (2017)	Positive
	16	Corruption Perception Index (worst 0–100 best)	70	67 (2019)	Negative
China	16	Press Freedom Index (best 0–100 worst)	19.2	25.7 (2019)	Negative
	1	Poverty headcount ratio at $3.20/day (%)	7.0	2.0 (2020)	Positive
	11	Annual mean concentration of particulate matter of less than 2.5 microns in diameter (PM2.5) (μg/m³)	59.1	52.7 (2017)	Positive
Colombia	16	Corruption Perception Index (worst 0–100 best)	37	41 (2019)	Positive
	14	Ocean Health Index: Clean Waters score (worst 0–100 best)	60.0	63.5 (2019)	Positive
Costa Rica	5	Seats held by women in national parliament (%)	33.3	45.6 (2020)	Positive
	9	Population using the internet (%)	59.8	74.1 (2018)	Positive

Peru	5	Seats held by women in national parliament (%)	22.2	26.2 (2020)	Positive
	9	Population using the internet (%)	40.9	52.5 (2018)	Positive
Qatar	5	Seats held by women in national parliament (%)	0.0	9.8 (2020)	Positive
	9	Population using the internet (%)	92.9	99.7 (2018)	Positive
	11	Annual mean concentration of particulate matter of less than 2.5 microns in diameter (PM2.5) (µg/m³)	94.4	91.2 (2017)	Positive
	13	Energy-related CO_2 emissions (tCO$_2$/capita)	46.4	44.0 (2017)	Positive
	16	Corruption Perception Index (worst 0–100 best)	71.0	62.0 (2019)	Negative
	16	Press Freedom Index (best 0–100 worst)	36.0	42.5 (2019)	Negative
Singapore	3	Age-standardized death rate due to cardiovascular disease, cancer, diabetes, or chronic respiratory disease in adults aged 30–70	10.0	9.3 (2016)	Positive
	9	Population using the Internet (%)	79.0	88.2 (2018)	Positive
	13	Energy-related CO_2 emissions (tCO$_2$/capita)	10.7	11.9 (2017)	Negative
Vietnam	1	Poverty headcount ratio at $3.20/day (%)	9.3	3.5 (2020)	Positive
	9	Population using the Internet (%)	45.0	70.4 (2018)	Positive
	11	Annual mean concentration of particulate matter of less than 2.5 microns in diameter (PM2.5) (µg/m³)	32.5	29.6 (2017)	Positive
	16	Corruption Perception Index (worst 0–100 best)	31.0	37.0 (2019)	Positive

Notes

i The data used in this tabular analysis were downloaded from https://sdgindex.org/reports/sustainable-development-report-2020/ [6 February 2021].

ii The "sustainable development goals" were numbered in the 2015 Resolution adopted by the Heads of State and Government and High Representatives at the United Nations Headquarters in 2015.

judged to be performing poorly against the indicators in the 2016 report were still performing poorly in the 2020 SDG Index. It has already been noted that strategic state capabilities were correlated with the 2020 SDG Index. Given the high correlation between the 2016 and 2020 SDG Indexes, it is not surprising that the 2016 SDG Index was moderately and positively correlated with the strategic state index. So, strategic state capabilities were moderately correlated with the 2016 and 2020 SDG Indexes (Figure 8.3).

The bivariate analysis results suggested a very slight drop over the period 2015–2019 in the correlation between strategic state capabilities and performance on SDG indicators. Perhaps this reflected changes in the construction of the Index, but it might also be worth noting that there were a few cases where countries might be judged to be slightly exceeding expectations of their performance in the 2020 SDG Index based on their 2015 SDG Index position. These countries included Algeria, Bangladesh, Cambodia, Chile, China, Colombia, Costa Rica, Peru, and Vietnam. None of them were in the top ten for strategic state capabilities in this book's normal sample of 63 countries. In fact, Algeria, Cambodia, Chile, Peru, and Vietnam were in the lower ranked group of countries on the strategic state index. The evidence appeared, therefore, to be pointing to the conclusion that countries with the most well-developed strategic state capabilities were not outperforming other countries in the global partnership to accomplish the 2030 Agenda as might have been expected.

From a management perspective, the obvious follow-up question is: what conditions explain why the governments with the most strategic capabilities were not leading the way in implementing the 2030 Agenda?

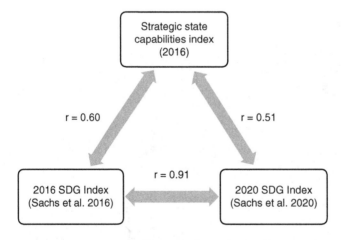

Figure 8.3 Bivariate analyses involving SDG Indexes and strategic state capabilities.

Note: Bivariate analysis was conducted for a sample of 63 countries.

There might have been a multitude of pertinent conditions at work and there could be many ways of linking them together in explanations. The ones selected here for attention are (i) the critical importance of the commitment of heads of states and governments to the delivery of the 2030 Agenda given the strategic autonomy of the national governments, and (ii) the complexities and challenges created by strategic issue tensions present in the sustainable development goals.

Strategic autonomy and national commitment

The existence of national-level commitment to the 2030 Agenda really mattered because the system of governance for the 2030 Agenda left individual countries with a lot of strategic autonomy (United Nations 2015, 6–7):

> We reaffirm that every State has, and shall freely exercise, full permanent sovereignty over all its wealth, natural resources and economic activity. ... All of us will work to implement the Agenda within our own countries and at the regional and global levels, taking into account different national realities, capacities and levels of development and respecting national policies and priorities. We will respect national policy space for sustained, inclusive and sustainable economic growth, in particular for developing States, while remaining consistent with relevant international rules and commitments.

Further on in the text of the adopted resolution it said, "that each country has primary responsibility for its own economic and social development" (United Nations 2015, 10). In line with this, governments were expected to set their own national targets and decide "how these aspirational and global targets should be incorporated into national planning processes, policies and strategies" (United Nations 2015, 13). It assumed that national parliaments would enact legislation and provide the funds needed. National governments would work with various stakeholders and institutions on implementation. And national governments would be in the lead role in monitoring progress, and would do this at national, regional, and global levels.

Given this system of governance, the 2030 Agenda would be very dependent on the commitment and enthusiasm of country leaders. So, their priorities and intentions would matter. What else would matter? It is possible that the commitment of a government to act on the 2030 Agenda will depend on public opinion. We have some evidence that public opinion in relation to environmental matters is massively variable. Table 8.3 shows public satisfaction with efforts to preserve the environment for a sample of countries.

Table 8.3 Public satisfaction with efforts to preserve the environment (2019)

Percentage satisfied	Countries
High (above 75%)	China, Saudi Arabia, and India
Medium (50–74%)	Germany and Canada
Low (less than 50%)	Russia, South Korea, Japan, the USA, and Iran

Notes

i Survey question – In this country, are you satisfied or dissatisfied with efforts to preserve the environment?

ii Source of data: Gallup World Poll, 2019.

iii Gallup (2020). Available at: https://news.gallup.com/opinion/gallup/308879/earth-day-world-satisfaction-environment.aspx [29 September 2021].

However, it is not clear if country leaders follow public opinion or influence and form public opinion. The evidence on public opinion with respect to environmental sustainability in Australia in recent years suggested that public attitudes changed in reaction to the policies and attitudes of the country's leaders.

Public opinion in Australia became increasingly dissatisfied with efforts to preserve the environment over the years from 2013 to 2019: dissatisfaction rose from 30% of Australians in 2013 to over 51% in 2019 (Reinhart 2020). The rise in dissatisfaction coincided with changing government policy on the environment. The Australian prime minister between 2013 and 2015 was Tony Abbott, leader of the Liberal Party. During his time as prime minister, a carbon pricing scheme was repealed even though it had succeeded in cutting emissions by 0.8% in the first year of its operation. The repeal of the scheme left Australia without legislation on policies to deliver reductions in greenhouse gas emissions (Taylor 2014).

In 2018, Scott Morrison became prime minister as well as leader of the Liberal Party. His policies on the environment showed continuities with those of Tony Abbott's (Reinhart 2020): "Morrison has been a vocal proponent of the coal industry and a critic of environmental activists". In 2021, Scott Morrison, still Australia's prime minister, and the head of a coalition government, explained a new government plan to achieve net zero emissions by 2050, which was published just ahead of an international summit on climate change. He stated in parliament that government "would pursue an "Australian way" that would not regulate or shut down industries" (Martin 2021). Support for this plan by Barnaby Joyce, the deputy prime minister, and leader of a party in coalition with the Liberal Party, seemed to rest on Australia continuing to produce and export gas and coal (Martin 2021):

"I'm very encouraged by making sure that, working with my National party colleagues, we talk about the continuation that we will remain one of the world's biggest producers and exporters of liquefied natural gas and this is a great outcome", Joyce said.

"It [the plan] talks about the ongoing use of coal. In fact, it talks about nearly a 6% decline over the near future. But that belies the fact that, currently, we're exporting more coal at a higher price than we ever have before".

Newspaper reports suggested that there was growing criticism that "Australia's climate policy lacks credibility" (Martin 2021). The plan was criticized for a lack of detail and for its assumptions about the role that technology will play in delivering the reduction of emissions.

Strategic autonomy for any head of government is limited by public opinion and pressure from the governments of other countries. Therefore, government strategy is, presumably, often the resultant of the interaction of the government's own priorities and intentions, public opinion, and external pressures from other governments. On this basis, the Australian plan of 2021 to achieve net zero emissions might be seen as a compromise between economic and environmental priorities. But for one critic the plan was not even a compromise (Martin 2021): "Climate advocate Mike Cannon-Brookes derided the updated plan as 'more bullshit', saying the government's claimed technology-driven approach was 'inaction, misdirection and avoiding choices'". Arguably, the implication was that the plan was not a real strategy but a ploy, that is, intended to deceive (Mintzberg 1987, 12).

Revision of national development agendas and arrangements

Some country leaders and their governments demonstrated commitment to the 2030 Agenda both in what was said and possibly even more by their revision of national priorities, strategies, structures, and partnerships.

It seems that the Prime Minister and the Government of Pakistan were receptive to taking responsibility for delivering the 2030 Agenda even before it had been officially adopted. "Pakistan 2025" was approved by the Prime Minister in 2014 and this strategy document contained the following statement (Government of Pakistan 2014, 3):

As we pass through an era of unprecedented change and complexity, it is imperative that we refresh our framework for national development. A renewed commitment to the founding vision is needed, both to address the current challenges and set out realistic and ambitious targets for the future – including ensuring that Pakistan succeeds in achieving the proposed Sustainable Development Goals (SDGs) of zero poverty and hunger, universal access to health services, education, modern energy services, clean water and sanitation, and join the league of Upper Middle Income countries by 2025.

It was suggested that the vision was building on the United Nation's Millennium Development Goals and would create the basis for delivering the 2030 Agenda. The seven pillars of the vision (which were labelled people first, growth, governance, security, entrepreneurship, knowledge economy, and connectivity) were seen as linked to the sustainable development goals. For example, in the vision statement "people first" was linked to, among other things, the first sustainable development goal (poverty).

The Pakistan Government's anticipation in 2014 of the goals that would be included in the 2030 Agenda, and their explicit linking of sustainable development goals to Pakistan 2025s seven pillars, was followed up in 2016 when a resolution of the National Assembly in the country's parliament adopted the Sustainable Development Goals as Pakistan's national development agenda (Government of Pakistan 2019).

The Federal Minister for Planning, Development and Reform outlined the structure that was going to be used to deliver the 2030 Agenda in Pakistan (Government of Pakistan 2019, 8):

> With the establishment of federal and provincial SDG units, Pakistan has instituted monitoring and evaluation processes that are critical for supporting the SDGs' implementation, horizontal and vertical coordination, and strengthened collaborations with development partners, civil society organizations, think tanks, academia and the private sector. To ensure an enabling institutional environment, Parliamentary Taskforces are operating in national and provincial assemblies, closely overseeing progress on the SDGs. All such efforts are expected to accelerate the pace of Pakistan's progress on the SDGs. ... The gigantic challenge of climate change alone requires intensive community mobilization efforts. Addressing these challenges means that we must take cue from the SDG wheel, which reminds us that development does not occur in silos – rather it is a sustained and integrated process dependent on creating synergies. A cornerstone of implementing the SDG goals is building on existing alliances and forging new partnerships... partnerships with a broad array of stakeholders including the private sector and the civil society, supported by international community, will continue to guide this process.

Not only had the Government responded by adopting the 2030 Agenda's sustainable development goals as its own, it had also, as we see, designed an infrastructure to govern delivery and to enable what looks very much like whole-of-government and whole-of-society approaches.

The commitment of the Government of South Africa to delivering the sustainable development goals might be seen as implicit in its statement in 2019 that it had played a role in developing the global agenda (on sustainable development goals) and that the Government approached its Vision 2030 agenda "with a sense of urgency" (Government of South Africa 2019, 19). Some degree of commitment to the 2030 Agenda was also evident in the following remarks on spending priorities (Government of South Africa 2019, 10):

> The National Development Plan (NDP), the Government's basic strategic document for economic development, which prioritises the elimination of poverty, reduction of income inequality and growing an inclusive economy by 2030, is closely aligned with the targets articulated in the SDGs. Government expenditures reflect the high priority accorded poverty, inequality and spending on SDGs. Spending on these Goals has increased markedly in real terms over the past three years.

The Government did not set up new structures for the delivery of the sustainable development goals, but it did identify the need to strengthen its capacity to implement development goals and to "strengthen partnerships between Government, the private sector, labour unions, CSOs and development partners" (Government of South Africa 2019, 30). This also suggested that responsibility for delivering sustainable development goals was taken seriously.

The Saudi Government publicly endorsed cooperation and international partnership to deliver the sustainable development goals (Kingdom of Saudi Arabia 2018). The Saudi Ministry of Economy and Planning was given responsibility for coordinating the sustainable development goals. Notably, it was assumed that existing strategies of government were "bound to promote" the sustainable development goals (Kingdom of Saudi Arabia 2018, 14):

> The Kingdom of Saudi Arabia is experiencing a dramatic and comprehensive transformation through Saudi Vision 2030 ... The Vision and related implementation programs, such as the National Transformation Program 2020, provide the foundations underpinning the integration of sustainable development goals into the national planning process. One key program of the Vision, namely life quality, has direct relevance to the sustainable development goals....

> In addition, Saudi Arabia has developed several strategies and plans that are bound to promote the seventeen goals of sustainable development. Among these are the National Environmental

Strategy, the National Strategy for Conservation of Biodiversity, the Vegetation Restoration Strategy in Riyadh region, the National Plan for Management of Natural Disasters, the National Marine Disaster Management Plan and the National Chemical and Bacteriological Incidents Management Plan.

... SDG-related activities will proceed hand-in-hand with the implementation of Vision 2030, which has already gathered significant momentum.

In the Saudi case, a massive political investment had been made in Saudi Vision 2030. This might have been so great that it seemed difficult to revise it formally to absorb the 2030 Agenda.

The examples of Pakistan, South Africa, and Saudi Arabia show varying degrees of response to the 2030 Agenda. These ranged from Pakistan Parliament's adoption of the sustainable development goals as the national development agenda, through the South African Government's setting of its financial priorities and its recognition of a need to strengthen its partnership capabilities and ending with Saudi Arabia's assumption that the 2030 Agenda could be delivered through Saudi Vision 2030. These examples suggest that at national level there has been a significant degree of commitment to the 2030 Agenda.

Complexities and challenges created by strategic issue tensions

The idea of integrated solutions has a long history. The case for integration was clearly made in the management and administration literature by Mary Parker Follett nearly a hundred years ago. She counterposed integration to compromise (Metcalfe and Urwick 1941, 35): "Compromise does not create, it deals with what already exists; integration creates something new ...". She argued that compromises are inherently unsatisfactory. It requires decision-makers to "give up" part of what they wanted, and sooner or later those who had to give up something to get a compromise will be looking for a way to achieve the whole of what they wanted. Whereas, by definition, an integrated solution means all objectives are accomplished. There is no sacrifice in terms of goals to be achieved.

The sustainable development goals are a statement of ideals for a better world. They are ambitious. They are presented in documents as a list, which might seem to imply they exist independently of each other. Le Blanc (2015) argued, in effect, that the goals are not independent and made the case for an integrated approach to strategies and implementation (Le Blanc 2015, 1):

Lack of integration across sectors in terms of strategies, policies and implementation has long been perceived as one of the main pitfall of previous approaches to sustainable development. Insufficient understanding and accounting of trade-offs and synergies across sectors have resulted in incoherent policies, adverse impacts of development policies focused on specific sectors on other sectors, and ultimately in diverging outcomes and trends across broad objectives for sustainable development.

The analytical answer to this argument is the use of management techniques such as interpretive structural modelling and strategic issue analysis (Nutt and Backoff 1992). In practical terms, the argument is answered by creativity, innovation, and negotiation.

Le Blanc presented his analysis of the sustainable development goals, in which he identified links between the goals. He did this by linking the sustainable development goals to the targets of the 2030 Agenda. This involved examining the wording of targets (and presumably the wording of the goals). Where targets linked to two goals, the goals were defined as being linked. He suggested that inequality, poverty, hunger, education, and sustainable consumption and production emerged from his analysis as at the core of the sustainable development goals.

Some years on from Le Blanc's analysis, it is possible to make the analysis of interdependence and linkages of sustainable development goals an empirical one. Using recently published data on the book's sample of 63 countries, bivariate analysis was carried out that had a bearing on two key areas – poverty (sustainable development goal 1) and climate change (sustainable development goal 13). A slight negative correlation ($r = -0.37$) was found between reductions in the percentages of people living in poverty and reductions of emissions of carbon dioxide during the years immediately following the adoption of the 2030 Agenda. As shown in Table 8.4, the five countries with the biggest reductions in poverty had increased their per capita emissions of carbon dioxide. The group of countries with the biggest reductions in emissions of carbon dioxide on a per capita basis had zero or very small reductions in poverty (varying between 0% for Norway and 0.1% for Estonia).

We might infer from this bivariate analysis that some governments in Asia were prioritizing tackling poverty (sustainable development goal 1) over climate action (sustainable development goal 13). This seems quite possible. For poor countries, faster economic growth may be seen as the answer to poverty. For example, the Government of Pakistan wanted to deliver more economic growth and explicitly identified an "Asian Tiger" model of development comprising rapid rates of economic growth, investment in human development, and the eradication of poverty (Government of Pakistan 2014, 6). One problem for Pakistan was obtaining the means of delivering high growth rates (Government of

Table 8.4 Poverty and carbon dioxide emissions

Country	Poverty (percent at $320 per day)			Carbon dioxide emissions (tons per capita)		
	2015 (%)	2020 (%)	Reduction	2015	2019	Reduction
Top five countries for poverty reduction:						
Bangladesh	53.22	31.01	22.21	0.466	0.627	−0.161
Cambodia	31.21	12.3	18.91	0.544	0.972	−0.428
India	39.96	24.61	15.35	1.72	1.915	−0.195
Pakistan	35.09	20.7	14.39	0.853	1.149	−0.296
Indonesia	33.7	22.19	11.51	1.962	2.282	−0.32
Top five countries for cutting carbon dioxide emissions:						
Singapore	1.08	1.06	0.02	11.111	6.71	4.401
Estonia	0.32	0.22	0.1	12.025	10.474	1.551
Germany	0.25	0.24	0.01	9.73	8.405	1.325
United Kingdom	0.22	0.21	0.01	6.415	5.477	0.938
Norway	0.33	0.33	0.00	8.721	7.89	0.831

Notes

i The poverty headcount data were obtained from Sachs et al. (2020).

ii The source of the carbon dioxide emissions data was Our World in Data. Available at: https://github.com/owid/co2-data [27 May 2021].

Pakistan 2014, 60): "Meeting the economic growth requirements to realize Pakistan Vision 2025 will demand enormous amounts of additional, reliable and cost-effective energy". It had big coal reserves and the government perceived coal as being a cost-efficient source of fuel. So, from the point of view of speeding up its economic growth rate, it might make sense to increase domestic coal production. But what would this mean for its emission of greenhouse gases? This surely placed the Government of Pakistan in a predicament? This also had an international context (Government of Pakistan 2014, 19): "While developed countries contribute disproportionately to greenhouse gas emissions, the developing world is beset with unsustainable exploitation of resources such as water, forests, and arable land".

Some richer countries were substantially reducing carbon dioxide emissions. Since they were not as troubled by problems of poverty, and since they were emitters of greenhouse gases, can we assume the richer countries had got their priorities right and were not suffering from a strategic angst? For them, the problem is otherwise, as the worst emitters of greenhouse gases they presumably ought to be vigorous in cutting greenhouse gas emissions. But they were facing a time pressure because of the climate crisis, and to bring global warming down to the target they needed a global effort on global warming. It would not be enough to bring down emissions just in their own countries. They were dependent on countries that had a different set of national priorities. Their dilemma was, it seems, they needed a stronger strategic and collaborative response to cutting global warming (Michel 2021):

> ... we are not all equally placed in the race against time where global warming is concerned. Industrialised countries bear a particular responsibility for supporting developing countries. Since the pledge to mobilise 100 billion dollars a year to finance the fight against global warming, few have paid their share.

Why had they not paid their share? What made this difficult? If we take the case of the UK, its fiscal position was weak because of sluggish economic recovery from the 2007 to 2009 crisis, its governments had been following austerity policies since 2010, trying to reduce public spending deficits and cut national debt. In 2020, it suffered a nearly 10% drop in real GDP. The governments of countries in this predicament might be reluctant to give money to developing and emerging economies to deliver on sustainable development goals. In fact, the UK ring-fenced its spending on finance for climate action but cut its overseas aid from 0.7% of GDP to 0.5% of GDP. A United Nations official was quoted in March 2021 as saying that the Cop26 UN Climate summit later that year needed to solve the fiscal dilemma holding back financing of climate action (Harvey 2021):

> What will be critical is to find a way to finance the acceleration of climate action and higher ambition on emissions. This must be a collective effort, a joint undertaking ...

In practice, therefore, it can be imagined that enormous amounts of strategic creativity and innovation might be essential for governments to overcome the strategic tensions they confronted, whether it was countries like Pakistan or like the UK. And we can speculate that if the global partnership was to deliver more transformation, the development of genuinely internationally coordinated and inter-dependent strategies to deliver sustainable development would be required and would only emerge after tough negotiations within the global governance of the 2030 Agenda.

Summary and conclusions

According to the 2030 Agenda, national governments were expected to set their own national targets and decide how to integrate them or incorporate them into national strategies and plans. They were also to work in partnership on implementation with various stakeholders and institutions within a country. They were given the central role in monitoring, which would take place at national, regional, and global levels.

The text of the resolution on the 2030 Agenda also said that national governments would be working in a global partnership to deliver the sustainable development agenda.

We saw earlier in the book that countries with strong strategic state capabilities were countries with strong national development achievements. Therefore, did this indicate that strong strategic state capabilities would be a cause of success in delivering sustainable development goals? The answer to this question might be difficult to find and prove for a variety of reasons. Countries varied massively in their initial starting point in 2015. Countries might have planned different trajectories in delivering progress, with some planning to make a slow start but building momentum all the time, whereas others might have intended to make a strong start on delivery that enabled them to coast at later stages, and so on. Countries could vary in the priorities they established with regards to the 17 sustainable development goals. They could vary in the profile of their progress on the 17 sustainable development goals.

In fact, analysis revealed a positive correlation between strategic state capabilities and the score achieved on the 2020 SDG Index. But there was also a positive correlation with the 2016 SDG Index. And the two indexes were very strongly correlated. The very strong correlation between the 2016 Index and the 2020 Index seemed to show that all countries were progressing equally. No evidence was found that governments with strategic state capabilities were massively outperforming other governments when it came to implementing the 2030 Agenda from 2015 onwards. If anything, the best "improvers" were countries that were not among the group with the most strategic state capabilities; but they were countries that had progressed a lot in terms of cutting poverty in their populations (e.g., Bangladesh, Cambodia, India, Pakistan, and Indonesia).

Countries with governance based on strategic state capabilities could have achieved relevant national social, environment, and economic developments prior to, or by, 2015. This appeared to be partially true in Sweden's case. Some countries certainly had national strategies relating to 2030 Agenda areas even before 2015. For example, the UK had strategies on energy and the environment before 2015, and even had become one of the top countries for cutting carbon dioxide emissions per capita.

While countries with governments that had strong strategic state capabilities might have been delivering green goals prior to 2015, they were the richer countries of the world and their previous social and economic development had also been damaging to the environment, for example, producing high levels of carbon dioxide emissions per capita. Indeed, governments with strong strategic state capabilities might have been trying to correct a problematic environmental record in the period prior to 2015.

It has been appreciated since the outset that linkages exist between the 17 sustainable development goals of the 2030 Agenda. Some years on from 2015 and the beginning of the implementation of the sustainable development goals, it is possible to study the linkages using empirical evidence. Using recently published data it was shown, using bivariate analysis, that there is a slight negative correlation between two areas of the 2030 Agenda – poverty and climate change. Countries with the biggest reductions in poverty had increased their per capita emissions of carbon dioxide. Countries with the biggest reductions in emissions of carbon dioxide on a per capita basis had zero or very small reductions in poverty. This suggested that the balancing of priorities among the sustainable development goals turned out differently for poor and rich countries. For poor countries, cutting poverty may have been given high importance and faster economic growth may have been seen by them as the best answer to the problem of poverty. This fast economic growth, and the energy inputs needed for it, would have placed an upward pressure on greenhouse gas emissions.

References

Department of Trade and Industry (2003) *Our energy future – Creating a low carbon economy*. Cm 5761. London: HMSO.

Gallup (2020) Earth day at 50: The world's satisfaction with the environment. Available at: https://news.gallup.com/opinion/gallup/308879/earth-day-world-satisfaction-environment.aspx [29 September 2021].

Gallup (2021) Environment. Available at: https://news.gallup.com/poll/1615/environment.aspx [29 September 2021].

Government of Denmark (2010) Denmark 2020. Available at: http://www.stm.dk/publikationer/arbprog_10_uk/Denmark_2020_knowledge_growth_prosperity_welfare.pdf [21 August 2018]

Government of Pakistan (2014) Pakistan 2025: One nation – One vision. Available at: https://www.pc.gov.pk/uploads/vision2025/Pakistan-Vision-2025.pdf [7 October 2021].

Government of Pakistan (2019) Pakistan's implementation of the 2030 Agenda for sustainable development: Voluntary national review. Available at: https://sustainabledevelopment.un.org/content/documents/233812019_06_15_VNR_2019_Pakistan_latest_version.pdf [7 October 2021].

Government of Singapore (2020) Charting Singapore's low-carbon and climate resilient future. Singapore: National Climate Change Secretariat Strategy Group, Prime Minister's Office. Available at: www.nccs.gov.sg [24 November 2020].

Government of South Africa (2011) National development plan: Vision for 2030. Available at: https://www.gov.za/documents/national-development-plan-vision-2030 [7 October 2021].

Government of South Africa (2019) South Africa's voluntary national review (VNR) report. Available at: https://sustainabledevelopment.un.org/content/documents/23402RSA_Voluntary_National_Review_Report__9_July_2019.pdf [7 October 2021].

Government of Sweden (2017) Sweden and the 2030 Agenda: Report to the UN high level political forum 2017 on sustainable development. Available at: https://sustainabledevelopment.un.org/content/documents/16033Sweden.pdf [21 August 2018].

Harvey, F. (2021) UK urged to take a lead in helping poor countries to fund climate action. The Guardian. 29 March 2021. Available at: https://www.theguardian.com/environment/2021/mar/29/uk-urged-take-lead-helping-poor-countries-fund-climate-action-cop26. [26 October 2021].

Hunt, M. (2021) Former diplomats challenge Australian government on climate change inaction. Global Government Forum. 30 September 2021. Available at: https://www.globalgovernmentforum.com/former-diplomats-challenge-australian-government-on-climate-change-inaction/ [1 October 2021].

Kingdom of Saudi Arabia (2018) Towards Saudi Arabia's sustainable tomorrow. *First Voluntary National Review*. Available at: https://sustainabledevelop ment.un.org/content/documents/20230SDGs_English_Report972018_FINAL. pdf [6 October 2021].

Le Blanc, D. (2015) *Towards integration at last. The sustainable development goals as a network of targets*. DESA Working Paper No. 41. March 2015. New York: United Nations.

Martin, S. (2021) Scott Morrison refuses to release net zero 2050 modelling amid condemnation of climate policy. *The Guardian*. 27 October 2021. Available at: https://www.theguardian.com/australia-news/2021/oct/27/scott-morrison-refuses-to-release-net-zero-2050-modelling-amid-condemnation-of-climate-policy [28 October 2021].

Metcalfe, H.C. & Urwick, L. (Eds.) (1941) *Dynamic administration: The collected papers of Mary Parker Follett*. Bath: Management Publications Trust.

Michel, C. (2021) Speech by President Charles Michel at the UN General Assembly. Available at: https://www.consilium.europa.eu/en/press/press-releases/2021/09/24/discours-du-president-charles-michel-a-l-assemblee-generale-des-nations-unies/pdf [26 September 2021].

Mintzberg, H. (1987) The strategy concept I: Five Ps for strategy. *California Management Review*, 30(1), 11–24.

Nutt, P.C. & Backoff, R.W. (1992) *Strategic management of public and third sector organizations*. San Francisco, CA: Jossey-Bass.

Reinhart, R.J. (2020) Majority of Australians unhappy with environmental efforts. 16 January 2020. Available at: https://news.gallup.com/poll/282701/majority-australians-unhappy-environmental-efforts.aspx?version= print [15 October 2021].

Sachs, J., Schmidt-Traub, G., Kroll, C., Durand-Delacre, D., & Teksoz, K. (2016) *SDG index and dashboards – global report*. New York: Bertelsmann Stiftung and Sustainable Development Solutions Network (SDSN).

Sachs, J., Schmidt-Traub, G., Kroll, C., Lafortune, G., & Fuller, G. (2019) *Sustainable development report 2019*. New York: Bertelsmann Stiftung and Sustainable Development Solutions Network.

Sachs, J., Schmidt-Traub, G., Kroll, C., Lafortune, G., Fuller, G., & Woelm, F. (2020) *The sustainable development goals and COVID-19*. Sustainable Development Report 2020. Cambridge: Cambridge University Press.

Secretary General (2021) Long-term future trends and scenarios: Impacts in the economic, social and environmental areas on the realization of the Sustainable Development Goals. Report to the Economic and Social Council of the United Nations. 5 May 2021. Available at: https://digitallibrary.un. org/record/3927759?ln=en#record-files-collapse-header [8 July 2021].

Taylor, L. (2014) Australia kills off carbon tax. *The Guardian.* 17 July 2014. Available at: https://www.theguardian.com/environment/2014/jul/17/australia-kills-off-carbon-tax [15 October 2021].

United Nations (2015) UN adopts new Global Goals, charting sustainable development for people and planet by 2030. Available at: http://www.un.org/apps/news/story.asp?NewsID=51968#.VgaegrSm3QM [26 September 2015].

United Nations (2017) 71/313. Work of the Statistical Commission pertaining to the 2030 Agenda for sustainable development. General Resolution adopted by the General Assembly on 6 July 2017. Available at: https://undocs.org/A/RES/71/313 [5 March 2020].

World Meteorological Organization (2021) *WMO atlas of mortality and economic losses from weather, climate and water extremes (1970–2019).* Geneva: WMO.

9   Strategic Crisis Management

Introduction

This chapter explores the strategic management of crises. What is meant here by the word crisis? It is too easy to stick the label "crisis" on any problem that feels like it is too much. According to one dictionary, the meaning of the word crisis has changed since its first use in the 15th century (Merriam-Webster 2021):

> Originally, crisis denoted "the turning point for better or worse in an acute disease or fever". Now it most commonly means "a difficult or dangerous situation that needs serious attention" ... .

There may be other connotations of the word crisis. For example, a crisis may be thought of as the malfunctioning of an institution or system (e.g., the 2021 Italian government crisis; the crisis in the global financial system in 2007–2009; the crisis of the climate system). By malfunctioning is meant that processes have been interrupted or have ceased to work as they normally do, and problems or dangers are increasing.

Presumably, crises often originate in the conditions under which an institution or system operates. Over time conditions may worsen and trigger more crises. At an open policy debate in Ireland in 2017, Aengus Collins, who was Practice Lead for Global Risks at the World Economic Forum in Geneva, said (Department of the Taoiseach 2017, 57):

> The process of assessing risks is becoming more difficult as deepening interconnectedness and uncertainty increasingly become the norm. Each year the World Economic Forum publishes the Global Risks Report to help this process by mapping the global risks landscape and drawing the attention of decision-makers in both the public and private sectors to potential sources of disruption. We track the perceived likelihood and impact of individual risks considered in isolation – and since 2007, our reports have shown a clear shift in focus from economic to environmental risks – but

DOI: 10.4324/9781351045797-9

increasingly our analysis focuses on the ways in which risks interact and on the feedback loops that can form between risks and our responses to them.

Crises vary in their nature. They can suddenly emerge and catch governments almost totally by surprise. Crises can be expected well in advance of their occurrence but still contain surprises. And sometimes a crisis is not surprising at all because it builds up slowly over a long period of time, and persists as a crisis because of issues that prevent effective responses happening. If crises are, or contain, surprises and if issues inhibit effective responses to crises, then crises are difficult to predict and control (Farazmand 2007, 150):

> Crises are ... often unpredicted and unexpected, but they develop with dynamic and unfolding events over months, days, hours, or even minutes. They disrupt the routine events of life and governance, disturb established systems, and cause severe anxieties; they produce dynamics that no one can predict and control.

Crises can also vary in the nature of the action required from government (Thomas 2021). Sometimes immediate government action is needed. Sometimes government communications matter a lot, as in a crisis when government is trying to avoid or reduce public confusion and panic, or trying to change the response of the public to the crisis. Sometimes the government response needs to have been planned by the government well before the crisis breaks.

This chapter begins with a case study of the coronavirus pandemic. One of the aspects of crisis management explored in this chapter is the use of strategic preparedness and strategic agility to minimize mortality rates. Then, international cooperation in a crisis is explored through the crisis of climate change. Towards the end of the chapter, the focus is broadened to include insights into crisis management generally and it concludes with some ideas on national strategies for crisis management.

The COVID-19 pandemic: strategic issues and capabilities

Were governments prepared?

According to a recent report by the OECD (2018, 100), it was typically the case that countries had suffered a crisis within the last twenty years for which they were not prepared. The world should have been prepared for a pandemic. Pandemics had occurred in the past and were expected to occur in the future. In 2019, the World Health Organization (WHO 2019, 2–3) quoted an authority in 2011 suggesting the world was not prepared:

In 2011, the Review Committee on the Functioning of the International Health Regulations (IHR) (2005) in relation to pandemic (H1N1) 2009 concluded, "the world is ill-prepared to respond to a severe influenza pandemic or to any similarly global, sustained and threatening public health emergency". Since the release of that report there has been a strong global movement to advance IHR (2005) compliance and the building of core capacities to strengthen pandemic preparedness and health security.

It is noteworthy that the 2011 warning referred not just to influenza pandemics but also to any similarly global health emergency. As it turned out, COVID-19 was not an influenza pandemic.

The WHO in 2019 said that governments had worked on preparing for a pandemic in the years that followed the 2011 report. Were the governments ready? To take one example, the UK Government appeared to be alert to the risk of a pandemic. It replaced its 2005 UK Influenza Pandemic Contingency Plan with a new strategy, the UK Influenza Pandemic Preparedness Strategy, in 2011. And, in 2016, the UK Government carried out "Exercise Cygnus" in 2016 which exposed issues around the governance of a pandemic. The dangers and possibility of a flu pandemic were brought once again to the attention of the UK Government cabinet by being rated as the top civil risk in the 2019 National Security Risk Assessment.

Of course, there were things the governments could not know about the next pandemic: not least, governments did not know exactly when the next pandemic would occur nor did they know with certainty just how dangerous it would be. When a pandemic did come, the amount of protection governments could provide citizens against infection and death would depend on at least four factors:

1 Their correct understanding of what they needed to do
2 Their capabilities as governments
3 How well they could mobilize and coordinate effort inside and outside government
4 Their commitment to protecting people from the health dangers of the pandemic

Some of these things could have been the subject of preparations and prior planning. It can be hypothesized that the second and third of the factors should have been possessed to a greater degree by governments with strategic state capabilities as compared to other governments.

Even though a pandemic had long been seen as a risk and preparations had been made some governments were not ready when COVID-19 struck. For some, it was because they were not ready for a threat as dangerous as COVID-19. It started at the end of December 2019 when the WHO was informed about cases of an unknown pneumonia in Wuhan City in Hubei Province of China and then the Chinese Government notified the WHO on 7 January 2020 that a new type of coronavirus had been isolated. A lot then happened in the space of a short few weeks (Box 9.1).

As can be seen, the countries that acted quickly included China (which had isolated the virus on 7 January 2020 and shared its genetic sequence by 12 January 2020), Thailand, Japan, Singapore, and the Republic of Korea. Within days these countries took measures such as screening and quarantining of travellers, and within days were finding cases of people who had been infected. From the point of understanding the possibilities of the strategic management of a crisis, we can ask about how they managed to react so quickly. Were they improvising (making it up as they went along) or had they a strategy and been prepared? In at least two cases – Singapore and South Korea – the governments seem to have been acting strategically and were well prepared.

Singapore handled the first few months well. By 18 May 2020, it had less than 29,000 cases and only 22 deaths. This was partly due to preparedness and this in turn seemed to be the result of its experiences of the Severe Acute Respiratory Syndrome (SARS) in 2003. Its preparations included pandemic response plans, regular exercises, and the creation of a 330-bed infectious disease management facility, which incorporated epidemiological, laboratory, and clinical functions. In January 2020, in addition to screening travellers from Wuhan, it set up a task force of relevant ministers on 22 January 2020, which was co-chaired by the Ministry of Health (MOH) and Minister of National Development (MND). After that, the following was done (Lee 2020, 209):

> When the COVID-19 task force was formed, the plans were quickly put into motion. The national strategy for pandemic response was to establish an effective community-wide surveillance system to detect, trace, and contain the disease (MOH 2014). To augment the tracing efforts and ensure public buy-in, a less invasive mobile phone app TraceTogether was launched with a fair level of voluntary adoption among citizens. SafeEntry was also deployed at venues with high human traffic or prolonged person-to-person interactions.

January to February was characterized by efforts to detect cases quickly through screening, and to follow this up with contact tracing and isolation. In the period of March to early April, the response centred on travel bans and encouraging physical distancing.

Celia Lee summed up the Singapore response as follows (Lee 2020, 218):

Box 9.1   COVID-19 events from 31 December 2019 to 30 January 2020

31 December 2019: WHO China Country Office informed about cases of an unknown pneumonia in Wuhan City, Hubei Province of China.

7 January 2020: Chinese authorities isolated a new type of coronavirus.

12 January 2020: Chinese authorities shared the virus's genetic sequence for countries to use in developing diagnostic kits.

By 20 January 2020: There had been only six deaths reported – all from Wuhan City. But confirmed cases of people with COVID-19 were reported by various countries. Thailand, Japan, and the Republic of Korea reported finding a total of four people who had been infected. Thailand screened over 18,000 people on direct flights from Wuhan between 3 and 20 January. Japan was taking enhanced quarantine and screening measures in respect of travellers from Wuhan from 7 January. The Republic of Korea enhanced its quarantine and screening measures for travellers from Wuhan from 3 January 2020 and contact tracing and other epidemiological work were begun. Singapore began screening travellers from Wuhan in early January.

22 January 2020: Dr Maria van Kerkhove at a WHO press briefing noted that the rapid sharing of the genetic sequence of the virus meant that labs all over the world could detect the virus in patients and said (WHO 2020): "… our recommendation is to ensure that individuals can be identified quickly, and isolated quickly. Tested quickly, cared for, and managed, so that they can prevent any further transmission".

23 January 2020: New cases were reported in Singapore and USA.

24 January 2020: New cases were reported in Vietnam and Singapore.

25–31 January 2020: New cases of people who were infected were reported in Australia, Nepal, France, Cambodia, Sri Lanka, Germany, United Arab Emirates, Philippines, India, Finland, Italy, and England.

30 January 2020: Dr Tedros Adhanom Ghebreyesus, Director-General WHO declared a Public Health Emergency of International Concern over the global outbreak of novel coronavirus.

Singapore did things right at the onset of the pandemic without closing schools and shutting down businesses, through rigorous screening, contact tracing, isolation orders, social distancing, safe measurements. These responses had earned Singapore early praises and was held as the model to emulate. (Bloomberg 2020)

South Korea was another country recognized for a successful response to the pandemic. It too seemed to have learnt from earlier experiences of coping with viruses (Im 2020, 223):

South Korea had experienced three different types of infectious virus spread in the recent years. Experiences from the SARS (Severe Acute Respiratory Syndrome) in 2003, and the MERS (Middle East Respiratory Syndrome) in 2015 and 2018 gave lessons to the Korean government on how confirmed patients should be treated, what kind of information should be shared with citizens, and which pools of experts group are immediately needed for policy decisions.

Its preparations included a new law in 2015 which addressed the cost of diagnosis and treatment related to infectious diseases and the recruitment of epidemiology specialists in 2018. It also took measures to enable communications with the public and to enable speedy action during a response to a pandemic (Im 2020, 223):

The Emergency Operations Centre (EOC), an organization that comprehensively controls quarantine sites in preparation for the outbreak of infectious diseases, was established, and after the MERS outbreak a system called "Crisis Communication Officer (spokesperson for KCDC)" was added to facilitate crisis communication with the public. A measure for speedily approving diagnosis and test kits has been institutionalized after MERS, which helped with early mass testing in the COVID-19 outbreak.

In fact, training on handling a pandemic took place in December immediately prior to the COVID-19 virus being identified and the first cases reported to the WHO in January 2020. As Im (2020, 224) put it, "South Korea's preparedness efforts were timely".

The quality of the civil service was identified as a positive factor in South Korea's response (Im 2020, 226):

The competent bureaucrats in South Korea, who intervened in a timely manner and effectively, were, arguably, a pivotal factor in the successful COVID-19 management. They worked within a competitive government that was characterized by competent civil servants in various agencies well aligned from the central government to street-level bureaucrats. The Korean bureaucrats provided proactive leadership, harmonizing central government and local government, and proved effective in dealing with this COVID-19 pandemic situation.

In fact, both Singapore and South Korea were perceived to have had effective governments for a very long time and, earlier in this book, both were classified as being highly developed in terms of "strategic state capabilities". But it is also clear from the reports of both Singapore and South Korea, there was a high level of preparedness. Lessons had been learnt by both governments from recent experiences (Joyce et al. 2020a, 11): "It appears to be easier to ensure preparedness where the danger is more vivid in the minds of government leaders".

Learning during the crisis

The United Nations described the COVID-19 situation as "unprecedented" and stressed the need for creativity. It said (United Nations 2020a, 1): "In the face of such an unprecedented situation in recent history, the creativity of the response must match the unique nature of the crisis – and the magnitude of the response must match its scale".

If something is unexpected and requires creativity governments have two main options. The first is haphazard action. It is based on hoping that something done spontaneously and randomly might just prove useful. This approach was extolled by some management theorists in the 1980s as appropriate for chaotic situations. The second option is to learn fast through evaluation and experimentation. This second approach for dealing with crises can be seen as overlapping with arguments for strategic agility to be used to either seize opportunities quickly or handle crises. It can be persuasively argued that strategic agility rests on an ability to recognize "weak signals" of an emerging opportunity or a crisis, the ability to take concerted action across ministries and with external stakeholders, and an ability to switch and reuse people, resources, and capabilities (Doz and Kosonen 2014). In an "unprecedented" situation, which means that government is operating in an unusual context, it is unlikely that agility can occur without some assistance from evaluation and experimentation. So, governments that can operate in a whole-of government manner, work in co-operation with citizens and external stakeholders, and experiment, evaluate and adapt, might be expected to be better at learning fast in a crisis. In other words, governments with strong strategic state capabilities should cope better with a crisis. Was this true in the case of the COVID-19 pandemic?

Strategic states and responses to COVID-19

Using once more the Institutional Profile Database (2016) and also COVID-19 mortality data for the period from July 2020 to January 2021, it is possible to examine the possible importance of strong strategic state capabilities in a pandemic.

As shown by Table 9.1, strategic state capabilities did not seem to matter in relation to countries that had a low mortality rate in July 2020 and had seen only a small increase in the mortality rate in the

Table 9.1 Strategic state capabilities and COVID-19 mortality rates

COVID-19 mortality rate in July 2020 & increase in rate over 6 months to 11 January 2021	*Extent of strategic state capabilities 2016 (Institutional Profiles Database)*		
	Low	*Medium*	*High*
High rate in July 2020 and medium increase		Ireland	Canada, Denmark, Germany, Netherlands, Sweden
Medium rate in July 2020 and low increase		Qatar	Finland, Norway
Low rate in July 2020 and low increase	Algeria, Cambodia, Egypt, Nigeria, Pakistan, Venezuela, Vietnam	Bangladesh, Ghana, Malaysia, Mozambique, New Zealand, UAE	Australia, China, Japan, South Korea, Singapore
Low/medium rate in July 2020 and medium/high increase	Romania, Greece, Poland, Tunisia, Kuwait, Paraguay	Hungary, Argentina, Costa Rica, Czech Republic, Georgia, Ukraine, Bahrain, Estonia, Oman, Russia, Saudi Arabia, Turkey, India, Indonesia	Austria, Slovenia, South Africa, Lithuania
High rate in July 2020 and high increase	Chile, Peru	Brazil, Colombia, France, Italy, Spain	Belgium, Portugal, United Kingdom, United States

Note
Countries were classified as low, medium, and high both in relation to their cumulative COVID-19 mortality rate in July 2020 and in relation to the change in their mortality rate between 11 July 2020 and 11 January 2021. They were also classified as low, medium, and high in terms of strategic state capabilities using data from the Institutional Profiles Database for 2016.

following six months. There were some notable examples of countries in this category that had high scores for strategic state capabilities (e.g., Australia, China, Japan, South Korea, and Singapore). These were countries that were held up as examples of successful government responses to the pandemic. But high scores on strategic state capabilities did not seem to be essential for a country to be in this group of countries with a low mortality rate in July and a low increase in the rate over the next six months.

Two groups of countries looked as though they might have been learning how to respond more effectively to the pandemic. The first consisted of three countries that had a medium mortality rate in July 2020 but had then seen only a low increase in the mortality rate over the next six months. The second group consisted of six countries, and they had a high mortality rate in July 2020 but then had only a medium increase in the mortality rate over the next six months. Seven out of nine of these countries had governments defined as strongly developed in terms of strategic state capabilities. The remaining two governments were assessed as being in the medium range for strategic state capabilities. This seems to offer us some evidence that strategic state capabilities can be useful when a government wants to achieve at least a partial turnaround in its performance in responding to a pandemic.

A third group, which had high mortality rates in July 2020 and a high increase in mortality rates over the next six months, could be described as failing to learn. Four of the 11 countries in this group were judged to possess strong strategic state capabilities. They were Belgium, Portugal, the United Kingdom, and the United States. Why did the governments of these four countries not use their capabilities to slow the increase in mortality rates over the six months from July 2020 to January 2021? Possible and plausible explanations are that they suffered from poor leadership, leaders had made errors, or that the leaders were not committed to making the reduction of mortality rates their single most important target.

Risky strategic compromises (stuck in the middle strategies)?

It became obvious within the first four or five months of the pandemic that successfully managing the crisis required confronting a very difficult issue, the linkage between two crises. The crises were the threat to human life and the threat to economic activity. It also became evident that governments could choose to handle the two linked crises either by prioritizing one over the other or attempting to deal with them simultaneously. What, it might be asked, is so special about two crises being linked: is it an issue of limited government attention being stretched by having two crises to resolve or is it more complicated than that?

We could loosely refer to any problem or concern as an issue, but some authorities in the technical literature of strategic analysis and planning have attempted to set out particular ways of clarifying or "expressing" the structure of a strategic issue. Nutt and Backoff 1987 (47) were among those who tried to do this for the public and third sectors:

> Issues are framed (fashioned or formed) in terms of opposing forces pulling or pushing the organization in various directions and away from idealized images of its future. These forces identify the under-lying tensions at work on the organization. This format for expressing issues illustrates polar opposites or contradictions within the organization or between it and external actors.

The threat to life was immediately obvious when the virus aggressively spread round the world. If a government responded to surging infection through stopping international travel to their country and through a national lock down (closing workplaces, schools, public transport systems, etc.) the longer these measures were continued, the greater the interruption would be to normal economic activity. If a government had decided to completely ignore the spread of infection within its borders, economic activity might be sustained to a greater extent, but the mortality rate would increase unchecked. Moreover, economic activity was still hurt to some degree as illness caused absences from work and disruption of activities in workplaces. Governments did have the option of trying a compromise response: that is, choosing to slow the spread of the virus without really trying to suppress it in the hope that economic activity could be kept going as much as possible in the circumstances. In effect, government leaders would be asking or expecting their citizens to tolerate the occurrence of some pandemic cases and COVID-19 deaths. There was one other possible response, which was the closest thing imaginable to an integrative solution. This is the one that the World Health Organization advised, which in principle offered a creative response to the issue – this was to act aggressively to suppress the virus though testing, tracing, and isolating measures. If done well, and with adequate resources, this response might have meant that lock downs could be avoided. A lock down would then be a back-up measure only needed if the virus got out of control.

If governments were slow to respond and failed to provide effective test, trace, and isolate measures the consequences could be high levels of infection and death, and this could pressurise governments to reluctantly order lock downs. For example, the UK was very slow to react to the warnings of the World Health Organization and struggled to create an effective test, trace, and isolate system. The result was reliance on lock downs as the only tool available in the pandemic toolbox. By the end of

2020, the UK had a very high total COVID 19 mortality rate. And its economy was also severely disrupted. The rollout of vaccines in 2021 did allow the UK Government to bring about a reduction in the seriousness of the pandemic as measured by mortality rates.

Figure 9.1 shows that there was a moderate negative correlation (r = –0.61) between the total (cumulative) COVID-19 mortality rate and the change in GDP for 2020. Countries like China, New Zealand, Australia, and Norway followed a more aggressive suppression strategy and thereby minimized loss of life and managed to emerge at the end of 2020 with a slightly bigger GDP or with only a small drop in GDP. Countries with high total mortality rates were likely to have a substantial decline in GDP.

The strategic lesson was therefore as follows: if a virus is aggressive and life threatening, as in the case of COVID-19, it is better for governments to use measures that control and suppress the virus rather than merely slow down its spread. This enables time for vaccines to be developed and rolled out. And in the meantime, if the virus is supressed, economic activity can be encouraged. It is better to start by aiming to save as many lives as possible rather than to start by aiming to keep economic activity at as high a level as possible.

It can be imagined that the governments which chose to compromise between saving lives and saving the economy could have been attempting to manage a very complex balancing act and could be taking some ethically challenging decisions. Logically speaking, the balancing act would involve trying to mitigate the rise in the number of cases so that economic activity could go on, but also trying to ensure that the flow of serious cases did not overwhelm the hospital system, because if the latter happened public support for the government could be strained and could lead to panic. Ethically, the government leaders would have to decide what rates of cases and deaths were acceptable to maintain some economic activity. In the absence of a focus on saving lives then even governments with good strategic state capabilities might find the balancing act too complex and might resort to chaotic muddling through that may have then produced high mortality rates (Joyce 2021).

Climate change and international cooperation during a crisis

So far in this chapter, the focus has clearly been on national governments. However, some crises might be better handled if governments cooperate. In years to come when the experiences of managing the COVID-19 pandemic are evaluated it may be concluded that more should have been done to get international cooperation in responding to it. But in 2021, there was evidence that international cooperation was not strong enough to deal with another crisis affecting the

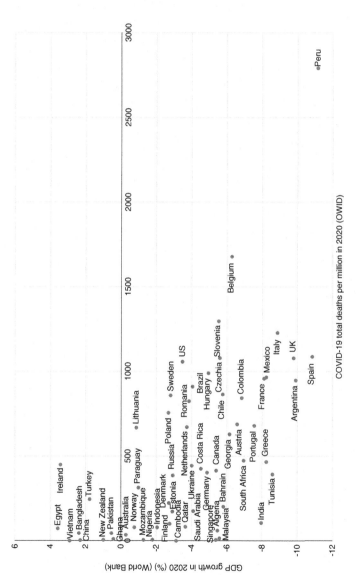

Figure 9.1 GDP growth in 2020 was negatively correlated with COVID-19 total mortality rates.

Notes:

The COVID-19 data was downloaded from https://github.com/owid/covid-19-data/tree/master/public/data [18 October 2021]. The GDP growth data was data from the World Development Indicators database and was downloaded from https://databank.worldbank.org/ [18 October 2021].
The bivariate correlation was r = −0.61.

whole world – the crisis of global warming. The United Nations doubted that any single government could deal with the climate crisis by itself, without working with other governments (United Nations 2020b, 30):

> Climate change is a global threat that requires a global response from all sectors of society. No nation can tackle climate change on its own ...

Why might it be difficult to get the necessary level of cooperation internationally? The Australian Government in 2021 can (again) serve as a mini-case study. It was in two minds over committing the country to a policy of net zero emissions by 2050. The government was said to be split. Then, in the summer of 2021, it published a plan to achieve net zero emissions which appeared to resolve the matter (Chapter 8). Here we focus on what was delaying the government making the commitment and what that might tell us about one of the limits on international cooperation in a crisis.

The prime minister of Australia was put under pressure to make a commitment to reduce emissions ahead of the UN Climate Change Conference scheduled for late 2021. A large group of former Australian diplomats made the point that plans are important but that commitment by leaders at the top of government is essential (Hunt 2021):

> "Actions, plans and policies are of course vitally important, but without a commitment to targets at the highest levels of government, no-one will believe that we are serious about pulling our weight on reducing emissions of CO2 and other greenhouse gases", the diplomats said.

The simple point here is that a plan is logically speaking more likely to be effective when its country's leaders are committed to its delivery by doing all they can to ensure that resources are provided and by monitoring that it is kept on track despite the problems that emerge along the way.

The hesitancy at the top of Australian Government to give its commitment appeared not to be caused by following public opinion since the public wanted greenhouse gas emissions to be cut and wanted action on climate change (Hunt 2021). So, if it was not public opinion causing the government's hesitancy, what was it? It could have been that leading politicians were delaying making a commitment because of the impact they thought it might have on economic growth and employment, which was reported to be the concern for at least one important political leader (Hunt 2021):

> Treasurer Josh Frydenberg and other Liberal ministers are in favour. Deputy prime minister and Nationals leader Barnaby Joyce is

against, having raised concerns about short-term job and income losses in regional Australia.

Governments might be adopting "free rider" strategies, doing nothing while hoping all other governments would act to cut greenhouse gases and reduce global warming. If successful free-rider strategies could give them the benefits of global action on temperature warming without them having to take risks with economic prosperity.

The Australian example shows that however potent public opinion is in the last instance, in the meantime a government may follow their own priorities and delay their cooperation in international efforts to deal with a crisis.

In general, how do governments manage a crisis?

Looking at recent writing on natural disasters, pandemics, emergencies, and crises, some key points can be made about crisis preparation and management (Ansell and Boin 2019; Boin and t' Hart 2003; Farazmand 2007; Joyce et al. 2020a; Joyce et al. 2020b; Joyce 2021).

(i) Leadership

Conventional wisdom says the quality of leadership is critical factor in a crisis. This is often thought to be a context in which "commanders" excel in leadership roles. Grint (2005, 1468):

> The assumption that successful leaders are those who respond most appropriately to the demands of the specific situation is common-place. When all is calm successful leaders can afford to relax, seek a consensus and make collective decisions at a leisurely pace. But when a crisis occurs the successful leader must become decisive, demonstrate a ruthless ability to focus on the problem and to ignore the siren calls of the sceptics and the cynics.

As we see, the assumption is that a crisis calls for command-and-control leaders and top-down decisions because there is little time and speed is of the essence. Not everybody agrees with this. For example, strategic crisis managers might need to be pragmatic and experimental (Ansell and Boin 2019, 1089):

> Strategic crisis managers should treat strategies as provisional and subject to continuous revision as new information becomes available. Pragmatic crisis leaders treat their decision as a hypothesis: Once it is made and "enacted", decision makers should carefully monitor the impact (or lack thereof) of their decision and adapt

where necessary. A series of small decisions in adaptive fashion will help decision makers wrestle down the imperatives of uncertainty. Rapid feedback allows for subsequent refinement of strategy.

(ii) Preparedness strategy

Strategic agility in response to a crisis may depend in part on the preparations and investments made under a preparedness strategy. Excessive application of a proportionality mindset to a preparedness strategy may cripple strategic agility in a crisis (Joyce 2021).

(iii) Open to learning

It may be important to learn from the experiences of your own country, but it is also important to learn from other countries. The Hurricane Katrina crisis was said to provide this lesson; governments should be prepared to "learn from other nations and global best practices" (Farazmand 2007, 156). In the early phases of the COVID-19 crisis, Norway was identified as a country that was open to learning (Joyce et al. 2020b, 580):

> In the case of Norway, the Government responded to the pandemic in a manner that showed receptiveness to learning, that was collaborative and pragmatic. They learnt from Asian countries (e.g., South Korea and China), from what had happened in Italy, and from bodies such as WHO and Imperial College London. Being receptive to learning from others may have been especially significant in explaining the government's choice of a suppression strategy. So, receptivity to learning, combined with strong public finances, pragmatic decision making (rather than ideological decision making?) and a collaborative decision-making style may create the best possibilities for agility and adaptability.

(iv) Complexity and creativity

A time of crisis may be made more complex by the existence of not one but multiple and linked crises. Indeed, government responses to one crisis may be the cause of additional crises. Government may also need to think about whether the crises need to be tackled sequentially and in what order.

(v) Whole-of-society approaches

Sometimes a whole-of-society approach is needed. On the day that the World Health Organization declared COVID-19 was a pandemic, its Director-General extolled the use of such an approach to it (WHO 2020, 8):

> I had a very good discussion with His Excellency, Prime Minister Pedro Sanchez of Spain two days ago and I was very much impressed by his commitment. ... We discussed that approach mobilising the whole society and making the response everybody's responsibility and we hope to see progress in Spain too.

The OECD has also highlighted the importance of partnerships for going beyond a whole-of-government approach to crisis management (OECD 2018, 91):

> Governments cannot manage crises alone. Developing trusted partnerships with the private sector, civil society organisations and volunteers, as well as international partners, is fundamental ... many countries have started partnering with operators of critical infrastructure to better assess vulnerabilities and define resilience measures. But engaging them in the crisis management processes also requires specific partnerships.

(vi) Resilience

If crises cannot be prevented, then government must try to lessen the impacts and danger they create and ensure quick recovery. Germany was impacted by heavy rains in July 2021, leading to deaths and the destruction of homes and villages. Newspaper reports linked the record rainfall in Western Europe, including in Germany, to the crisis of climate change. The Chancellor of Germany in July 2021 was reported as agreeing that the extreme rainfall was the result of climate change and saying that Germany must improve its tackling of its impact (Reuters 2021).

(vii) The public expects government will act to protect them

One lesson for policymakers from crises is that the public expects (or hope) their government will protect them. During the COVID-19 crisis in 2020 and 2021, public opinion polls showed public approval of the UK Government's handling of the crisis went up and then down dramatically. The approval for the government went up when the first lock down was ordered in March 2020 – the public wanted the protection of their lives that the lock down would bring. The public's approval went down when the Government failed to deliver personal protective equipment (PPE) to hospital personnel and exposed them to greater risk. It went down when the UK Government began easing the lock down in May 2020 more quickly than many members of the public thought would be safe (Joyce 2021).

It is not certain whether the handling of a crisis will just cause short-term fluctuations in public satisfaction with the government or whether more serious and longer-lasting damage to public trust in the government or the public sector is the result of a government failing to protect the public.

Evidence from the United States seems to be consistent with the thesis that the public expects government to protect them and save lives in a pandemic. Reductions in opinion poll approval ratings of Republic Governors between April 2020 and September 2021 may have been because they did not put saving lives first during the COVID-19 pandemic (Kamarck 2021):

> ... with two exceptions, the top 10 governors who have suffered the largest losses are Republican. Most of these governors have opposed masking, schools being shut down, quarantines, vaccine mandates, and tolerated anti-vaxxers. The real-world results have been horrific. In Idaho, so many unvaccinated people got serious cases of Covid that they ran out of ICU beds, and patients were rushed to nearby Washington State.

(viii) Responsibility, accountability, and the "blame game"

It is often difficult for political leaders to escape responsibility for how well a crisis is handled (OECD 2018, 88):

> The ultimate responsibility lies at the highest levels of government, which have a key role to play to fulfil these crisis management functions effectively, from inter-agency co-ordination to decision-making and communication. This is fundamental for maintaining public trust, which is particularly tested during emergencies: citizen's trust in government is directly affected by how quickly, efficiently and transparently government decisions are taken in crisis situations. Political leadership is considered accountable for good or poor crisis management.

Attributing success or blame is a big part of public debate during and after a crisis. Blaming is intertwined with both learning and accountability. Post-mortems after a crisis has passed may centre on whether spending and actions were "proportionate" (no more than they need to be) or whether the precautionary principle (erring on the side of caution) had been followed. As Boin and t' Hart (2003) comment, while the public expects to be safeguarded, government efforts to prevent a crisis and mitigate the harm of a future crisis earn politicians little political credit. It might be said that politicians walk a political "tightrope" in terms of preparing for and managing crises, or as Boin and t' Hart (2003, 547) express it:

> Leaders sit precariously, then, between a rock and hard place. If they implement crisis prevention, they are chastised for doing too much too soon. If they ignore crisis prevention, they are scolded for having done too little, too late.

In the following excerpt of a parliamentary committee's interview of Gus O'Donnell, formerly the UK's top civil servant, he is challenged about whether there had been a proportionate response to the swine flu pandemic, there are suggestions that there had been "failure", and views are expressed on where "blame" properly rested (Public Administration Select Committee 2011):

> Paul Flynn [Public Administration Select Committee member]: "... The Cabinet Office produced a report on the swine flu pandemic that never was ... The result was that 450 people died with swine flu but only 150 died of swine flu. Does that sound like a proportionate response or were the Government panicked into overreacting? ... Britain spent £1.2 billion. The Polish Health Minister, Ewa Kopacz, who is a medical person, decided to spend about seven zlotys on it, refused to buy the vaccine, didn't trust it, and refused to frighten the population. The result was half the number of deaths from swine flu in Poland that we experienced here. Was it still a proportionate response?
>
> Sir Gus O'Donnell [formerly in the top job of the UK's civil service]: Imagine if it had been a slightly different variant. Imagine if the worst case had come out and imagine if I were the Cabinet Secretary for the Polish Government. What kind of questions would you be asking me now? ...
>
> Paul Flynn:... but haven't the Cabinet Office failed us by not taking a critical look at what was a very foolish decision? There might have been good reasons and the main blame should rest with the World Health Organisation ... I believe that the Cabinet Office has that role to act at one stage removed from other government departments; didn't it fail as far as swine flu was concerned?

National strategies

No doubt the acceptance of the need to get better at the strategic management of crises is strongest in the immediate aftermath of crises. But if a government wishes to get better at strategic crisis management, what should it do?

First, a government could formulate a national risk management strategy and include within that strategy how it will improve and maintain "government's crisis management architecture" and "increase community resilience to threats and hazards" (OECD 2018, 27). The strategy could also specify in some detail how exercises and "drills" will be used to deliver preparedness when it is needed.

Second, a government could improve its capabilities for "identifying novel, unforeseen or complex crises" (OECD 2021, 6). This probably should mean continuous and proactive surveillance which is looking for weak signals that provide early warning of a crisis. This would be in addition to a national risk register.

Third, the national risk register could be set up to engage with the public and to design processes to avoid the group think that may have led to some countries making mistakes in the response to the COVID-19 crisis. The Government of Ireland had a system for examining trends that might produce crises at a national level of government. This was undertaken by the Department of the Taoiseach (Prime Minister's Office). In addition, a strategic overview of national risks was carried out on an annual basis, and this encompassed civil emergencies that could become crises. The annual overview was facilitated by the Department of Taoiseach in a process designed to be inclusive of others beyond government (Department of Taoiseach 2017, 2–3):

> One of the original impetuses behind the National Risk Assessment process was to avoid the possibility of 'group think' when identifying strategic risks to the country. As such, the National Risk Assessment process involves several stages, including collaboration with government departments and agencies, and open public consultation to gauge whether there are any significant risks that have been overlooked or underplayed. As in previous years, a draft list of risks was drawn up in collaboration with a Steering Group, which comprises representatives from government departments and agencies, and is chaired by the Department of the Taoiseach. The draft list was then discussed and debated in the course of an Open Policy Debate held in the Department of the Taoiseach on 24 April 2017, which was attended by senior representatives from across government departments and agencies, as well as representatives from a wide range of public bodies, universities, think-tanks, NGOs and other civil society groups … a preliminary assessment of high-level risks facing Ireland was prepared by the Department of the Taoiseach in collaboration with the Steering Group. The draft National Risk Assessment 2017 was published and laid before the Houses of the Oireachtas in June as the basis for a further public consultation exercise."

Fourth, the national strategy could provide for a regular capability review of the government and its partners in relation to strategic crisis management.

Fifth, the strategy could include a plan and preparations for whole-of-government responses to a crisis, testing out different approaches. Comparisons of different countries show there is not a single whole-of-government model (OECD 2018, 90–91):

> ... in France each ministry has a high-level civil servant in charge of security and defence, and they together form an inter-agency network which can directly be activated when a crisis occurs. In Finland, the Security Strategy for Society has created a large multi-sector engagement. It identifies seven vital functions necessary in all situations and 49 strategic tasks of the government which contribute to securing these functions. The strategy has assigned responsibilities to ministries for each of these tasks.

Sixth, the strategy could provide a basis for planning and maintaining partnerships needed for the response networks led by governments in a crisis. These "response networks" can be seen as core parts of the delivery chain for strategic crisis management. The design of the response network should include the scope for using "common principles and interoperable tools" to support flexible co-operation (OECD 2018, 92–93).

Seventh, the strategy could plan government's system for crisis communication with the public to ensure that it met the highest standards for honesty, transparency, and openness.

Summary and conclusion

This chapter was first and foremost concerned with assessing the advantages that a government with strong strategic state capabilities might have during the COVID-19 pandemic (at least in the period up to early 2021). The COVID-19 pandemic was a crisis that proved difficult to manage because the virus was aggressive and deadly, much worse than a flu pandemic anticipated by so many governments. It was a complex crisis because of its scale and duration. Countries with reputations for an effective responsive to the first part of the pandemic included countries with strong strategic state capabilities. But reports about two of these countries – Singapore and South Korea – suggested that they were well prepared when the crisis struck and were able to act quickly and decisively. It was also evident that some countries that had avoided high mortality rates were not strong in terms of strategic state capabilities. So, for countries that had very low mortality rates, it cannot be concluded that strategic state capabilities were the key factor in their performance.

But there was evidence that strategic state capabilities made a difference. During the crisis, countries had to contend with waves of infection. It was theoretically possible, therefore, for governments to engage in strategic learning. Data were analysed and found to be consistent with the proposition that governments with strong strategic state capabilities were faster at learning during the crisis and thus were able to achieve partial turnarounds in their mortality rates. So, it is possible that strong strategic state capabilities were important for their strategic agility in the crisis. Such capabilities included being good at evaluation, experimentation, and adaptability to new contexts. Surely, some governments may have evaluated their initial responses, experimented with new approaches and new tools, and then adapted to better meet the challenges of the crisis.

It was also seen that some governments with strong strategic state capabilities continued to experience high total mortality rates in the six months from July of 2020. Why did they continue to experience them? Why did they not use their capabilities? It was speculated that this was explicable by factors such as leadership errors or a leadership decision against making the infection and mortality rates the top targets by which to measure the effectiveness of the government's response to COVID-19.

It became evident to governments during the crisis that some measures (i.e., lock downs) designed to protect citizens from death were harming the economic activity of the country. An analysis conducted in the chapter showed that countries with high total mortality rates were also countries with the poorest performance in terms of GDP growth. It seemed that a country that wished to have the best economic growth possible in the circumstances was right to prioritize saving lives, since controlling the virus permitted greater economic activity to be resumed. Countries with low total mortality rates and a better record of economic growth in 2020 included Australia, China, New Zealand, and Turkey. On this occasion, the experiences of 2020 suggested that governments that were trying to compromise (that is, save lives and keep the economy going, or restore it again quickly) could end up in an unsatisfactory compromise.

This chapter also looked at the issue of international cooperation in relation to the global warming crisis, and identified the perniciousness of national-level free-rider strategies from the point of view if international solidarity. It looked more generally at all types of crisis, and underlined the existence of factors such as government openness to learning, public expectations to be protected by government actions, and the intertwining of the "blame game" with learning and accountability. It ended with a section highlighting some of the elements of a national strategy for strategic crisis management, and this featured the use of an inclusive process of national risk assessment by the Irish Government.

References

Ansell, C. & Boin, A. (2019) Taming deep uncertainty: The potential of pragmatist principles for understanding and improving strategic crisis management. *Administration & Society 2019*, 51(7), 1079–1112.

Bloomberg (2020) As Asia panics over coronavirus, Singapore wins praise for its approach. 11 February 2020. Available at: https://www.japantimes.co.jp/news/2020/02/11/asia-pacific/science-health-asia-pacific/asia-coronavirus-singapore/ [29 October 2021].

Boin, A. & t' Hart, P. (2003) Public leadership in times of crisis: Mission impossible? *Public Administration Review*, 63(6), 544–553.

Department of the Taoiseach (2017) *National risk assessment 2017: Overview of strategic risks.* Dublin: Government of Ireland.

Doz, Y. & Kosonen, M. (2014) *Governments for the future: Building the strategic and agile state. Sitra studies 80.* Erweko, Helsinki: Sitra. Available at: https://media.sitra.fi/2017/02/23222725/Selvityksia80.pdf [30 October 2021].

Farazmand, A. (2007) Learning from the Katrina Crisis: A global and international perspective with implications for future crisis management. Public Administration Review, December 2007, Special Issue, pp. 149–159.

Grint, K. (2005) Problems, problems, problems: The social construction of 'leadership'. *Human Relations*, 58(11), 1467–1494.

Hunt, M. (2021) Former diplomats challenge Australian government on climate change inaction. *Global Government Forum.* 30 September 2021. Available at: https://www.globalgovernmentforum.com/former-diplomats-challenge-australian-government-on-climate-change-inaction/ [1 October 2021].

Im, T. (2020) COVID-19 national report on South Korea. In Joyce, P., Maron, F., & Reddy, P.S. (Eds.) *Good public governance in a global pandemic.* Brussels: IIAS, pp. 221–230.

Joyce, P. (2021) Public governance, agility, and pandemics: A case study of the UK response to COVID-19. *International Review of Administrative Sciences.* January 2021. doi:10.1177/0020852320983406

Joyce, P., Maron, F., & Reddy, P.S. (2020a) A dangerous virus: Introduction to IIAS special report. In Joyce, P., Maron, F. & Reddy, P.S. (Eds.) *Good governance in a global pandemic.* Brussels: IIAS, pp. 5–26.

Joyce, P., Maron, F., & Reddy, P.S. (2020b) Managing global pandemics: Public governance matters. In Joyce, P., Maron, F. & Reddy, P.S. (Eds.) *Good governance in a global pandemic.* Brussels: IIAS, pp. 567–591.

Kamarck, E. (2021) Pandemic politics: Red state governors are in trouble for their Covid leadership. Brookings. 19 October 2021. Available at: https://www.brookings.edu/blog/fixgov/2021/10/19/pandemic-politics-red-state-governors-are-in-trouble-for-their-covid-leadership/?utm_campaign=Governance%20Studies&utm_medium=email&utm_content=172981441&utm_source=hs_email [20 October 2021].

Lee, C. (2020) Responses of Singapore to COVID-19 pandemic: The whole-of-government approach. In Joyce, P., Maron, F. & Reddy, P.S. (Eds.) *Good public governance in a global pandemic.* Brussels: IIAS, pp. 205–219.

Merriam-Webster (2021) Crisis. Available at: https://www.merriam-webster.com/dictionary/crisis [29 October 2021].

MOH (2014) MOH pandemic readiness and response plan for influenza and other acute respiratory diseases (Revised April 2014). Available at: https://www.moh.gov.sg/docs/librariesprovider5/diseases-updates/interim-pandemic-plan-public-ver-_april-2014.pdf [29 October 2021].

Nutt, P.C. & Backoff, R.W. (1987) A strategic management process for public and third-sector organizations. *Journal of the American Planning Association*, 53(1), 44–57.

OECD (2018) *Assessing global progress in the governance of critical risks, OECD reviews of risk management policies*. Paris: OECD Publishing.

OECD (2021) *Government at a glance 2021*. Paris: OECD Publishing. doi:10.1787/1c258f55-en

Public Administration Select Committee (2011) Examination of witnesses (Question Numbers 1–123). Sir Gus O"Donnell KCB, and Ian Watmore. 28 October 2010. Available at: https://publications.parliament.uk/pa/cm201011/cmselect/cmpubadm/555-i/10102802.htm [15 October 2021].

Reuters (2021) Merkel says Germany must do more to tackle climate change. Euronews. 18 July 2021. Available at: https://www.euronews.com/2021/07/18/us-europe-weather-germany-climate?utm_source=newsletter&utm_medium=en&utm_content=us-europe-weather-germany-climate&_ope=eyJndWlkIjoiYTE1NmMyNjM2ODRiNTBmYWMzNTQzNGMyYTIw-M2UyNDIifQ%3D%3D [18 July 2021].

Thomas, A. (2021) The government's confused communications have worsened the fuel crisis. Institute for Government. 30 September 2021. Available at: https://www.instituteforgovernment.org.uk/blog/government-communications-fuel-crisis [30 October 2021].

United Nations (2020a) Shared responsibility, global solidarity: Responding to the socio-economic impacts of COVID-19. March 2020. Available at: https://unsdg.un.org/sites/default/files/2020-03/SG-Report-Socio-Economic-Impact-of-Covid19.pdf [25 June 2020].

United Nations (2020b) Climate change: Annual report 2019. Available at: https://unfccc.int/annualreport [7 December 2020].

WHO (2019) *Global influenza strategy 2019-2030*. Geneva: World Health Organization.

WHO (2020) WHO emergencies coronavirus EC meeting. 22 January 2020. Available at: https://www.who.int/docs/default-source/coronaviruse/transcripts/ihr-emergency-committee-for-pneumonia-due-to-the-novel-coronavirus-2019-ncov-press-briefing-transcript-22012020.pdf?sfvrsn=b94d86d9_2 [7 April 2020].

10 Strategic Leaders

Introduction

Much of the research conducted into leadership has been preoccupied with leaders and followers and how leaders direct and motivate followers. This is a rather narrow framing of leadership for the case of leaders in a public governance setting and can be too abstract. Conceptualizing the work of leaders in public governance must take account of the public as well as the people who work for government, and the fact that leaders work with and through constitutions and institutions that are part of public governance systems. If we take this an intellectual step further, leaders in public governance systems in which there are well-developed strategic state capabilities can be thought of as directors of government's strategic effectiveness and strategic crisis management, and re-designers of institutional capacity and institutional changes.

The first section of this chapter deals with three (ideal) types of leaders: transformational leaders, democratic populist leaders, and adaptive leaders. It then looks at how leaders operate as designers of institutional capacity and changes. Finally, the chapter builds a composite picture of the work of strategic leadership, which is elaborated by adding some comments on country leaders, ministers, and civil servants. The chapter's exploration of strategic leadership addresses both the "is" of leadership and the "ought" of leadership.

Transformational leaders

What are transformational leaders? How does this type of leadership work? The idea of transformational leadership is often introduced by going back to the writing of James MacGregor Burns in the 1970s. In one article Burns focused on political leadership. He built his arguments not using empirical evidence and analysis but from a discussion of a conceptual framework that he proposed. He began by discussing ideas of leaders and followers, the difference between wants and needs, a

DOI: 10.4324/9781351045797-10

hierarchy of needs ranging from lower needs to higher needs, hopes and values, and so on. He also offered a definition of leadership (Burns 1977, 274):

> I define leadership as leaders inducing followers to act for certain goals that represent the values and the motivations - the wants and needs, the aspirations and expectations - of both leaders and followers. And the genius of leadership lies in the manner in which leaders see and act on their own, and their followers', values and motivations.

He said that leaders helped followers to get to a higher need level (Burns 1977, 274):

> But more typically, the leader may operate at a motivational level higher than the follower's, in part because persons acting as leader usually have satisfied their own lower need levels and are seeking to satisfy "higher" ones, such as the need for self-realization or efficacy. But whatever the relative motive levels, the test of leadership is the capacity to help gratify follower's need and, by thus extinguishing it, help the follower move to a higher need level ...

He endorsed leaders having an uplifting effect on followers (Burns 1977, 275):

> The common perception of leadership that it should inspire and elevate the public is quite correct. Revolutionary leaders may seek to appeal to the egalitarian ideals of followers at the same time that they satisfy their needs. Ministers urge their parishioners to rise above Mammon and materialism and to pursue more principled missions. Moralizing politicians seek to bring out "the best in us" in following some cause.... Hence, despite all the abuses and perversions and hypocrisy, the call for moral leadership, as it was issued by a founding father of this [American Political Science] Association, Woodrow Wilson, ... is still the noblest cry that can be sounded on this planet.

Irrespective of the empirical credentials of Burns theories, the 1980s and 1990s saw a substantial interest in researching transformational leadership and an alternative known as transactional leadership. Bass (1999, 9) described transformational leaders as ones who "uplift the morale, motivation, and morals of their followers". How did they do this? He suggested that they did this by (Bass 1999, 11):

> ... moving the follower beyond immediate self-interests through idealized influence (charisma), inspiration, intellectual stimulation,

or individualized consideration. It elevates the follower's level of maturity and ideals as well as concerns for achievement, self-actualization, and the well-being of others, the organization, and society.

The transactional leader was conceptualized as someone who succeeds by linking results to contingent rewards for followers. (Presumably reinforcing selfishness and not addressing the individual's concern for the well-being of others?) Other species of transactional leadership were termed management-by-exception and laissez-faire leadership. In fact, empirical studies have found contingent reward leadership did correlate with leadership effectiveness but not as strongly as the five factors of transformational leadership. Bass (1999, 22) concluded on this point:

> ... of the 200 reports to date, a large majority reconfirm the "correlational hierarchy". The transformational factors are usually found more highly correlated with outcomes in effectiveness and satisfaction of colleagues than is contingent reward. Contingent reward is ordinarily more highly correlated with outcomes than is managing-by-exception, particularly passive managing-by-exception. Finally, laissez-faire leadership is almost uniformly negatively correlated with outcomes.

So, reviews of large numbers of studies, including studies in the public sector, have found that transformational leadership and the use of contingent rewards to motivate followers are effective. Other writers and researchers have supplemented and even challenged this perspective. For example, Kotter (1990) made some influential suggestions about leadership and management as functions. He envisaged individuals might be both active in leadership and management but stressed their separate conceptualization. He claimed that American business was overmanaged and underled. Leadership was needed for making changes and management was needed for handling complexity. Leaders set direction, communicate, empower, motivate, coach, act as a role model, and recognize and reward success. Whereas, managers prepare plans, decide budgets, organize (design and set up structures), recruit, and control. At various points in his argument, Kotter underlines the difference between the work of leaders and managers. The theories of Bass could be integrated with the conceptualization of leadership and management by Kotter.

Two UK researchers (Alimo-Metcalfe and Alban-Metcalfe 2006) have cast doubt on the proposition that transformational leadership as conceived in the transformational literature applies to the UK public sector. They were specifically doubtful about the causal impact of charisma and vision. Based on very large UK surveys and inductive analysis, they examined what they termed "nearby" leadership, meaning respondents were asked about leaders with whom they were in day-to-day contact. They report (Alimo-Metcalfe and Alban-Metcalfe 2006 300) that a factor called "showing genuine concern for others" mattered most, explaining 60% of the variance in a leader's impact on staff motivation, staff satisfaction, performance, and so on:

> This scale reflects a variety of individual-focused behaviours, and attitudes, which include showing a genuine interest in staff as individuals, being interested in their needs and aspirations, and how they feel about working in the organisation; valuing their contributions, developing their strengths; coaching, mentoring; and having positive expectations of what staff can achieve.

Democratic populist leaders

Gustafson (2008) apparently tried classifying three Prime Ministers of New Zealand as transformational or transactional. But his description of them ended up making use of the concept of populism (Gustafson 2008, 107):

> They all accepted that leaders like themselves recognise, meet, manipulate and mobilise but do not initially create collective forces of social change or voter discontent or aspiration. They all sought to balance their ability to absorb, understand and utilise knowledge with their intuitive common sense and feel for public opinion. As leaders it was essential to understand people as well as policies and processes. As a result they tended towards populism and were anti-elitist. All were adept at using rhetoric, bargaining and manipulation.

This observation can be built on to define "democratic populist leadership". These are leaders who take as their starting point the discontent that exists in the citizenry, seeks to understand the discontent, and then uses it through manipulation with the intention of mobilizing support. Logically, therefore, populist leaders present themselves as anti-elitist (sometimes described as being anti the governing establishment) even if they are in government and even if they are a prime minister.

Any political party seeking power must make some populist appeal, and all governments seek to shore up their power by mobilizing public opinion to support them once in office. What distinguishes democratic populists from other democratic politicians is that having secured a mandate through elections or referenda they also make it clear in words and deeds that they do not like or accept the value of constitutional checks and balances or approve of widening consent to what they are doing. Accordingly, it can be argued that Bauer and Becker (2020) are wrong to link populists in government with "democratic backsliding' and right when they say, "Present-day populists are not fascists" (Bauer and Becker 2020). It might be said that democratic populists are in favour of democracy but are opposed to liberal pluralist democracy. Populist leaders perceive all impediments caused by checks and balances as evidence that the people forming the "elite" (or "the establishment") are using their positions in governance structures to impede their progress in delivering the changes the people want.

When populist politicians are elected to positions of authority in government, they may begin to centralize decision-making and eliminate resistance to their democratic mandate. Examples of centralization tendencies can be identified in countries such as Brazil and Hungary (Aldane 2021; Bauer and Becker 2020, 25). In Weberian language, they tend towards monocratic leadership, that is one-person leadership, with government completely in the hands of a prime minister or president. Peters and Pierre (2019, 1528) link centralization and the building of personalized control:

> ... we should expect some centralization of power in the president or prime minister and more personalized control. Although seemingly the antithesis of the adoration of "the people", most populist governments have tended to centralize, or at least attempt to centralize, power (Papadopolous, 2002). This move to centralize may arise from the feeling of isolation in a "system" that is hostile, or because of a felt need to impose a program of change on that system, but it does tend to be characteristic of populists in the government. That centralization is almost by definition more apparent in authoritarian versions of populism, and also appears to occur in more democratic versions.

If archetypal democratic populist politicians mobilize electoral support through their use of rhetoric and manipulation, can this sometimes cross a line in terms of honesty and trustworthiness? Can rhetoric and manipulation become plain dishonesty? According to an article in *The Washington Post*, the President of the United States, Donald Trump, frequently and increasingly made false claims (Kessler et al. 2021): "What is especially striking is how the tsunami of untruths kept rising the longer he served as president and became increasingly unmoored from the truth". Johnson, who became UK prime minister in 2019, was often seen as a leader who had won support in and for his political party by his gifts in rhetoric. His party's campaign in the 2019 general election was based on antagonism to the European Union and the need to control UK borders, which were said to be admitting too many immigrants (Campbell 2021). Did he win the 2019 election and succeed with taking the UK out of the European Union because of his skills in rhetoric and manipulation? Some commentators have written about Johnson's truthfulness. For example, Kuenssberg (2021) wrote:

> The prime minister's relationship with the truth is under intense scrutiny at the moment.... It is not the first time in Boris Johnson's long career that he has faced questions about his conduct and character.... He famously wrote two versions of his newspaper column, one backing Leave [the European Union], the other Remain, arguing through all the options to be completely sure.... Another source told me Mr Johnson has a "genuinely selective memory" and that "'I choose to remember certain things or not remember others'" is his default way of dealing with the pressures of life at No 10.... An insider told me: "He frequently leaves people with the belief that he has told them one thing, but he has given himself room for manoeuvre", believing that, "the fewer cast iron positions you hold the better, because you can always change political direction".

The Leader of the Opposition queried Johnson's believability in the House of Commons in June 2021 (House of Commons 2021, 274):

> The British people do not expect miracles, but they do expect basic competence and honesty.... After all these failures and mistakes, why should anyone believe the Prime Minister now?

Polling in Great Britain in September 2021 found that 61% of those surveyed thought the Prime Minister was "untrustworthy" (YouGov 2021).

In some countries, populist leaders secured their power base by polarizing the public. If they pleased their own supporters in the electorate, the chances were that another major part of the electorate was antagonized.

Adaptive leaders

Heifetz (1994) defined leadership as an activity. He saw leaders as engaged in "mobilizing" others to do things. He was especially interested in how leaders mobilized people to do adaptive work (Heifetz 1994, 22):

> Adaptive work consists of the learning required to address conflicts in the values people hold, or to diminish the gap between the values people stand for and the reality they face. Adaptive work requires a change in values, beliefs or behavior. The exposure and orchestration of conflict – internal contradictions – within individuals and constituencies provide the leverage for mobilizing people to learn new ways.

What is the source of adaptive work? Heifetz et al. (2009) said an organization may be falling short of its aspirations and thus adaptation is required.

How is adaptive work managed? Formally speaking, managing change may look quite conventional. It may begin with a leader presenting their vision, goals, strategy, timelines for making an important change. Heifetz et al. (2009) recommend that the leaders do this concretely so others can see what is intended. But alongside the formal structure of managing adaptive work is a spirit of managing. This is a spirit of managing change by experimentation. Consequently strategic plans are used in an open-minded way and leaders approach implementation open to learning (Heifetz et al. 2009, 107):

> People view the latest strategic plan as today's best guess rather than a sacred text. And they expect to constantly refine it as new information comes in.

Managing change means managing conflict. Heifetz and colleagues recommended that leaders appreciate that others will have their own priorities and advised them to negotiate their purposes and priorities. They suggested compromise might be needed.

They recommended that leaders "surface conflicts" to understand how differences in perspectives were impeding the organization from achieving its aspirations. Leaders should offer interpretations that make the conflictual aspects public. They must encourage conversations. The conversation includes which losses are negotiable and those which are not. The aim is to allow new adaptations to be discovered. Obviously, this means there is a need for leaders to be people who are tolerant of conflict as the process of finding adaptations is pursued.

Differences between stakeholders may be the source of creative tensions that lead to innovative adaptive solutions (Heifetz et al. 2009). We might infer from what Heifetz and his colleagues were saying that leaders seeking a new synthesis might strike a better compromise or balance between the losses and gains and how they are distributed. And maybe a new experiment may be suggested by a leader to show stakeholders how a proposal might work or to get them to give it a try for a period. In effect, this idea of working through differences implied that an adaptive leader needed not only a tolerance of conflict but also good persuasion and negotiation skills.

Adaptive leaders at the very least cause "disturbance". Heifetz and colleagues assume that people avoid dealing with "adaptive problems" and get stressed when they are forced to do so. So, it is the job of the adaptive leader to move people out of a state of feeling comfortable and satisfied. But if this is done too much, the stress becomes too high and adaptive work is impeded. So, there is a range of increased stress that is optimum. They called this the "productive zone of disequilibrum" (Heifetz et al. 2009, 30):

> Within the productive zone, the stress level is high enough that people can be mobilized to focus on and engage with the problem they would rather avoid.

The leader must keep pursuing the change intervention, keeping the amount of stress within the productive zone, and that means the change must be carefully paced. It requires persistence, openness, and flexibility (Heifetz et al. 2009).

The role of the adaptive leader is evidently a demanding and even dangerous one. Being such a leader calls for a capacity for being reflective, tolerant of conflict, and resilient. If applied to public governance, it would provide a perspective on how the rigidity of pathological forms of bureaucracy might be challenged.

The three types

The discussion of the three ideal types of leaders suggests that they are to some degree conceptual alternatives. Transformational leaders are thought to carry out their role in a superior way by inspiring individuals to put aside their self-interests and to give their support to an uplifting strategic vision. Laissez-faire leaders are the least effective type of leader; they do not inspire the followers, and do not improve their morals. The democratic populist leaders succeed when they mobilize the public, or rather a proportion of the public, sufficiently to give the populist leader a democratic victory in elections. These leaders then have democratic legitimacy and formal governmental power to make changes. Their clout is based on legitimacy. This in turn reflects rhetorical capabilities to win the support of "the people". They are inclined to respond to conflict by seeing it as undemocratic resistance by "the establishment". The adaptive leaders achieve superior performance by being prepared to confront difficult problems (adaptive problems) and to confront potential conflicts arising from the losses that might be incurred by stakeholders. At their best, adaptive leaders are tolerant of both uncertainty and conflict, using experimentation and negotiation to achieve the adaptive change that is desired. See Table 10.1 for a summary and a comparison.

Each of the ideal types has features that make them appealing. Transformational leadership is linked to the promotion of creativity and innovation. The democratic populist leadership acknowledges the important relationships with the public and with the "elite" that is in control of public governance. Adaptive leaders are open to experimentation and negotiation and recognize that they manage relationships with multiple stakeholders.

Table 10.1 Types of leaders

Dimensions	Transformational leaders	Democratic populist leaders	Adaptive leaders
Key relationship(s) Source of conflicts	Followers (usually employees) Conflict between self-interest of followers and a higher purpose championed by the leader	The public and the elite Conflicts between populists and the "elite" who have been governing the country [Are senior civil servants a part of the elite?]	Stakeholders Conflict occurs because of "many competing visions, values, and views", and there is a pluralistic situation with various stakeholders' interests present.
Organizational intervention	Leaders inspire "followers" with a vision of the future and "uplift the morale, motivation, and morals of their followers".	Leaders centralize decision making and eliminate resistance to executive's exercise of a democratic mandate (monocratic leadership)	Leaders make changes by disturbing employees and maintaining the trajectory of change in a "productive zone of disequilibrium".
Nature of change	Leaders' intellectual stimulation of followers leads to creative and innovative change	Democratic change is made through imposition of mandates provided by electoral outcomes ("will of the people")	Experimentation
Personal characteristics of leaders	Leaders must have higher morality than followers because they set an example and inspire them with a vision of the future; from UK research it appears leaders have empathy and concern for the individual follower.	Leaders are good at recognizing public discontent and public emotions and attitudes that have been ignored. They are good at rhetoric and manipulation.	Leaders require many personal characteristics, including patience, persistence, being open to reflection, tolerant of conflict, and resilient.

The limited empirical evidence we have suggests leaders are more effective when they communicate visions, strategies, and rationales for new programmes or reforms (Gabris et al. 2000). Transformational leaders might be assumed to score highly on such communications. If democratic populist leaders feel they have a democratic mandate and feel that this fully legitimizes their giving of orders, they may be weak communicators of rationales for change and reform. There is evidence that successful leaders empower employees (Gabris et al. 2000). Adaptive leaders are advised by Heifetz et al. (2009) to keep "giving back" responsibility to people to find the solutions to problems; perhaps this indicates an orientation to empowering employees. Democratic populist leadership are said to centralize decisions and favour monocratic governance; presumably, they would not be keen on empowerment. There is evidence that effective leaders keep their promises (Gabris et al. 2000). If transformational leaders offer moral leadership, then presumably they would be assumed to be likely to keep their promises and would be seen as trustworthy by their followers. If populist leaders rely on rhetoric and manipulation to form their power base, then the democratic populist leaders might be prone to making false promises or over-promising and under-delivering.

Re-designing and changing Institutions

The words "institutions", "systems", and "structures" are often used in discussing governance and public management. All can be seen as implying something that constrains people, something that people fit into, whether this "fitting in" is conceived as being a process of socialization into roles, or the application of rewards and sanctions, or the exercise of control over individuals. In discussing leadership and the institutionalization of public organization, Boin and Christensen (2008, 272) refer to organizations with institutional characteristics as being "remarkably durable, surviving environmental turbulence while preserving their identity". They also say that they withstand external pressure to their way of working. The withstanding of external pressures can be positive.

But research does not show that all withstanding of external pressures is a positive thing. Public administration may be based on bureaucracy which is exhibiting rigidity rather than learning and adaptability (Crozier 1964). Leaders may be needed to change and develop institutions (or systems or structures). Public governance can be imagined, therefore, as involving interactions between, on one side, an institution of public governance that has capabilities that could be used for the well-being of citizens, and, on the other side, the strategic leaders that choose how to use and adapt that institution to ensure the citizens' interests are being served as well as possible.

There are many examples now of the argument that the institutions of governance and administration need to change. The Chief Human Resources Officer at the Treasury Board of Canada Secretariat has argued there is now a need for more agility from government. She defined agility as requiring the Canadian civil service to "embrace uncertainty and learn through experimentation" (Ross 2021). She said, "Today's top managers ... operate in an environment where stakeholder management, co-design and citizen engagement are becoming ever more important". She presented this as a movement away from a hierarchical world to an interconnected world with distributed powers. What did this mean for leaders? She suggested it meant "very complexified leadership roles, and very complexified expectations of our leaders ..." (Ross 2021).

Consistent with this call for more agility, the Chief Innovation Officer of the State of New Jersey in the United States, Beth Simone Noveck, set out the following portrait of civil service leaders (Abramson 2021):

> But I would like to see more mission-driven leaders who are agile, data driven, and human centered. I have a vision of civil servants as public entrepreneurs who are passionate about solving problems. Many civil servants do have these characteristics. But many civil servants are still burdened by rules and hidebound by culture. I would like to see public servants who work with other sectors to get things done quickly and innovatively. I would like to see the passion of public servants unleashed. I would like to see them use data in new ways and increase their use of public-private partnerships. I would also like to see more agile implementation, more collaboration, and more measurement of what works.

In summary, leadership work involves adapting and modifying public governance and public administration to keep them as effective as possible. In terms of the advice given by the OECD, and reviewed at earlier points in this book, leaders need to move away from New Public Management reforms. They may need to build more capacity for strategic management and partnership working and create more effective arrangements for the existence, and work, of centres of government. And they may need to take a personal interest in the vitality of experimentation, evaluation, and learning within government and administration to enable higher levels of adaptability and agility.

What strategic leaders do

Ideally, as envisaged in the Canadian Management Accountability Framework, leaders improve government outcomes for the public (Government of Canada 2015). But this is not inevitable. Poor leadership exists. This seemed to be the opinion of Reddy (2016) who commented on the unsatisfactory state of local public service delivery in South Africa (Chapter 7). The existence of poor leadership was the conclusion of a study of government failures by Light (2014). So, in outlining what strategic leaders do it is not intended that their job should be seen as easy or that they can ever be infallible.

1　A strategic leader makes decisions.
　　Leaders do make decisions as well as communicating and acting as a role model. They do so using their knowledge of and insights into situations (Follett 1941). In the case of leading a public sector turnaround, leaders need to know the "business" and know and understand key stakeholders (Borins 1998).
2　A strategic leader should develop compelling strategic visions.
　　Country leaders may be expected to create consensus in a country around compelling visions (World Bank 1997, 155):

> Venezuela's reforms under Carlos Andrés Perez were a political failure because there was no coherent vision to help sell the reforms.... . In Malaysia, by contrast, Prime Minister Mahathir Mohamad's policy initiatives in the 1990s were packaged in his Vision 2020, which set the eye-catching target of raising Malaysian living standards to industrial-country levels by 2020.

It is sometimes argued that strategic visions should be based on evidence and analysis (Pettigrew et al. 1992) and that visions should be deliverable (Heymann 1987). In other words, they are not the results of inexplicable acts of imagination. Nor are they mystical or messianic creations (Kotter 1990, 105):

> Most discussions of vision have a tendency to degenerate into the mystical. The implication is that a vision is something mysterious that mere mortals, even talented ones, could never hope to have. But developing good business direction isn't magic. It is a tough, sometimes exhausting process of gathering and analyzing information. People who articulate such visions aren't magicians but broad-based strategic thinkers who are willing to take risks.

When strategic visions are implemented they will eventually get tested by reality, including the reality of the variety of interests and cleavages in society. Ron Heifetz, in his book on adaptive leadership, argued the importance of realism (Heifetz 1994, 24):

> To produce adaptive work, a vision must track the contours of reality; it has to have accuracy, and not simply imagination and appeal.

If we were trying to place strategic visions on a continuum between totally subjective or totally objective, then the preference should be for them to be as close to the objective end as possible. The aim, or ideal, should be to formulate a strategic vision based on some judgment of what is possible. Hence, strategists may want to revise strategic visions and goals after they have completed a situational analysis.

3 Institutional strategic leaders define strategic priorities and lead medium-term strategic planning.

According to the OECD (2020), institutional leaders should be defining the strategic priorities and leading medium-term strategic planning to deliver them. They should base the priorities on the long-term strategic vision for the country.

4 A strategic leader should be persistent but approach strategic planning and the delivery of strategic plans with an experimental mindset.

Leaders should persist in pursuing their agenda over the long run and this takes "single-minded discipline" (Barber 2015). On the other hand, leaders must be experimentally minded and open to learning. Experimentation and learning are key capabilities (Pettigrew 2012, 1311):

So execution is analysis and implementation also has to be formulation. Putting a concept into practice leads to valuable clarification of the original but only if the participants have a developed capacity for learning, experimentation, and inventiveness.

Heifetz et al. (2009) in their book on adaptive leadership also underlined learning from implementation of strategic plans.

5 A strategic leader should be inclusive when preparing strategic visions and plans.

The work of the strategic leader may be to synthesize the opinions and preferences of a diverse set of people and interests (Bennis and Nanus 1985, 103):

If there is a spark of genius in the leadership function at all, it must be ... a kind of magic, to assemble – out of all the variety of images, signals, forecasts and alternatives – a clearly articulated vision of the future that is at once simple, easily understood, clearly desirable, and energizing.

Hamel (2002) writing on management in the business sector called on senior managers to rethink their strategy-making processes so new voices can be heard in strategic conversations. In an earlier chapter (Chapter 5), we noted the occurrence of experiments to involve the public in systematic ways. Two of the examples were Botswana and Mexico. As a third example, we can mention the Eleventh Five Year Plan for China covering the period 2006–2010 which "was prepared with participation from various levels of government representatives, National People's Congress (NPC) deputies, scientific and economic experts as well as ordinary Chinese citizens" (Wang and Lin 2007, 25).

6 Strategic leaders build leadership capability at all levels.
   Building leadership capability includes creating an effective top leadership team (Moore 1995). But it does not stop there. When asked about his experiences of leading changes at Tactical Air Command in the United States (1978–1984), General Creech mentioned, among other things, the following success factors (Osborne and Gaebler 1992, 258): "We think it was a new spirit of leadership at many levels-making good things happen".

7 A strategic leader ensures coherence, coordination, and alignment.
   An empirical study by Andrew Pettigrew and others, based on case studies in the UK's National Health Service, emphasized coherence as a key concept in their model of strategic change (Pettigrew et al. 1992, 28):

   The most robust strategies also considered questions of coherence between goals, feasibility and implementation requirements and the need to complement service strategies with other functional strategies (such as finance or human resources).

To give just two examples, leaders should ensure coherence by aligning strategic decisions and decisions on finance; they also need to create coherence over time by showing persistence in delivering a vision and a strategy, despite difficulties.

Leaders go to great lengths to ensure coherence. As we saw in the case of the President of Russia's involvement in monitoring and evaluation in 2013, the top leaders may want to personally check that coherence exists (Chapter 5).

8 Institutional strategic leaders decentralize decision-making as much as possible to increase responsiveness to the public.
   With the best will in the world, the top political leaders and civil service leaders know relatively little about the diverse circumstances of government departments, agencies, communities, service users, and citizens affected by the government's strategic visions and medium and long-term strategic plans. It may be better if they decentralize decision making to leaders at "lower levels". If these lower-level leaders are interacting with the public and service users,

they may understand better what the priorities should be to serve the public (Osborne and Gaebler 1992, 277):

> The closer a government is to its citizens, polls show, the more they trust it. The closer it is, the more accountable its officials tend to be and the more likely they are to handcraft solutions rather than create one-size-fits-all programs.

9 Institutional strategic leaders build continuous learning loops involving feedback from the public.
   Crozier (1964) investigated pathology in bureaucracy and his main conclusion seemed to be that when a bureaucracy malfunctions it is because it has become incapable of learning from the feedback it gets from its environment. A strategic leader should, therefore, make it a priority to maintain, and if necessary, create, feedback loops so that government is clear about the public's thinking, about its preferences and concerns. Good strategic leaders would be ones that created open communication channels with society and stimulated interactions with the public and stakeholders that allowed government to carry out more continuous learning and partnership with civil society.
10 Strategic leaders communicate visions and strategies, allocate and distribute authority to deliver them, incentivise cooperation and support, and act honestly and with integrity.

Strategic leaders communicate visions and strategies. They need to be believable (Gabris et al. 2000). Hence, the importance of their personal honesty and integrity. They encourage support for the visions and strategic plans, which they do by rewarding and recognizing those that contribute to their delivery. They support effectiveness in delivery by allocating and distributing authority appropriately.

Country leaders

In some countries, maybe all countries, leading politicians who want to lead their country must offer a vision. Their vision is a "pitch" for the support and confidence of the public, and of others. Masciulli et al. (2009, 4) suggest the vision may be important in relation to culture:

> Both leaders and followers are involved in a circular process of motivation and power exchange that is often difficult to break up into a causal sequence (Wildavsky 2006). Still 'politics as leadership' (Tucker 1995) does occur, however complex it is to conclude about the significance of its causal role: leaders mobilize a significant number of followers to accept their diagnosis of, and policy

prescriptions for, collective problems or crises. Moreover, leadership is a symbolic activity mediated by culture, for leaders as 'identity entrepreneurs' are engaged in providing myths/visions to create, reshape or enhance national and other political cultures.

They go on to say (Masciulli et al. 2009, 10):

Successful leaders are those who have demonstrated their ability to move their society tangibly in the direction that seemed clearly supportive of their suggested 'grand design'. Unsuccessful leaders are those whose efforts to move their society in the direction of their choosing have backfired or brought about results clearly destructive of their propagated strategic vision.

Senior civil servants can observe political leaders at work, and they will notice that there is more to being a leader than creating and selling visions. Gus O'Donnell was the head of the UK civil service under three consecutive Prime Ministers. Here he is talking about Tony Blair's approach to being Prime Minister and then summing up in general what it takes to be a good Prime Minister (O'Donnell 2013):

When I came in as Cabinet Secretary for Tony Blair, Tony Blair had been Prime Minister for a number of years and I was a new, green, Cabinet Secretary ... So, you know, he'd kind of established the way he was going to do the job of Prime Minister by then, and so you're working with a working style which he had already established and which, after eight years, he wasn't going to change fundamentally.... And he was also, of course, a very passionate moderniser, and he wanted to move on, and he wanted public services to be better and more citizen focused, so you needed to find ways of working with him. You know, he was very much into stock takes to determine delivery, you know, were we on track? Had we hit the milestones? All of that. So he had that style of you know, rolling up his sleeves, getting down and saying 'I want to know the street crime numbers for these streets, and come back in a week and tell me precisely how many ...' You know, he got very much into detail ... So that was his style.... the key thing [for a Prime Minister] is having that strategic vision, thinking about what's right for the country in the long term and just sticking to your guns on those things. That's what makes a great Prime Minister....

Strategic vision and persistence are important. But presumably leaders all have their own style of leading and doing the work of leadership. As we can see from the quote, Tony Blair not only had a desire to see change and modernization and good quality public services that were citizen-centric but also had his own style, which emphasized paying attention to the detail of delivery. Monitoring and evaluation were given great weight by government when he was Prime Minister. Presumably, he would have set an example that was quite influential at all levels of the civil service and public services generally.

Leaders can have different styles because there is always a degree of choice for the individual in how they play their role of leader. The choices individuals make will in part be caused by what has worked for them in the past and the conscious lessons they have drawn from that experience. Those country leaders who are in position for long periods of time may have more opportunities to revise their ideas about how best to provide strategic leadership; but on the other hand, over time country leaders may become committed to a specific style of strategic leadership and find it difficult to adapt it as circumstances change.

Perhaps the individual choices of leaders may go some way to explaining why the government of some countries have highly visible long-term strategic visions for the country and the governments of other countries have weak long-term visions but very strong prioritization of strategic goals.

Ministers and senior civil servants leading ministries

In relation to public governance, leadership can be political or administrative. In the following definition, administrative leadership is linked with governance objectives, change, and relationships (Gerson 2020, 9):

> The concept of leadership, in this report, refers to the way senior civil servants work towards governance objectives through/with others. This implies two basic dimensions. First, leadership is about achieving objectives which change and improve upon the status quo, implying some kind of change, innovation and/or transformation. Second, leaders don't achieve objectives alone. Leadership is an interpersonal phenomenon, and so leadership is about the relationship between individuals or groups.

Governments vary in how the work of strategic leadership is divided between politicians and civil servants. In the UK, in the period 2004–2007 the intention was that ministers created and owned the strategies for major policy sectors (education, health, criminal justice, and so on) and the civil service leadership focused on delivery by developing the strategies and executing them. One of three stated objectives of the programme of Capability Reviews began during the third term of the Blair Government (2005–2007) was to check that the "civil service leadership [of government departments] is suitably equipped to develop and execute Ministerial strategies" (UK Government 2007). Nowadays, in many countries, civil servants are often expected to be strategic thinkers and advisers on strategy; and they may formally or informally have a major role to play in the creation of long-term strategic visions and strategies.

The Blair model with ministers taking the lead on strategic thinking but relying on their civil servants to lead on the execution of strategic plans can be contrasted with models in which the civil servants take the lead in formulation as well as delivery of strategic plans (Joyce 2014). In the case of Turkey, a law passed in 2003 led to a model in which civil servants were in the driving seat of strategic planning. This was the Public Financial Management and Control Law, which was adopted in late 2003. According to Article 9 of this law, public administrations, civil servants and not politicians, were to prepare strategic plans, measure performance, and monitor progress (Republic of Turkey 2010, 6–7):

> Public administrations shall prepare strategic plans in a cooperative manner in order to form missions and visions for future within the framework of development plans, programs, relevant legislation and basic principles adopted; to determine strategic goals and measurable objectives; to measure their performances according to predetermined indicators, and to monitor and evaluate this overall process.

The "top managers" were to be "responsible for preparation and implementation of the strategic plans and budgets of their administration in conformity with the development plan, annual programs as well as with the strategic plan and performance objectives and service requirements of the administration" (Republic of Turkey 2010, 8–9). The Ministry of Finance and the Undersecretariat of the State Planning Organization were to be involved in setting performance indicators, which were intended to matter for decisions on budget and resource allocations. Under the Law the top managers were expected to ensure preparation and implementation of the strategic plans and budgets, and were accountable to their Ministers for what they did. The intended importance of these strategic plans can be inferred from the fact that the 2003 Law stated that budget and resource allocations would be made based on the strategic plans. This system had some resemblance to the United States system for strategic planning by federal agencies established in 1993. According to this system, the agency leaders produced strategic plans that were monitored and evaluated by the United States Congress. The role of the politicians in both Turkey and the United States was essentially one of oversight.

The success of a Turkish-style model will depend greatly on how seriously the ministers take the strategic planning of their ministry.

If they see it as unimportant, then they might be inclined to "rubber stamp" a strategic plan. The downside of this is that it might be difficult to get the ministers to authorize strategic projects proposed by officials that were costly or carried too much political risk.

Generalizing about the strategic role of civil service leaders is difficult. As Althaus and Wanna summed it up (2008, 128):

> Public servants also provide strategic vision, policy expertise and innovative risk-taking flair, but not in isolation. They do so within a relationship with their political masters that cannot be neatly compartmentalised and which can vary from minister to minister and from government to government.

Timmins and Davies (2015) illuminated some of the variations between ministers when they wrote about the role of cabinet ministers. They analysed interviews of ten former health secretaries of state in the UK. They quoted one secretary of state, Alan Milburn, who instigated massive strategic changes in the National Health Service of England (Timmins and Davies 2015, 51):

> Now I might have been either a terrible secretary of state, or I might have been just an aberration, but reform didn't come from the system. 'Why do people, whether it's right or wrong, why do they now rather, through rose tinted glasses, look back fondly on my time? Why? Because they feel that there was clarity. There was energy. There was determination. And there was shared mission because actually we were smart enough, I hope, to construct a shared view of what we wanted to do. It was because politics was driving it. So I think you've just got to be a bit careful with this debate [about depoliticising public services] because it can very easily turn into – "if only the politicians got out of this, everything would be wonderful". If they do, [nothing] would happen because what do systems do? What do bureaucracies do? They don't change. By definition they don't change so you've got to have a shock. Politics should be able to provide shock.

The title of Timmins and Davies' study refers to window-breakers and glaziers, meaning that some ministers attempt to reform the "system", whereas others aim to "implement, or to enhance, or to adapt a broad thrust of policy that had already been agreed" (Timmins and Davies 2015, 36). That is, some government ministers want to make major changes, and some are content to preside over a period of incremental development. The leaders within the civil service and individual ministries and agencies then find they are operating in a climate of radical and possibly turbulent change or more gentle evolution.

The implication of Milburn's reflections on his experience is that ministerial led strategic planning may be more ambitious and transformative than strategic planning led by civil servants. One other observation may be worth making here. Alan Milburn's comments on the inertia of a public service system can be compared with Crozier's ideas about bureaucratic pathology: Milburn said bureaucracies do not change by themselves and Crozier referred to their rigidity and delaying of change.

Summary and conclusions

While much previous research concentrated on how leaders motivate and produce good performance by employees, the work of leaders in public governance should be understood in relation to the public as well as the people who work for government and should give attention to the work they do with and through constitutions and institutions that are part of public governance systems.

There are many different perspectives on leadership. This chapter explored the nature of leadership in terms of three ideal types of leaders: transformational leaders, democratic populist leaders, and adaptive leaders. The transformational leader is primarily seen as someone who succeeds by enhancing the morality of followers and getting them to put aside their self-interests. Many studies have suggested that transformational leadership works, although it has been demonstrated that leaders who use contingent rewards can be effective. Populist leaders in a democracy succeed when they mobilize a sizable section of the public to give them a victory in elections. They centralize decision-making and eliminate resistance to the executive's exercise of a democratic mandate. Adaptive leaders mobilize people to work on adaptive problems, they handle conflicts, and seek to maintain the trajectory of change in a "productive zone of disequilibrium". Each ideal type illuminates aspects of leadership activity but fare variously when compared to evidence on successful leadership in government (Gabris et al. 2000).

Strategic leaders at times redesign and change the institutions of governance and administration. Durability and rigidity of institutions may be two sides of the same coin of institutional effectiveness. Public governance can be thought of as involving interactions between institutions and strategic leaders who use and adapt institutions to serve the public as well as possible. In recent times there are repeated calls for institutional innovation to deliver more agility and partnership working by government. As noted by the OECD, the move towards agility is a move away from New Public Management reforms. The implications for leadership roles are profound. Leaders would spearhead agility, problem-solving, innovation, the use of public-private partnerships and more agile implementation.

Strategic leaders should improve government outcomes for the public. They need to communicate a vision. And they need to know operational processes and details and understand the main stakeholders. They move vision on by defining strategic priorities and leading strategic planning. They should be persistent and experimental.

Leaders can have different styles because there is always a degree of choice for the individual in how they play their role of leader. Correspondingly, perhaps, some countries have highly visible long-term strategic visions for the country and the governments of other countries have very strong prioritization of strategic goals.

The strategic leadership role within ministries is normally divided between politicians and civil servants. In those countries and times where ministers take the lead on strategic thinking then their civil servants need to focus on the execution of strategic plans. In other cases, civil servants, through their advisory function, take the lead in formulation as well as delivery of strategic plans.

References

Abramson, M.A. (2021) How government is failing public servants. Government Executive. 20 October 2021. Available at: https://www.govexec.com [26 October 2021].

Aldane, J. (2021) Brazil's public sector reform bill advances through congress. Global Government Forum. 27 September 2021. Available at: https://www.globalgovernmentforum.com/brazils-public-sector-reform-bill-advances-through-congress/ [28 September 2021].

Alimo-Metcalfe, B. & Alban-Metcalfe, J. (2006) More (good) leaders for the public sector. *International Journal of Public Sector Management*, 19(4), 293–315.

Althaus, C. & Wanna, J. (2008) The institutionalisation of leadership in the Australian Public Service. In 't Hart, P. & Uhr, J. (Eds.) *Public leadership perspectives and practices*. Canberra: ANU E Press, pp. 117–131.

Barber, M. (2015) *How to run a government: So that citizens benefit and tax-payers don't go crazy*. UK: Allen Lane.

Bass, B.M. (1999) Two decades of research and development in transformational leadership. *European Journal of Work and Organizational Psychology*, 8(1), 9–32.

Bauer, M.W. & Becker, S. (2020) Democratic backsliding, populism, and public administration. *Perspectives on Public Management and Governance*, 2020, Vol. 3, No. 1, 19–31.

Bennis, W. & Nanus, B. (1985) *Leaders: The strategies for taking charge*. New York: Harper & Row.

Boin, A. & Christensen, T. (2008) The development of public institutions: Reconsidering the role of leadership. *Administration & Society*, 40(3), 271–297.

Borins, S. (1998) *Innovating with integrity; how local heroes are transforming American government*. Washington, DC: Georgetown University Press.

Burns, J.M. (1977) Wellsprings of political leadership. *The American Political Science Review*, 71(1), 266–275.

Campbell, A. (2021) Boris Johnson: The sado-populist prime minister. The New European. 15 July 2021. Available at: https://www.theneweuropean.co.uk/brexit-news/westminster-news/boris-johnson-and-sado-populism-8136296 [17 July 2021].

Crozier, M. (1964) *The bureaucratic phenomenon.* Chicago: The University of Chicago Press.

Follett, M.P. (1941) Some discrepancies in leadership theory and practice. In Metcalfe, H.C. & Urwick, L. (Eds.) *Dynamic administration: The collected papers of Mary Parker Follett.* Bath: Management Publications Trust.

Gabris, G., Golembiewski, R., & Ihrke, D. (2000) Leadership credibility, board relations, and administrative innovation at the local government level. *Journal of Public Administration Research and Theory*, 11(1), 89–108.

Gerson, D. (2020) *Leadership for a high performing civil service: Towards senior civil service systems in OECD countries.* OECD Working Papers on Public Governance No. 40. Paris: OECD Publishing.

Government of Canada (2015) Management accountability framework. Available at: http://www.tbs-sct.gc.ca/hgw-cgf/oversight-surveillance/maf-crg/index-eng.asp [28 December 2015].

Gustafson, B. (2007) *Kiwi Keith: A biography of Keith Holyoake.* Auckland: Auckland University Press.

Gustafson, B. (2008) History, biography and leadership: Grasping public lives. In 't Hart, P. & Uhr, J. (Eds.) *Public leadership perspectives and practices.* Canberra: ANU E Press, pp. 103–113.

Hamel, G. (2002) *Leading the revolution.* Boston, MA: Harvard Business School Press.

Heifetz, R.A. (1994) *Leadership without easy answers.* Cambridge, MA: The Belknap Press of Harvard University Press.

Heifetz, R., Grashow, A., & Linsky, M. (2009) *The practice of adaptive leadership.* Boston, MA: Harvard Business Press.

Heymann, P. (1987) *The politics of public management.* New Haven and London: Yale University Press.

House of Commons (2021) *Parliamentary debates (Hansard).* 16 June 2021. London: House of Commons. Available at: https://hansard.parliament.uk/commons/2021-06-16 [17 June 2021].

Joyce, P. (2014) Different political management structures and coherence issues in the Centre of Government. In Joyce, P., Bryson, J.M., & Holzer (Eds.) *Developments in strategic and public management: Studies in the US and Europe.* Basingstoke, UK and New York, United States: Palgrave Macmillan, pp. 93–107.

Kessler, G., Rizzo, S., & Kelly, M. (2021) Trump's false or misleading claims total 30,573 over 4 years. The Washington Post. 24 January 2021. Available at: https://www.washingtonpost.com/politics/2021/01/24/trumps-false-or-misleading-claims-total-30573-over-four-years/ [5 October 2021].

Kotter, J.P. (1990) What leaders really do. Harvard Business Review, May-June 1990, 103–111.

Kuenssberg, L. (2021) Boris Johnson: What is the PM's relationship with the truth? BBC News. 2 May 2021. Available at: https://www.bbc.co.uk/news/uk-politics-56624437 [3 May 2021].

Light, P.C. (2014) A cascade of failures: Why government fails, and how to stop it. Available at: https://www.brookings.edu/research/a-cascade-of-failures-why-government-fails-and-how-to-stop-it/ [4 March 2019].

Masciulli, J., Molchanov, M.A., & Knight, W.A. (2009) Political leadership in context. In Masciulli, J., Molchanov, M.A., & Knight, W.A. (Eds.) *The Ashgate research companion to political leadership*. Aldershot, Hampshirer: Ashgate. pp. 3–27.

Moore, M. (1995) *Creating public value: Strategic management in government*. London: Harvard University Press, pp. 3–27.

O'Donnell, G. (2013) Former Cabinet Secretary Lord O'Donnell Interview with Lord Hennessy Wednesday 30th February 2013 at 10 Downing Street. Available at: http://www.cabinetsecretaries.com/_lib/pdf/Former%20Cabinet%20Secretary%20Lord%20ODonnell%20Interview%20with%20Lord%20Hennessy.pdf [30 July 2015].

OECD (2020) *Policy framework on sound public governance: Baseline features of governments that work well*. Paris: OECD Publishing.

Osborne, D. & Gaebler, T. (1992). *Reinventing government: How the entrepreneurial spirit is transforming the public sector*. Reading, MA: Addison Wesley Publishing Company.

Peters, B.G. & Pierre, J. (2019) Populism and public administration: Confronting the administrative state. *Administration & Society*, 51(10), 1521–1545.

Pettigrew, A., Ferlie, E., & McKee, L. (1992) Shaping strategic change. Public Money and Management, July-September, 27–31.

Pettigrew, A.M. (2012) Context and action in the transformation of the firm: A reprise. *Journal of Management Studies*, 49(7), 1304–1328.

Reddy, P. S. (2016) The politics of service delivery in South Africa: The local government sphere in context. *The Journal for Transdisciplinary Research in Southern Africa*, 12(1), a337. http://dx.doi.org/10.4102/td.v12i1.337.

Republic of Turkey (2010) *Public financial management and control law*. No. 5018. August 2010. Ankara, Turkey: Ministry of Finance Strategy Development Unit, Republic of Turkey.

Ross, M. (2021) Enter the era of enterprise: Leadership in the 2020s. Global Government Forum. 5 September 2021. Available at: https://www.globalgovernmentforum.com/entering-an-era-of-enterprise-leadership-in-the-2020s/?utm_source=Non-Government+Bulletin+Sign+Ups&utm_campaign=e28be98db0- NonGov+email+newsletter&utm_medium=email&utm_term=0_1184a8b56c-e28be98db0-194625861 [6 September 2019].

Timmins, N. & Davies, E. (2015) *Glaziers and window breakers: The role of the secretary of state for health, in their own words*. London: The Health Foundation.

Tucker, R.C. (1995), *Politics as leadership*, 2nd edition. Columbia, MO: University of Missouri Press.

UK Government (2007) Capability reviews. Last updated 8 November 2007. Available at: https://webarchive.nationalarchives.gov.uk/ukgwa/20090104

152549/ http://www.civilservice.gov.uk/about/accountability/capability/back
ground.asp [2 October 2021].

Wang, M. & Lin, X. (2007) China: Towards results-based strategic planning.
In *Emerging good practice in managing for development results*, 2nd edition.
Available at: www.mfdr.org/%5c/Sourcebook.html [2 April 2014].

Wildavsky, A. (2006) *Cultural analysis: Politics, public law, and administration*,
Volume 1. New Brunswick, NJ: Transaction Publishers.

World Bank (1997) *The state in a changing world*. Washington, DC, USA:
Oxford University Press.

YouGov (2021) Is Boris Johnson trustworthy? Available at: https://yougov.co.
uk/topics/politics/trackers/is-boris-johnson-trustworthy [25 September 2021].

11 A Moment of Renewal

Introduction

Analysis presented in earlier chapters showed that national performance (measured by combining indexes of human development and environmental performance), the quality of public services, and sustainable development (measured by SDG indexes for 2016 and 2020) were correlated with the strength of strategic state capabilities. In Chapter 9, it was shown that the COVID-19 mortality rates between July 2020 and January 2021 were partially turned around for countries with governments that had strong strategic state capabilities. If these partial turnarounds were the result of fast learning and adaptation then this would be consistent with the argument that agile states have strengths in policy evaluation, policy experimentation, and adapting policies to changing social and economic contexts, which are aspects of a strategic state capability.

To these conclusions, we can also add the observation that there was a slight positive correlation between strategic state capabilities (in 2016) and public confidence in government (in 2018). This is shown in Figure 11.1.

A combination of the threat of the climate crisis caused by global warming and the hopes of a better world, as expressed in the 2030 Agenda, together spell a big challenge for the effectiveness of governments and the contribution that strategic state capabilities might make to the future of citizens all around the world.

In this final chapter, we reflect on the findings presented in the preceding chapters. We touch on optimism and pessimism about the civil service and change. We end on a philosophical note and reject the possibility of a closed system of concepts to understand the problems of public governance and the future of the strategic state.

Vanguards of progress?

Over the decade 2010–2019 governments with strong strategic state capabilities were making efforts to act on global warming. The examples

DOI: 10.4324/9781351045797-11

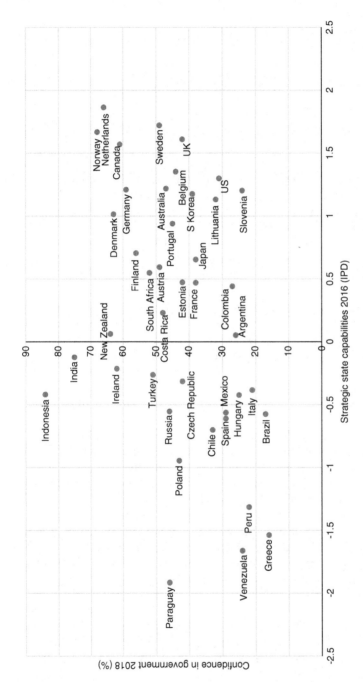

Figure 11.1 Confidence in government (2018) by strength of strategic state capabilities.

Notes:
1 Data from OECD (2019). Most of the data on confidence in government was downloaded in an Excel spreadsheet from: https://doi.org/10.1787/888934033137 [31 October 2021]. Rest of data from https://www.oecd-library.org/sites/50c07fc2-en/index.html?itemId=/content/component/50c07fc2-en [6 March 2021].
2 Data refer to the percentage who answered "yes" to the question, "Do you have confidence in national government?"
3 Data for Peru and Venezuela are 2017 rather than 2018.

of Singapore and Germany in five years from 2015 to 2019 showed very clearly that big reductions in a major greenhouse gas (carbon dioxide) were possible when a government with strong or relatively strong strategic state capabilities decided to act. These two countries provided a "coercive comparison" for all other governments with strong strategic state capabilities.

Based on analysis of the book's sample of 63 countries it was not countries with strong strategic state capabilities that were in the forefront of progress in the decade to 2019. The countries that had progressed most in terms of national performance (measured by a combination of the Human Development Index and the Environmental Performance Index) were, in rank order, Bahrain, Mozambique, United Arab Emirates, China, Nigeria, Pakistan, South Africa, Bangladesh, Oman, and Turkey. No country in the top ten for improved national performance over the years 2010–2019 was also in the top ten of countries with governments that had strong strategic state capabilities. It was the case that three of the fastest improving performances were by countries with moderately strong strategic capabilities: China, South Africa, and the United Arab Emirates. But overall, the correlation between strength of strategic state capabilities and improvement in performance over the decade was negligible.

Of course, these observations make no reference to the conditions that might have made progress more difficult for the governments with strong strategic state capabilities, but they do suggest that they had no grounds for complacency as they faced the challenges of the years up to 2030.

Optimism and pessimism inside public administration

On some occasions when civil servants come together to discuss how to make government strategies more effective, the tone is optimistic, supercharged with a "can do" spirit. The optimism is very exaggerated. They may mention the need for strategic leaders who can be visionary, think the unthinkable, and imagine futures by using thought experiments that alter assumptions about the way things must be. They think, in other words, about the need for "contrarians". They may speak with "evangelical" zeal and call for civil servants to have "passion". They may discuss the importance of working to deliver the aspirations of ministers and government priorities. They may stress the value of using fashionable or "on trend" management tools.

But there can be a different side to the civil service. There can be a mood of pessimism. This is a mood that says change is extremely difficult. Surveys of civil servants may show that there is a perception that change is not well managed in government. The pessimistic mood is only too well aware of the problems that create barriers to change.

One problem of managing change is the problem of getting "buy in" to government strategic plans by managers closer to the front line of government's delivery chains. At a recent webinar for civil servants a senior civil servant talked about the responsibility that the "strategy team" had towards "middle managers" (Global Government Forum 2021):

> With some managers inevitably engaging "through gritted teeth", it is the job of the strategy team to make managers feel empowered and listened to, he said. "We engaged [middle managers] at the start. And as we went through the re-iteration of objectives and deliverables, they were absolutely part of that discussion. So that they felt, and hopefully can see, some of their contributions both being recognised and then played back to them".

The problem of the middle managers can be seen as a symptom of reform or change fatigue. Over the last twenty years or so, governments have proclaimed the importance of serving the public or empowering the public. Inside the public administration structures, this is sometimes resented. Sometimes serving the public better means disruption and losses for civil servants (Chapter 10).

Another problem is resourcing government effectiveness let alone ensuring resources are available for strategic changes. This is a long-recognized problem and may be more serious in some contexts than others. A World Development Report included references to weaknesses in public administration in developing countries (World Bank 1997, 83):

> Central capacity is weak, stretched thinly among a handful of senior officials who must attend to numerous tasks. These strains are compounded by problems in the bureaucracy: low pay at senior levels, rampant political patronage, and an absence of meritocratic recruitment and promotion.

Governments that have been through years of austerity policies and subject to major reorganizations carried out as part of the cutting of public administration may find the flexibility and resilience of the civil service much reduced.

A third problem is poor alignment of management systems to ensure focus and persistence in delivering strategic goals. Governments that have set out on the path of developing strategic capabilities may plan for budgetary systems to be tightly coordinated with ministry or departmental strategic plans but are not always able to make this happen. Governments that are serious about the development of strategic state capabilities will not give up on this requirement and will persist until strategic priorities are backed up by budgetary allocations.

Some messages for the future might be to make more effort to build ownership of strategic agendas within public administration; look for ways to consult and listen to managers and employees; and conduct evaluations of the extent to which budgetary systems and allocations are reinforcing strategic priorities and plans (see Chapter 6 on the evaluations of the Lithuanian National Audit Office).

Social capital and consensus

Public support is now considered by many governments to be vital if they are to be successful in delivering a strategy. And support may be easier to mobilize where there is a high degree of social capital (Demmke and Moilanen 2012, 37): "Putnam has defined social capital as 'features of social organisation, such as trust, norms, and networks, that can improve the efficiency of society by facilitating coordinated actions'".

In practice, in the last decade, the civil service of many countries found a rising tide of populism – which can be authoritarian populism or democratic populism. In the latter case, where there is a greater development of democratic populist parties the social capital of a society may be partially eroded. In the book's sample of 63 countries, there were three cases of countries with strong strategic state capabilities which also had relatively strong populist parties in 2019, as shown by their percentage share of the vote in the most recent elections. These countries were the United States, the UK, and Lithuania. It was noticeable that the same three countries had relatively low percentages of the public expressing confidence in their governments in 2018 compared to their counterparts with similar strengths of strategic state capabilities. President Trump (in office 2017–2021) in the United States polarized American society with his various policies (including those on immigration). According to Quirk et al. (2020, 16): "Though opposed by most Americans, Trump's xenophobic rhetoric and his draconian – often unconstitutional – immigration measures have been popular with his base, the roughly 40% of those citizens who approve of his performance". The UK electorate became polarized because of a populist movement focused on bringing about a referendum on leaving membership of the European Union. In late 2019, a populist UK prime minister, also leader of the right-wing Conservative Party, was elected on a slogan of getting Brexit done. Problems of polarization have also been reported for Lithuania in the period leading up to 2019 (Nakrosis et al. 2019, 7):

> Party polarization remains a major obstacle to finding cross-party agreements in policymaking. ... It appears that both parties often clash publicly on issues in order to mobilize their voters,

reducing the space for potential cross-party agreements on long-term reforms. This type of conflictual behavior became increasingly visible with municipal and presidential elections approaching in 2019.

If society is polarized and social capital is damaged, and if cross-party policy agreements are difficult to negotiate, the prospects for sustainable progress may be lessened. Barber (2015) linked sustainability, which he called irreversibility, and consensual traditions in politics (Barber 2015, 244):

> ... in some countries the democratic process has developed a consensual tradition ... they expect to work together, sometimes in coalition and sometimes simply because that is the way the political culture expects them to behave. This is often true, for example, in the way Germany goes about fundamental reform ... The result is often slower, more deliberate change, but also change with much better prospects of lasting longer and becoming irreversible.

From the point of view of civil servants, an increase in populism in society might lead to increased perceptions of the advantages of stressing a more legalistic approach to strategic policymaking.

Political context

Very often, in the past, assumptions have been made about the design of constitutions or the best forms of regime for the delivery of national development. One hundred years ago this might have been debated in terms of whether communism or capitalism was better at helping a society industrialize. In recent years, the terms of this debate have changed to being a discussion of the relative merits of liberal democracy and authoritarian models of governance. This is apparent in the following contribution to discussions about how the Gulf States in the middle east might modernize (Khonker 2011, 306):

> Consider Singapore, where the leadership's disillusionment with liberal democracy is shared by a large number of populace who are cognizant of both the value as well as the cost of Western-styled liberal democracy. Singapore's remarkable economic growth and its success in creating a safe, stable society receive much attention in the Gulf.... a tacit acceptance of the position that there are multiple roads to modernization seem to have gained grounds. A careful scan of the world will reveal that the path to modernity is not single but multiple.

Dreze and Sen (2013) touched on the same debate in some brief comments they made on India and China. They were critical of aspects of the situation in India, pointing to problems of corruption and the "persistent ineptitude and unaccountability in the way the Indian economy and society are organized" (Dreze and Sen 2013, 11). However, they considered India's democratic institutions to be relatively healthy and described China's system as having "relatively little scope for democratic pressure from below" (Dreze and Sen 2013, 14). They suggested that authoritarian systems had the inherent problem that leadership errors can be made so quickly and so easily. In contrast, they thought policy-making in a democratic system can be hard work because of political pressures and public demands but was less liable to error (Dreze and Sen 2013, 16):

> ... governments, especially one made up of a coalition such as the present government in New Delhi, have to respond to the priorities set by political pressures and public demands, which can take widely diverse forms and which all compete for governmental attention and resources. Cultivating democratic engagement can be a harder task than convincing a handful of political leaders of the need for a policy change. On the other hand, if a norm of this kind is democratically established, it is less subject to the fragility to which all authoritarian decisions remain vulnerable.

In reflecting on these various assessments of strengths and weaknesses of different governance systems, it should be noted that copying other country's governance systems is not an easy thing to do. For example, Barber (2015) thought that some countries had combative political cultures that would impede attempts to be more consensual.

These are all interesting arguments and to them can be added the point that authoritarian systems may need to be combined with high levels of government competence and honesty if the performance of Singapore is to be copied. Long ago the World Bank remarked that governments of East Asian countries worked well with the private sector and deployed their capability in optimum ways for government effectiveness. Economic growth was perceived to result from these governance characteristics. It was commented (World Bank 1997, 163), "many East Asian countries have experienced remarkable growth (with some improvement in equity) under authoritarian regimes". The World Bank, at that time, considered that some African countries suffered from ineffective authoritarian regimes, and that these regimes were associated with economic decline.

If the World Bank's view in 1997 was correct and is still correct, then the important thing for national development is the competence and effectiveness of government, not whether it is authoritarian or not. The implication here is that whatever the type of governance system, improving the capabilities of government – including strategic state capabilities – is important if national development is to take place successfully.

It remains to be seen whether the assessments of governance systems by commentators such as Dreze and Sen (2013) and Barber (2015) are important too, raising the possibility that governance systems involving democracy and consensual forms of democracy have untapped or underexploited resources for human development and further progress. It also remains to be seen if the experiences of governments working in a global partnership to deliver the 2030 Agenda and relief from global warming can engender interactions and learning that will generate new syntheses of public governance from the configurations which prevail now. We did not reach the end of history in the last twenty or thirty years. Nor will we in the next twenty or thirty years. We should expect the problems of public governance and the future of the strategic state to continue to evolve, and to evolve in ways and directions that will depend on what governments and people do now. As Max Weber (1949, 84) put it:

"The stream of immeasurable events flows unendingly towards eternity. The cultural problems which move men [and women] form themselves ever anew and in different colors, and the boundaries of that area in the infinite stream of concrete events which acquires meaning and significance for us ... are constantly subject to change. The intellectual contexts from which it is viewed and scientifically analysed shift."

References

Barber, M. (2015) *How to run a government: So that citizens benefit and tax-payers don't go crazy.* UK: Allen Lane.

Demmke, C. & Moilanen, T. (2012) *Effectiveness of ethics and good governance in central administration of EU-27: Evaluating reform outcomes in the context of the financial crisis.* Frankfurt: Peter Lang.

Dreze, J. & Sen, A. (2013) *An uncertain glory: India and its contradictions.* London: Allen Lane.

Global Government Forum (2021) *Find your northstar: How to build impactful public sector strategies.* Available at: https://www.globalgovernmentforum. com/find-your-northstar-how-to-build-impactful-public-sector-strategies/?utm_ source=GGF+Global+Subscriber+List&utm_campaign=503d50f92c-EMAIL_ CAMPAIGN_2020_03_30_12_48_COPY_01&utm_medium=email&utm_ term=0_be045faa37-503d50f92c-196905661 [25 March 2021].

Khonker, H.H.K. (2011) Many roads to modernization in the middle east. *Society*, 48, 304–306.

Nakrosis, V., Vilpisaukas, R., & Jahn, D. (2019) *Lithuania report: Sustainable governance indicators 2019.* Gutersloh: Bertelsmann Stiftung.

OECD (2019) *Government at a glance 2019*. Paris: OECD Publishing.

Quirk, P.J., Lammert, C., & Thunert, M. (2020) *United States report: Sustainable governance indicators 2020*. Gutersloh: Bertelsmann Stiftung.

Weber, M. (1949) The methodology of the social sciences. Translated and edited by Edward A. Shils & Henry A. Finch. New York: The Free Press.

World Bank (1997) *World development report 1997: The state in a changing world*. New York: Oxford University Press.

Appendix: Data Sources

The data used for the analysis presented in this book came from a variety of sources including the United Nations, the World Bank, the French Government, etc. The core data sources are shown below.

Average Subjective Wellbeing Score in 2018. Source: Sachs, J., Schmidt-Traub, G., Kroll, C., Lafortune, G., Fuller, G., Woelm, F. (2020). Sustainable Development Report 2020. Cambridge: Cambridge University Press. Data downloaded from: https://sdgindex.org/reports/sustainable-development-report-2020/ [6 February 2021].

BTI Data. Source: BT Transformation Index. Data downloaded from: https://www.bti-project.org/en/meta/downloads.html [10 February 2021].

Carbon dioxide emissions data. Source: Our World in Data. Data downloaded from: https://github.com/owid/co2-data [27 May 2021].

Confidence in Government in 2018. Source: OECD. Most of the data were downloaded as an Excel spreadsheet from: https://doi.org/10.1787/888934033137 [31 October 2021]. The rest of the data was downloaded from: https://www.oecd-ilibrary.org/sites/50c07fc2-en/index.html?itemId=/content/component/50c07fc2-en [6 March 2021].

COVID-19 total deaths per million in 2020. Source: Our World in Data. https://github.com/owid/covid-19-data/tree/master/public/data [18 October 2021].

COVID-19 mortality data for 11 July 2020 and 11 January 2021. Source: Johns Hopkins University and Medicine. Mortality data were downloaded from: https://coronavirus.jhu.edu/data/mortality [11 July 2020 and 11 January 2021].

Environmental Performance Index. Source: Wendling, Z. A., Emerson, J. W., de Sherbinin, A., Esty, D. C., et al. (2020). 2020 Environmental Performance Index. New Haven, CT: Yale Center for Environmental Law & Policy. https://epi.yale.edu/. The data were obtained from: https://epi.yale.edu/epi-results/2020/component/epi [20 August 2021].

GDP growth data. Source: World Development Indicators. https://databank.worldbank.org/ [18 October 2021].

Government effectiveness data. Source: Worldwide Governance Indicators. https://databank.worldbank.org [4 July 2020].

Government long-term vision. Source: World Economic Forum Global Competitiveness Index. https://govdata360.worldbank.org/indicators/h5b74eef6?country=B [11 April 2021].

Government outsourcing in 2016. Source: OECD (2017), Government at a Glance 2017. Paris: OECD Publishing. Data downloaded from StatLink: http://dx.doi.org/10.1787/888933532029 [17 September 2021].

Human Development Index. Source: Human Development Report Office. The data were reported in the 2020 Human Development Report. The data were obtained from: http://hdr.undp.org/ [20 August 2021].

Ireland Foreign Direct Investment. Source: World Development Indicators. Available at: https://databank.worldbank.org [7 January 2021].

Political attitudes of citizens in 2008. Source: Thomas Denk, Henrik Serup Christensen, and Daniel Bergh (2015) The Composition of Political Culture—A Study of 25 European Democracies. St Comp Int Dev, 50:358–377.

Public administration data. Source: CEPII 2016. Institutional Profiles Database (IPD). http://www.cepii.fr/institutions/EN/ipd.asp [28 August 2018].

SGI Index and sustainability indicators data. Source: Sachs, J., Schmidt-Traub, G., Kroll, C., Lafortune, G., Fuller, G., Woelm, F. (2020). Sustainable Development Report 2020. Cambridge: Cambridge University Press. The data used in a tabular analysis were downloaded from: https://sdgindex.org/reports/sustainable-development-report-2020/ [6 February 2021].

Index